BRENDAN BEHAN

To Moyra

Brendan Behan

Cultural nationalism and the revisionist writer

JOHN BRANNIGAN

FOUR COURTS PRESS

Set in 10 on 13 point Janson for
FOUR COURTS PRESS LTD
Fumbally Lane, Dublin 8, Ireland
e-mail: info@four-courts-press.ie
and in North America
FOUR COURTS PRESS
c/o ISBS, 5824 N.E. Hassalo Street, Portland, OR 97213.

A catalogue record for this title
is available from the British Library.

ISBN 1–85182–669–6

Printed in England
by MPG Books, Bodmin, Cornwall

Contents

Acknowledgements

I have many people to thank for their advice, encouragement and assistance during the course of researching and writing this book. My first debt of gratitude goes to the University of Luton, particularly to Adrian Page, Tim Boatswain, Ian Beckett, and Martin Gray, for their kind support. The Institute of Irish Studies at the Queen's University of Belfast awarded me a research fellowship in 1999/2000, which provided the funds and congenial surroundings to enable the book to be written. My thanks to Brian Walker and Catherine Boone, in particular, for their generous assistance. I owe much gratitude to the librarians and staff of the British Library, the National Library of Ireland, the libraries of the Queen's University of Belfast, Trinity College Dublin, University College Dublin, University College Cork, University of London, and the University of Luton, the British Newspaper Library at Colindale, RTE Sound Archives, and Trevor White and Mrs Kavanagh at the BBC Written Archives Centre at Caversham. I would like to thank *Eire-Ireland*, *JNT: Journal of Narrative Theory*, and *Irish Studies Review* for publishing early versions and drafts of parts of the book, and Graeme Harper for publishing a draft of chapter five on *Borstal Boy* in *Colonial and Postcolonial Incarceration* (Continuum, 2002). The arguments formulated here were rehearsed in many seminars and discussions at the University of Luton, University of Sussex, University of Dundee, and Queen's University of Belfast, and I am grateful to Adrian Page, Alan Sinfield, David Marriot, Julian Wolfreys, Brian Walker and Clare McManus for giving me the opportunities to do so. Lastly, this book would never have been written without the constant encouragement and love of my partner, Moyra Haslett, who is always generous with her support and wise with her counsel.

Introduction: Brendan Behan and Irish literary revisionism

A nation once again

There is a story, perhaps apocryphal, that after the Abbey theatre burned down in 1951, Brendan Behan set up office in its derelict shell. He placed a sign on the door which advertised 'The Town Office of Brendan Francis Behan,' and held court there for months before the Abbey's director, Ernest Blythe, discovered and duly evicted him.[1] It is a story which, if not actually true, certainly resonates with symbolic significance. Behan had submitted his early plays to the Abbey, only to have them dismissed by Blythe.[2] The young writer compared himself to Synge and O'Casey in his prison letters,[3] but could only become part of the theatre which first gave expression to their dramatic talents by squatting in its ruins. Ironically, Blythe and the Abbey company, who were roundly criticised at the time, and since, for peddling a steady diet of mediocre nationalist dramas, became sitting tenants in the Queen's theatre, the theatre which had provided Behan with a sound education in the techniques of Victorian melodrama and music hall. It is a story of symbolic appropriation and ironic dislocation which, even if dubious, tells us much about Behan's mercurial relationship with Irish culture and society at the mid-century.

The life of Brendan Behan (1923–1964) coincides roughly with a period of political consolidation and cultural conservatism in modern Irish history, from the Irish civil war in the early twenties to the beginnings of liberal reform and international co-operation in the sixties. His adult life was spent almost entirely in what historians came to call 'the age of de Valera,'[4] characterised by its powerful fusion of conservative nationalism with the moral and educational prescriptions of the Catholic Church. The economic stagnation, cultural insularity, and social restraint of those years prompted Sean O'Faolain to reflect in an editorial in *The Bell* on the intellectual poverty of independent Ireland. 'We are discovering,' he wrote, 'that phrases like "a free Ireland", "an independent Ireland", a "self-contained Ireland", mean very much less than we thought.'[5]

---

1 S. McCann (ed.), *The Wit of Brendan Behan* (1968), p. 9.   **2** Behan submitted both *The Landlady* (only a part of the manuscript remains in the Abbey's archives) and *Casadh Súgáin Eile* (*The Twisting of Another Rope*), which eventually became *The Quare Fellow*, to the Abbey, but Blythe rejected them both.   **3** E.H. Mikhail (ed.), *The Letters of Brendan Behan* (1992), p. 24, p. 27.   **4** G. Ó Tuathaigh and J.J. Lee (eds), *The Age of de Valera* (1982).   **5** S. O'Faolain, 'Editorial: New Wine in Old Bottles', *The Bell*, 4, no. 6 (1942), p. 381.

Behan's writings were forged in the spirit of this deflated and broken idealism, in which the nationalist icons of the previous generation were invoked continually, only to serve as constant reminders of the belatedness of his own age. As Christopher Ricks noted, the weary sardonic question, 'Where were you in nineteen-sixteen?,' recurs all too frequently in Behan's writings.[6] It does so, however, with good purpose, since it illustrates that sense of the constraining force of history which pervades the writings of Behan's generation.

'We in Ireland are all in a sense children of the revolution,' wrote F.S.L. Lyons,[7] a point which registers both the indebtedness of state nationalism to the insurgents, and indeed the obsession with the mythology of revolution which Fintan O'Toole evokes in his childhood memories of the 1966 commemoration ceremonies.[8] Behan demonstrates this mesmeric hold of the 1916 Rising in his short sketch for the *Irish Press*, 'The family was in the Rising.'[9] He begins by quoting Yeats' 'Sixteen Dead Men,' which itself gives voice to the notion that the death of the insurgents should induce silence among the living. Instead, in Behan's pub scenes, the living do nothing but talk of the Rising, and, more importantly, their various, highly fictionalised roles in it. Behan's sketch acknowledges the Rising as a potent mythical event, a piece of pure theatre, which, as Yeats' poetic representations suggest, owed more to the aesthetic than the political imagination:

> 'To take as a headquarters the most prominent target in the whole city,' said a man in a middle-aged growl, 'what ridiculous strategy.'
> Old George Roberts took the tumbler from his little full lips and stroked on his beard. 'But what taste – what impeccable taste,' said he.
> Me life on you, said I: for I knew what he meant. Hadn't I stood in the Queen's Theatre, with the frenzied Saturday night crowd, for the 'Transformation Scene: Burning GPO,' while the very amplifiers carrying Pearse's oration over the grave of Rossa were deafened in a mad roar of cheering that went on till the darkness came down and we had till the end of the next act to compose our features and look at our neighbours without embarrassment?[10]

The Rising, replayed scene by scene in the popular theatres of Dublin, forms a cathartic night of frenzied entertainment for Behan and his fellow theatre-goers, who, it seems, are transformed themselves by the 'Transformation Scene.' Behan describes this theatrical event as an experience of dislocation,

6 C. Ricks, 'Bee-keeper', *New York Review of Books*, 11, no. 12 (1964), p. 9.   7 F.S.L. Lyons, *Culture and Anarchy in Ireland, 1890–1939* (1979), p. 1.   8 F. O'Toole, 'The Southern Question', *Letters from the New Island*, ed. D. Bolger (1991), p. 15.   9 B. Behan, 'The family was in the Rising', *The Dubbalin Man* (1997), pp 75–8.   10 Ibid., p. 75.

from which the audience have to recover, to compose themselves. As such it dramatises the temporal dislocation of the post-independence generation, who, steeped in the association of Irishness with the mythology of sacrifice and struggle, can only watch through the medium of melodrama the moment at which Irish national identity is supposedly affirmed and fulfilled.

'There was nothing remote about it,' writes Behan, reflecting on the paradoxical currency of the 1916 Rising with his own time:[11]

> When I was nine years old I could have given you a complete account of what happened from Mount Street Bridge out to the Battle of Ashbourne, where I was giving Tom Ashe and Dick Mulcahy a hand. I could tell you how Seán Russell and I stopped them at Fairview, and could have given you a fuller description of Easter, 1916 than many an older man. You see, they were mostly confined to one garrison – I had fought at them all.[12]

Behan's recollection of his heroic role in the Rising is anamnesis, *par excellence*, of course. 'I have learned enough arithmetic to know that I could not possibly have taken part in the Rising, which happened seven years before I was born,' he writes, yet still he can recall the events of the Rising more vividly than its actual participants.[13] His representation of 'total recall' of the Easter Rising is indicative of what might be called a 'memory crisis' in the nationalist discourses of the mid-century. On the one hand, memory functions characteristically to distance its referent, and to register loss or absence. On the other hand, the continual evocation of the formative events in the evolution of state nationalism produces the effect of constant presence. This is particularly the case when, as Francis Mulhern argues, the bankruptcy of official nationalist ideologies under de Valera 'meant, in effect, the obsolescence of "the Irish nation" as a sustainable cardinal value.'[14] De Valera's failure to 'complete' the nationalist revolution, and more importantly his legitimising embrace of the counter-revolutionary ideologies of state nationalism, left cultural nationalism in the mid-century with nothing but its memories. As Homi Bhabha argues of the nation-state in general, 'the language of culture and community is poised on the fissures of the present becoming the rhetorical figures of a national past.'[15] Bhabha suggests, as indeed does Richard Terdiman, that the displacement enacted in such communal experiences of memory serves to 'bring the entire problem of representation into focus.'[16]

---

11 Ibid., p. 75.   **12** Ibid., p. 75.   **13** Ibid., p. 75.   **14** F. Mulhern, 'A Nation, Yet Again', *The Present Lasts a Long Time: Essays in Cultural Politics* (1998), p. 157.   **15** H. Bhabha, 'DissemiNation: time, narrative, and the margins of the modern nation', *Nation and Narration* (1990), p. 294.   **16** R. Terdiman, *Present Past: Modernity and the Memory Crisis* (1993), p. 70.

Behan's anamnetic imagination of the Rising, then, is indicative of the failure of modern nationalism, and, in situating nationalist heroism firmly in the past, thus implies the end of the nationalist project. This is a recurring theme in Behan's writings. In *The Hostage* the nationalist characters are figured as anachronistic, particular in the character of Monsewer who, perhaps like Behan in his sketch, believes that he is still fighting in the war of independence. The hanging of 'the quare fellow,' in the play of that title, figures the tragic repetition of the social, political and cultural structures of colonialism under the nationalist state, and so brings into focus the process by which nationalism fails to inaugurate a new time, fails to enact the temporal logic of revolution. *Borstal Boy* is remarkable for its evasion of any considered account of Behan's nationalist convictions, and instead dresses Behan in the clothes of the 'dead generations.' Behan compares himself to Thomas Clarke and Terence MacSwiney, and follows the conventions of the nationalist prison narrative, but by the end of his autobiographical novel his justifications for nationalist war have been exhausted. Behan has learned to love the English, and simultaneously recognises the ideological limitations of nationalism as an emancipatory discourse.

Behan's writings enact a sustained engagement with the literary and cultural legacies of the Irish nationalist revival, but in doing so they bring into focus the disjunctive, volatile foundations of both state and fugitive nationalism in the mid-century. Read through the revisionary lenses of Behan's writings, the formative texts and events of cultural nationalism begin to register a crisis in the representation of nationalism itself. It was a crisis, moreover, which was becoming more clearly visible to Behan's generation, as the fissure between political rhetoric and social reality became more apparent. O'Faolain gave expression to this view in *The Bell*, in which his editorials persistently returned to the failure of modern Irish politics to progress beyond an atavistic and myopic nationalist agenda. One could argue, as John Hutchinson does, that the emergence of modern historiography in Ireland in the 1930s was constructed 'in conscious reaction against the excesses of nationalist history, then politically embodied in de Valera's constitution that declared Ireland as Gaelic, Catholic and indivisible.'[17] To evoke continually the legitimising force of history is to risk becoming confined to that history. Patrick Kavanagh argued that literature and culture had been impoverished by state-nationalism when he declared in the first issue of *Kavanagh's Weekly* that political liberty had resulted in nothing more than a new regime of mediocrity, defined by its social and cultural anomie.[18] Nationalism became increasingly dependent during the years of cultural insularity on

17 J. Hutchinson, 'Irish Nationalism', in D. G. Boyce and A. O'Day (eds), *The Making of Modern Irish History: Revisionism and the Revisionist Controversy* (1996), p. 101. 18 P. Kavanagh, 'Editorial: Victory of Mediocrity', *Kavanagh's Weekly*, no. 1 (1952), p. 1.

repetitive representations of its historical validity, which exposed it more fully to revisionist literary and historical criticism. Behan's writings, I will argue throughout this book, participated in the construction and working through of revisionist perspectives on Irish culture and society. The next section will situate Behan in relation to the critical debates and arguments of the period.

Criticism in the age of de Valera

'Criticism,' Terry Eagleton argues, 'is a reformative apparatus, scourging deviation and repressing the transgressive.'[19] The emergent critical discourses of mid-century Ireland qualified but did little to refute nationalist narratives of literary and cultural history. Both literary and historical revisionists depended upon their relation to nationalism, and, insofar as they assumed the nation as the basic unit of social and cultural experience, were 'methodological nationalists.'[20] The revisionism which is now commonly associated with Sean O'Faolain, T.W. Moody and Ruth Dudley Edwards, then, might be best understood in terms of what Peter Bürger calls 'dialectical criticism,' which, Bürger explains, 'enters into the substance of the theory to be criticized and derives decisive stimuli from its gaps and contradictions.'[21] Much of Behan's writings might be theorised in these terms, simultaneously embedded in, and deeply critical of, cultural nationalism. O'Faolain, in particular, was an instructive role model for Behan, in this regard, in his earlier transition from militant nationalism to revisionist criticism. At the time at which O'Faolain became Behan's mentor in Mountjoy prison, he had become a key figure in the formation of a critical intellectual culture in Ireland, and perhaps exemplified more than most the relationship of antagonistic dependence between nationalism and revisionism.

Behan's arrival on the Irish literary scene was coterminous with the emergence of contentious debates about the condition and shape of Irish literary criticism, and indeed about the 'social mission' (to borrow Chris Baldick's term)[22] of criticism in Irish society more generally. The intervention of the Irish state in cultural production, the most obvious manifestation of which was the censorship programme introduced in 1929, attempted to yoke culture into the service of defining and policing state ideology. In contrast, the prevailing tendencies of Irish literature after independence tended towards revisionist politics. Sean O'Faolain, who Behan facetiously referred to as his 'father confessor, nursemaid, and prison visitor,'[23] argued in *The Bell* that the time for

---

19 T. Eagleton, *The Function of Criticism: From* The Spectator *to Post-Structuralism* (1984), p. 12. 20 Hutchinson, 'Irish Nationalism', p. 101. 21 P. Bürger, *Theory of the Avant-Garde*, trans. Michael Shaw (1984), p. liv. 22 C. Baldick, *The Social Mission of English Criticism, 1848–1932* (1983). 23 B. Behan, 'Sermons in Cats, Dogs and Mice', *Hold Your Hour and Have Another* (1988), p. 188.

nationalist symbols had passed: 'these belong,' he wrote, 'to the time when we growled in defeat and dreamed of the future.'[24] O'Faolain's ensuing campaign against the censorship of writers took the form of a contest between liberal and conservative nationalism, however, rather than a strictly post-nationalist critique of state nationalism. Nevertheless it served to identify culture as a major site of contest in post-independence Ireland.

Behan shared with O'Faolain a sense of indignation at the process of state intervention in acts of cultural production, not merely because of the assault on his own artistic liberty, but because of the more insidious attempt to prescribe and control cultural values and tastes.[25] 'The literary censorship ... was an effort to codify certain alleged native instincts about literature,' wrote O'Faolain, 'and what has been the result? Time has proved that these alleged instincts are *not* native.'[26] For O'Faolain and Behan, censorship attempted to dictate and delimit the meaning of Irishness, to define some cultural expressions as native and natural and others as foreign and corrupt.

In practice, censorship was the regressive materialization of a strain of Irish literary criticism which Eamonn Hughes has characterised as the school of 'Irish exceptionalism,'[27] and which we can trace in the critical attempts of Douglas Hyde, Thomas MacDonagh, W.B. Yeats and Daniel Corkery to seek out the authentic 'Irish note.'[28] The 'Irish note,' in the hands of the literary censorship, was synonymous with puritan strains of Catholic nationalism, marked by its prim morality and what Elizabeth Bowen called 'a heavy trend to the Right.'[29] Behan seemed to take peculiar delight in mocking and transgressing the edicts and values of this culture, in his satirical depiction of puritanism in *The Hostage*, for example, or his emphatic representation of Ireland as the site of incorrigible cultural hybridity in his sketches and anecdotes for the *Irish Press*. Much of his writing either articulates or implies revisionist and postcolonial critiques of the post-independence state, characterised by its incessant dialogue with and revision of the nationalist myths of the revival. O'Faolain argued in *The Bell* that this was

24 S. O'Faolain, 'Editorial: This is Your Magazine', *The Bell*, 1, no. 1 (1940), p. 5. 25 Behan is reported to have been furious when he heard the news that *Borstal Boy* had been banned. He did, however, compose a short comic song to the tune of *MacNamara's Band*: 'My name is Brendan Behan, I'm the latest of the banned/ Although we're small in numbers we're the best banned in the land,/ We're read at wakes and weddings and in every parish hall,/ And under library counters sure you'll have no trouble at all'. Quoted in M. O'Sullivan, *Brendan Behan: A Life* (1997), p. 243. 26 S. O'Faolain, 'Editorial: Standards and Taste', *The Bell*, 2, no. 3 (1941), p. 7. 27 E. Hughes, 'Forgetting the Future: An Outline History of Irish Literary Studies', *The Irish Review*, no. 25 (2000), pp 1–15. 28 See D. Hyde, *A Literary History of Ireland from Earliest Times to the Present Day* (1899); W.B. Yeats, 'Nationality and Literature', in M. Storey (ed.), *Poetry and Ireland since 1800: A Source Book* (1988), pp 85–92; T. MacDonagh, *Literature in Ireland: Studies Irish and Anglo-Irish* (1916); D. Corkery, *Synge and Anglo-Irish Literature* (1931). 29 Quoted in Robert Fisk, *In Time of War: Ireland, Ulster and the Price of Neutrality, 1939–45* (1983), p. 371.

a necessary phase in the evolution of a modern independent culture, in which writers were engaged in clearing away 'the briars and the brambles' of history in order to make way for the new reality.[30]

O'Faolain thus defined Irish literature in the post-revival period as necessarily a revisionist literature, which must 'eschew abstractions,' and begin to experiment with describing the day-to-day reality of 'young and earnest' Ireland.[31] *The Bell* retreated from idealism, perhaps understandably at a time when Europe was at war, and Ireland's isolation intensified the dominance of conservative nationalism. But it went further than this too, and co-opted the rhetoric of empiricism for what it heralded as an emergent field of experimental literary and cultural criticism, just as the rising generation of poets and novelists in England were poised to do.[32] As the magazine's subtitle proclaimed, as it turned out only in the first five issues, *The Bell* sought to be 'a survey of Irish life,' and O'Faolain advocated methods for cultural and political analysis which were akin to the principles of new criticism. Ireland was to be known neither through abstraction nor through the legacy of its dead generations, but through rigorous description of its individual component parts, its 'little platoons,' in Burke's phrase. This gave *The Bell* an anthropological impetus, at least in its early years, which sought to find a voice for those 'hidden' Irelands which remained uncharted in the cultural and political imagination of the post-independence state.

The Bell published Behan's first serious attempt at literature, his short story 'I Become a Borstal Boy,' which appeared in June 1942. The significance of O'Faolain's journal for Behan was not as an outlet for publication, however. The objects of O'Faolain's ridicule and invective in his editorials, 'bourgeoisie, Little Irelanders, chauvinists, puritans, stuffed-shirts, pietists, Tartuffes, Anglophobes, Celtophiles, *et alii hujus generis*,' became with equal force the targets of Behan's derision.[33] Behan would attack the culture and intellectual legacy of censorship and monologic nationalism in much of his writing, and continued to represent 'hidden' Irelands throughout his literary career. In particular, Behan gave expression to the cultural dispossession of working-class Dubliners, who found themselves ostracised from the political visions of successive Free State governments, and dislocated in the slum clearances of the thirties. There was, however, less idealism in Behan's writings, and in his critiques of the post-independence state, than in O'Faolain's invective, perhaps because the flurry of critical journals and writings of the forties had already foundered when Behan emerged fully on the literary scene in the fifties.

---

30 Sean O'Faolain, 'Editorial: This is Your Magazine', p. 7. **31** Ibid., p. 7. **32** See B. Morrison, *The Movement: English Poetry and Fiction of the 1950s* (1980). **33** S. O'Faolain, 'Editorial: Signing Off', *The Bell*, 12, no. 1 (April 1946), p. 5.

O'Faolain believed that *The Bell* had failed to define and create the new Ireland, and in his final editorial bemoaned both the aridity of cultural debate and the apparent antipathy of the state towards intellectuals.[34] In 1952, six years after O'Faolain ceased to be editor of *The Bell*, Patrick Kavanagh would echo those criticisms in his final editorial of the short-lived *Kavanagh's Weekly*, when he argued that the reasons for the demise of his journal were not financial but cultural. There was no demand, he argued, for a critical journal in Ireland, which lacked the reading public necessary to sustain an organ of critical and creative thought. It was Kavanagh's parting editorial snipe at the intellectual vacuum of modern Irish society. John Ryan's *Envoy* found the same fate, folding after just twenty issues in 1951. All three journals were not merely forums for new writings and ideas, but implicit in the editorial disposition of each was an idealistic aspiration to create the critical reading public which each editor in turn argued was lacking in Irish culture. 'Readers unused to the critical mind may think us destructive,' wrote Kavanagh, 'but this is because they are accustomed only to the flabby unthinking world of the popular newspaper.'[35]

As Richard Kearney argues, Irish intellectuals in the 1940s and 1950s attempted to foster discussion about the relationship between literature and politics, and specifically 'to conscript the dual vehicles of political and literary debate into the service of a new communal identity.'[36] There were significant variations between them, of course, in the kind of new community they aspired to create. Kavanagh wavered between a kind of vague regionalism and outright anglophilia; Ryan dispensed the Shavian conviction that nationalism was a sickness from which all good poets needed to wrestle themselves free; O'Faolain and his fellow editor Peadar O'Donnell, meanwhile, were intensely engaged in staging an argument between the progressive nationalism which they espoused and the puritan nationalism enshrined in the post-independence state. *The Bell*, in particular, and the other journals in less palpable ways, as Gerry Smyth argues, returned repeatedly to the role that literature and literary criticism could play in generating and moulding into shape the cultural conditions for the community it valued.[37]

A debate in the Jesuit journal, *Studies*, in 1955, between Denis Donoghue, Donald Davie and Vivian Mercier, called attention to the impoverished status of criticism in Ireland. 'Nothing is more striking in the Anglo-Irish literary tradition,' Davie observed, 'than the absence of any true critic at all, certainly of any critical tradition.'[38] Davie interpreted Donoghue's appeal to the universal, professional aspirations of the new criticism as a strategic response to the frustrating mesh of literature, politics and morality in mid-century Ireland, but

---

34 Ibid., pp 5–8. 35 P. Kavanagh, 'Editorial', *Kavanagh's Weekly*, no. 3 (April 26th 1952), p. 1. 36 R. Kearney, *Transitions: Narratives in Modern Irish Culture* (1988), p. 263. 37 G. Smyth, *Decolonisation and Criticism: The Construction of Irish Literature* (1998), p. 117. 38 D. Davie, 'Reflections of an English Writer in Ireland', *Studies*, 44 (Winter 1955), p. 440.

gently rebuked the Irish critic for implicitly endorsing a doctrine of specialised aesthetic criticism 'doomed to shore up poetry as the reserve of trained specialists.'[39] What is perhaps most significant about this debate is that Davie interpreted Donoghue's advocation of the objective methods of new criticism within the contexts of ideological dispute between Irish nationalism and its revisionist critics. Davie was thus, apparently unwittingly, echoing sentiments expressed by O'Faolain in *The Bell* more than ten years earlier which had explicitly associated the lack of literary criticism with a more pervasive problem in Irish society in the relationship between cultural and political authority.

This problem of the relationship between authority and criticism was the subject of one especially resourceful editorial in *The Bell*. O'Faolain compared the judgements of three book reviewers in national newspapers when reviewing Kate O'Brien's *The Land of Spices* with the judgements of the five men on the censorship board on the same novel. The reviewers warmly praised the book, even when two of them duly noted the objections which a Catholic doctrine of morality would have with one sentence. The censorship board, however, banned O'Brien's novel on the basis that it was 'in its general tendency indecent.'[40] 'Clearly that is a lie,' declared O'Faolain:

> The five gentlemen of the Board of Censors disagree violently; obviously so violently that they ban the book absolutely. Patently, nothing could be more controversial than the question here raised. In other words, Standards and Taste are not established at all here, yet, and one man's opinion is just as good as another's, and the Censors, certainly, cannot be taken as authorities.[41]

The standards of the censorship board were, it seemed, so violently different to those of the liberal intelligentsia represented in the press and the arts, that it cast doubt on the whole fabric of social, cultural, and ultimately also moral authority of the state and church nexus. Implicit in O'Faolain's argument is the view that the regressive tendencies of state nationalism undermine its own authority, and foster a condition of cultural anomie. There are no critical standards in Ireland, and thus the argument goes that there are also no critical or cultural authorities.

The answer for O'Faolain, however, was not to turn to the apparent rigour of new criticism, which he disdained for its separation of the artwork from its context. 'Wherever else art is today,' he argued, 'it is in the market-place, the pub, the queue, the bus, the office, the parliament and the press, in the kitchens and the hospital, as happy painting frying pans as writing of potato stalks. Art is

---

39 Ibid., 444.   **40** S. O'Faolain, 'Editorial: Standards and Taste', *The Bell*, 2, no. 3 (June 1941), p. 8.   **41** Ibid., p. 8.

no longer something separate; it is what it always was in the great ages ... a vital part of common life.'[42] In passages like these, O'Faolain seems to pre-empt the critical writings of Raymond Williams, prescribing and bringing to life the conditions for the emergence of Irish cultural studies, as much as he was shaping Irish literary criticism. If art could be found amidst common life, so too must criticism, hence O'Faolain's call in *The Bell* for writing which articulated the uncharted corners of Irish society. These were important themes in *Kavanagh's Weekly*, but more important to the commingling of criticism and everyday life was Kavanagh's style as an editor. As Gerry Smyth observes, Kavanagh 'digresses rapidly from pseudo-analysis to pseudo-theory to evaluation and back again ... The effect is more like a pub monologue than a reasoned textual response – rambling, anecdotal, impulsive and occasional.'[43] This style is, of course, no accident, nor simply the result of haste on Kavanagh's part. Like the apparent casual tones of Behan's writing, it is a crafted pose of spontaneity and capriciousness, a technique in the art of narrative and critical seduction by which Kavanagh assumes a position of critical authority.

Kavanagh was attempting to invent the role and style of critic anew, reflecting what W.J. McCormack argues was the case for literary and cultural criticism generally during this period. In surveying the critical landscape of post-1945 Ireland, McCormack notes that 'The impact of *Scrutiny* and *Horizon*, even of T.S. Eliot's *Criterion*, is nowhere evident,' the consequence of which, he argues, was that 'the study of Irish literature was to work out its own procedures and methods.'[44] There is room for some qualification in McCormack's argument. *The Bell* shared some of *Scrutiny's* emphasis on the value and morality of literature and criticism, although it considered a much wider range of cultural and social issues than Leavis' journal. *Envoy*, in its short life, emulated to some degree the European outlook of *Horizon*, and sought to open the intellectual debates of its own society to more cosmopolitan approaches. But, in general, the critical debates of the 1940s and early 1950s in Ireland were marked by a proprietorial spirit, which assumed the need to develop an independent sphere of Irish critical endeavour.[45] The moment for an Irish literary studies, it seems, had arrived, and began to stake a claim to its own critical terrain.

---

42 S. O'Faolain, 'The New Criticism', quoted in G. Smyth, *Decolonisation and Criticism*, p. 116. **43** G. Smyth, *Decolonisation and Criticism*, p. 112.   **44** W. McCormack, 'Convergent Criticism: The *Biographia Literaria* of Vivian Mercier and the State of Irish Literary History', *Bullán: An Irish Studies Journal*, 2, no. 1 (Summer 1995), p. 85.   **45** V. Mercier declared at the time that Irish critics should either 'put up or shut up': 'either write better books than Levin and Ellmann and Kenner or stop jeering at them'. Vivian Mercier, 'Dublin's Joyce', *Irish Writing*, no.35 (Summer 1956), p. 79.

Literature, criticism, nation

The debates surrounding the emergence of an Irish literary studies in the forties and fifties were largely preoccupied with the interrelations between literature, criticism and nation. In this respect, as Gerry Smyth observes, the critical agenda of Behan's time was still being set by the events and concerns of the revolutionary period, 1916–22.[46] This leads Smyth to argue that *The Bell* and other contemporaneous organs of intellectual debate were enmeshed in the complex cultural process of decolonisation, which was both the logical completion and the critical revision of prevailing discourses of cultural nationalism. O'Faolain thus argued in his editorials in *The Bell* that the process of rethinking and reimagining Ireland had to be worked out independently, in terms and methods which were distinctively and verifiably 'our own.'[47] Behan's writings, I will argue, diverge from O'Faolain on this point, in opening up questions about the analogous cultural experiences of Irish and English peoples.

Perhaps the most surprising aspect of Behan's representation of Irish cultural identities was his insistence in *Borstal Boy* and in *Brendan Behan's Island* that Ireland was *de facto* an Anglophone culture: 'the two nations are inextricably mixed up,' he wrote, 'and little in the way of national characteristics divide them.'[48] This was particularly the case in urban cultures, Behan argued in *Borstal Boy*, in which he compared his experiences in Dublin to those of his working-class contemporaries in Manchester, Liverpool, Glasgow and London: 'All our mothers had all done the pawn – pledging on Monday, releasing on Saturday. We all knew the chip shop and the picture house and the fourpenny rush of a Saturday afternoon, and the summer swimming in the canal and being chased along the railway by the cops.'[49] Behan's weekly column in the *Irish Press* similarly opened up questions about the analogous cultural experiences of Irish and English peoples, and, perhaps more importantly, gave expression to the legacy of British army culture among the Dublin working class:

> On Wednesdays and I a child, there were great gatherings of British Army pensioners and pensionesses up on the corner of the North Circular, in Jimmy-the-Sports.
>
> When the singing got well under way, there'd be old fellows climbing up and down Spion Kop till further orders and other men getting fished out of the Battle of Jutland, and while one old fellow would be telling of how the Munsters kicked the football across the German lines at the

46 Smyth, *Decolonisation and Criticism*, p. 114.   **47** S. O'Faolain, 'Editorial: 'Answer to a Criticism', 1, no. 3; 'Standards and Tastes', 2, no. 3; 'New Wine in Old Bottles', 4, no. 6. *The Bell*.   **48** B. Behan, *Brendan Behan's Island* (1965), p. 190.   **49** B. Behan, *Borstal Boy* (1961), p. 241.

Battle of the Somme, there'd be a keening of chorused mourners crying from under their black shawls over poor Jemser or poor Mickser that was lost at the Dardanelles.[50]

The subculture Behan depicted in these sketches included not just the folk songs and stories of British army experiences, which swept images and anecdotes of India, South Africa, the Dardanelles, and the Somme into the purview of Behan's 'ordinary Dubliners,' but it also acknowledged the significant value of British army pensions to the economic conditions of post-independence Dublin.[51] Such a vibrant subculture frequently found itself, in Behan's depictions at least, diverging from the rhetoric of self-sufficiency.

Behan returns to the persistence of British army culture in working-class Dublin culture frequently, if often only briefly, in the course of his writings for the *Irish Press*, juxtaposing the sense of a Republican tradition with the history of participation in the British army. In March 1956, Behan described the way in which scenes from the Great War dominated the imagination of his Dublin, as much as the 1916 Rising. 'I'm now going to give my eyewitness account of my father's death in action at the Dardanelles,' he began, then describing a scene in which he sat among army widows as they watched a documentary film, *Gallipoli*, or *Tell England*, as it was called when shown in England:

> The picture got off to a good start, with the fellow in the orchestral stalls knocking hell out of his drum during the bombardment of the shore batteries. The next thing we saw was what we were waiting for – the soldiers charging down the gang-planks of the landing-craft. From every part of the gods the screeches went up, 'Oh, there's our Mickser.' Other old ones screeched: 'Oh, take me out, I can't stick it. There's me husband in the water.' Granny Carmody was not to be bested and let a roar out of her that you'd hear in Gallipoli, 'Oh, me own sweet onion, there he is, me poor first husband's brother.' As the face that appeared close up that moment was that of a bearded Indian, I was very much impressed by the Granny's relations.[52]

Behan then proceeds to let out his own roar, claiming to see his father being killed in the picture, 'for the good reason,' he says, 'that you might as well be

50 B. Behan, 'Up and Down Spion Kop', *Hold Your Hour and Have Another* (1965), p. 85.   **51** S. O'Faolain recorded statistics from a Banking Commission in 1938 that two of Ireland's largest sources of income were emigrants remittances and British pensions. British pensions were worth £3.25 millions in 1931 and just below £3 millions in 1935. See O'Faolain, 'Editorial: New Wine in Old Bottles', *The Bell*, 4, no. 6 (Sept. 1942), p. 382.   **52** Behan, 'My Father Died in War', *Hold Your Hour and Have Another*, p. 89.

out of the world as out of the fashion.'[53] As Behan's suspicion of his Granny's relations and his own dubious vision of his father being killed suggest, there is some cause to doubt whether the expressions of grief voiced in the picture house are entirely genuine. Like other scenarios Behan depicts in his *Irish Press* column, this might be another attempt by the outcast Dubliners of Behan's writings to forge the illusion of remembrance in order to arrogate some degree of attention and authority to themselves. Nevertheless, what is interesting here is both the objects of their remembrance, and the implication, which is repeated frequently in various forms through the writings of Behan and many of his contemporaries, that their own time is infinitely impoverished in comparison to the generations immediately preceding them.

One could argue that Dublin lent itself to a critical view of the isolationist ideologies of cultural nationalism. Joyce and O'Casey had each mined this vein of subcultural antipathy to the dogmas of nationalism. Louis MacNeice wrote of the city in 1939, 'She is not an Irish town/ And she is not English,' a salutary reminder of the city's cultural ambiguity,[54] while just a few years later Hubert Butler wrote in *The Bell* that a stroll along O'Connell Street and up as far as Parnell Square would reveal that 'the culture of Ireland is still overwhelmingly Anglo-Saxon, nakedly or in word for word translation.'[55] So too, Behan's characters were caught up in the city's inevitable hybridity, and were as likely to slip into Cockney rhyming slang as to stammer out the *cúpla focail*. Behan's Ireland was urban and modern; its modernity shaped and pulled 'Irishness' into a diversity of cultural identities and affiliations which extended beyond the confrontational terms of Catholicism and Protestantism, Irish and English, Colonial and Nationalist. Such oppositions were, in Behan's writings, both cancelled and complicated by the inflections of class, locality, gender, sexuality, and cultural custom.

The revisionism of Behan's time questioned the legacy of nationalist revolution, and perhaps most importantly, nationalist historiography, but did not interrogate adequately the variegated experiences of culture and society in mid-century Ireland. I have been arguing in this introduction that Behan's writings emerged alongside the critical revisionism of the forties and fifties to interrogate the meanings of independence and Irish national identities, but Behan extended revisionist critique further in returning insistently to issues of cultural hybridity and subalternity. By focusing attention on the subcultural heterogeneity of mid-century Ireland, Behan began to delineate the imaginative space of an Irishness which exceeded and weakened the claims of nationalism. In revisiting nationalism as a process of exclusion and amnesia, Behan's writings

---

53 Ibid., p. 91.   **54** L. MacNeice, 'Dublin', *Collected Poems* (1966), p. 164.   **55** H. Butler, 'The Barriers', *The Bell*, 2, no. 4 (July 1941), p. 40.

bear witness to culture as a contested zone of identity. By presenting life in modern, independent Dublin as analogous to the ex-army popular cultures of London or Liverpool, Behan was countering the exclusivist logic of nationalism with representations of the complex interplay of Irish and English cultures.

His own career made this impression forcibly and indelibly. Behan was absorbed easily into the literary culture and media frenzy of the Angry Young Men in England in the 1950s. His plays reflected and extended themes which featured so persistently in the English theatre of the time, complementing the work of John Osborne, Arnold Wesker, Shelagh Delaney, Frank Norman and John Arden. *Borstal Boy* touched on the common cultural experiences of the English and Irish working classes, and, on its publication in 1958, tapped into contemporary debates about delinquency, class identity, and emergent youth subcultures. A more attentive reading might also have discovered the resonances of then current notions of homosexuality in a homosocial environment, but no discussion of this theme emanated in the reception of Behan's autobiographical novel, either in Ireland or England. At the same time, Behan's successful absorption into English literary culture perhaps exaggerated the ambivalence with which he was treated in Ireland. The Abbey theatre, as Alan Simpson notes with some resentment, produced Behan's plays only after he had become a commercial and critical success in Stratford East and the West End in London.[56] Behan's writings and plays earned the critical acclaim of some of the most revered writers and critics of their time, in England and North America. Kenneth Tynan, Nancy Mitford, Norman Mailer, Christopher Ricks, Al Alvarez, Colin MacInnes, Cyril Connolly, Richard Ellmann and Harold Hobson were just some of the reviewers and critics who championed Behan's work. In contrast, as Ted Boyle argues, while Behan 'yearned for Irish approval; he received only a very grudging acceptance.'[57]

Behan's stage-Irish persona undoubtedly had much to do with the ambivalence with which he was received in Ireland. His alcoholism, exuberance and profanity perhaps offended the sensibilities of a modernising, middle-class Ireland, eager to show the world the signs of its maturity and respectability. His writings, however, were also deeply contentious, and interrogated Ireland for its varieties of cultural identities, its recalcitrant strands of irreverence, and for what Mulhern calls its 'shifting repertoire of social initiative and resistance.'[58] At a time when the emergent discourses of criticism in Ireland were gathering around the oppositional terms of nationalism and revisionism, Behan's writings began with imitations of nationalist ballads, but increasingly came to articulate dissident and subaltern perspectives on the nationalist state and its ideological

56 A. Simpson, *Beckett and Behan and a Theatre in Dublin* (1962), p. 56.   57 T. E. Boyle, *Brendan Behan* (1969), pp 35–36.   58 F. Mulhern, 'A Nation, Yet Again', p. 157.

foundations. His belated engagements with revival nationalism sought to dis-entangle the myths of Irishness fostered in the cultural nationalist hegemony of his time, and to remind Ireland of its variety, its hybridity, and its modernity. In doing so, Behan perhaps became a controversial beacon of dissidence and critic-ism for his own, if not later, generations.

1 / Tradition, transgression, and literary authority

The rage of Caliban

'Celtic primitive with sophisticated tendencies': this was Milton Shulman's summary appraisal of Brendan Behan's qualities as a dramatist in the English theatre.[1] Shulman was not alone in casting Behan in the role of the exotic, sometimes demonic, outsider, who embodied the virtues of irreverence, passion, aggression and primitive anarchy which were felt to be lacking in modern English culture. Kenneth Tynan, the theatre critic with *The Observer*, contrasted Behan's language – 'ribald, dauntless and spoiling for a fight' – with the miserly hoarding of words which dogged the English stage. 'It is Ireland's sacred duty,' he argued, 'to send over, every few years, a playwright to save the English theatre from inarticulate glumness.'[2] Tynan places Behan comfortably within a tradition of Irish writers whose work serves principally to shore up the flagging intellectual fortunes of English culture, whose 'sparklin' dialogue' and irreverent humour injects a ready fix of energy into the English theatre, in particular. Both Tynan and Shulman reiterate Arnoldian conceptions of the Celt in their praise of Behan's work, characterising it in terms which are antithetical to the rational, accomplished, pre-conceived art of the English intellectual, and pegging Behan's value as a dramatist on his 'sacred' role of reinvigorating the English theatre. These assessments of Behan's place in the English theatrical tradition, albeit the transient and brief impressions of two eminent reviewers, recapitulate a neo-colonial conception of Irish writing as a 'minor literature' which is bound to serve the more significant English literary and theatrical scene, but, more specifically, they take for granted the *desire* of the Irish writer to play this role. However appealing may be the rewards of serving the Irish theatre alone, the Irish writer is assumed to gravitate when required towards the greater attractions of entertaining and attending the audiences in London. Irish literature and culture is deemed to be *de facto* Anglocentric, even when it is not Anglophile.

The course of Brendan Behan's career as a writer seems to corroborate this notion. While in his youth he penned Republican verse, and later wrote plays and poems in the Gaelic language, he increasingly inclined towards writing in English for English audiences and readers. In *The Hostage*, in particular, which

1 M. Shulman, 'Mr Behan Makes Fun of the I.R.A.', *Evening Standard*, October 15th 1958, p. 13.
2 K. Tynan, 'The End of the Noose', *The Observer*, May 27th 1956, p. 11.

24

was first performed in 1958 to London audiences, Declan Kiberd argues that Behan exploited 'the foibles of a quaint island people for the amusement of a "superior" British audience.'[3] Behan became a 'middle-aged English play-wright,' in Kiberd's words, who 'had been converted almost imperceptibly from a major Gaelic dramatist into a music-hall Stage Irishman.'[4] It is not, however, an idiosyncrasy of Behan's career that he turned towards the greater attractions of success in London's West End, for as Gus Martin argued in one of the earliest serious critical treatments of Behan's work, published in the Belfast journal, *Threshold*, in 1963, '[Behan] could almost be said to be slavishly follow-ing a trail blazed by generations of his countrymen before him.'[5] For Martin, it was not simply a matter of Ireland 'sending over' its latest dramatist to be absorbed into English theatre history. Instead, Martin argues that 'it is almost necessary for Irishmen to detonate themselves in the centre of the field of English literature before they are noticed.'[6] The Irish writer apparently occu-pies a peculiar role, neither Shelley's unacknowledged legislator, nor yet Auden's secret policeman, but instead the cultural terrorist, detonating explos-ions in the heart of English literature. This is, of course, an especially apt, even if ill-advised, metaphor, in the case of Brendan Behan, whose writing career was infinitely more successful than his attempt in his mid-teens to become an IRA bomber. More importantly, it is a metaphor which lies hidden beneath many of the reviews and critical appreciations of Behan's writings, posing the question of how Behan continues or refuses the nationalist struggle in his works. Colbert Kearney argues, for example, that Behan's writings are the logical development of his involvement in a tradition of republican separatism,[7] while in contrast both Richard Wall and Ulick O'Connor hold that after Behan abandoned the Irish language and took his plays to London, he turned the icons of republican-ism into the stage-Irish figures he knew would delight and pander to his English audiences.[8] The terms which reverberate through the critical reception of Behan's work are those of 'tradition' and 'betrayal,' 'continuity' and 'abandon-ment,' intimating Behan's painful struggle with the demands of national belonging and the desire for cultural authority and acclaim.

The relationship between the writer and 'tradition' is a central focus of much literary criticism, partly due to the influence of seminal figures such as T.S. Eliot, F.R. Leavis and Harold Bloom, who have all invested heavily in the notion of tradition not only as genealogy of influences and forms, but also as the source of cultural authority. For each of these critics, 'great' writers borrowed and learned from the canons of Western literature, but could hold

3 D. Kiberd, 'The Fall of the Stage Irishman', *Genre*, 12 (Winter 1979), p. 466.   4 Ibid., p. 469.
5 A. Martin, 'Brendan Behan', *Threshold*, 18 (1963), p. 22.   6 Ibid., p. 22.   7 C. Kearney, *The Writings of Brendan Behan* (1977), p. 18.   8 R. Wall, '*An Giall* and *The Hostage* Compared', *Modern Drama*, 18 (1975), p. 171, and U. O'Connor, *Brendan Behan* (London: Abacus, 1993), p. 63.

their own ground within such canons too. Writers such as Yeats and Joyce borrowed extensively from literary traditions, but, in classic Bloomian terms, they also invented their own traditions, so that 'one can believe that they are being imitated by their ancestors.'[9] For a 'minor' writer such as Behan, however, constructed either as the exotic, witty servant of the English theatre, or the slavish disciple of those Irish writers who have blazed a trail before him, 'tradition' is the force which might sanctify and authorise his work. In a revealing passage in Anthony Cronin's account of his friendship with Behan in the early 1950s, the legitimating embrace of tradition appears to evade Behan, leaving him troubled by his lack of cultural authority, and consumed instead by jealousy of a 'greater' tradition:

> [Brendan] had in those days no vision of a form that might contain his stories, his imitations, his parodies and the anarchic glee and comic life-apprehension that lay behind them. He might have found something of what he was looking for in Irish writers as different as Carleton, Lever, and Somerville and Ross, but I do not think he had read these; and meantime he picked up *Pride and Prejudice* and looked into it with a sort of comic rage and dismay.[10]

Behan appears in Cronin's description as a Calibanesque figure, unlettered in the indigenous traditions of his island, peering with 'comic rage and dismay' into Prospero's books. His rage is explained as the consequence of his ignorance of the *Irish* traditions in which he might find the models for self-expression, the form in which he might properly and fully represent himself. In the meantime, left with Prospero's tradition, which, in George Lamming's terms, is to Caliban 'an unknown history of future intentions,'[11] Behan finds only consternation. Behan, apparently, cannot read himself into Jane Austen's *Pride and Prejudice*, and must instead await the messianic moment of encountering, and inserting himself into, the Irish literary tradition which is properly and wholly his own. Thus, Cronin suggests the scene which Homi Bhabha describes in his essay, 'Signs Taken for Wonders,' of the moment in which the English book is discovered in colonial contexts. Bhabha argues that the English book becomes 'an ambivalent text of authority,'[12] since it represents at first the word of the master, but when it has been read through the 'uncanny forces of race, sexuality, violence, cultural and even climatic differences,'[13] it emerges as a model of colonial hybridity. The discovery of the English book thus institutes 'a process of displacement, distortion, dislocation, repetition.'[14] This scene might become

9 H. Bloom, *The Anxiety of Influence: A Theory of Poetry* (1973), p. 141. **10** A. Cronin, *Dead as Doornails: A Chronicle of Life* (1976), p. 22. **11** G. Lamming, *The Pleasures of Exile* (1984 – orig. 1960), p. 109. **12** H. Bhabha, 'Signs Taken for Wonders', *The Location of Culture* (1994), p. 107. **13** Ibid., p. 113. **14** Ibid., p. 105.

the moment of Caliban's awakening, of rejecting the language of his coloniser, prior to reconnecting with his indigenous cultural inheritance. The authority of the English literary canon, of which Austen's novel stands as signifier, is troubled in Cronin's description, but I want to argue that Behan played a crucial role in troubling the authority and force of the Irish traditions which Cronin asserts are his own. For Behan, the Irish literary tradition was nothing if not a model of the enduring legacy of cultural hybridity produced through centuries of colonial rule. Hybridity was embedded in the language, folk culture and literary forms of Irish cultural nationalism, and symbolised for Behan the complex historical and cultural interchange between Irish and English cultures. 'Tradition,' as it was construed in the discourses of Irish cultural nationalism, therefore, could be equally as forceful, equally as distorting, as the rage-inducing authority of the English canon. It is the authority and force of Irish literary and cultural traditions and their impact on the writings of Brendan Behan with which I'll be concerned in this chapter.

To situate Behan within 'the Irish literary tradition' is apparently an easy matter. Brian Behan describes his brother as 'Boucicault crossed with O'Casey';[15] Michael O'Sullivan, his most recent biographer, places Behan as the heir of Joyce's 'unfettered linguistic elasticity';[16] Herbert Kenny argues that Behan 'carried on the irreverent tradition of Gogarty,' as well as Wilde and Shaw;[17] while Declan Kiberd sees Behan as the successor to the vaudeville routines and critical nationalism of O'Casey.[18] At stake in each of these comparisons is the vexed issue of 'belonging,' of the relationship between lines of literary descent and inheritance and a national culture. Each representation of Behan's place in relation to other Irish writers invokes the notion of an Irish literary tradition, and of the writer's indebtedness to a core of values, styles, attitudes or idioms which have been 'handed down.' Such invented traditions function largely to emphasise conservatism and continuity while subduing notions of rupture, upheaval and ambivalence, for, as Daniel Cottom has argued, the very notion of 'tradition' relies on 'the assumption that it transcends difference, individuality, and mortality.'[19] Hence, T.S. Eliot wrote in his essay on 'Tradition and the Individual Talent,' that the value of a writer could only be gleaned from '[setting] him, for contrast and comparison, among the dead.'[20] Behan surveyed the literary landscape around him in 1951 in despair, announcing that 'Joyce is dead and O'Casey is in Devon. The people writing here now have as much interest for me as an epic poet in Finnish or a Lapland

15 B. Behan, with Aubrey Dillon-Malone, *The Brothers Behan* (1998), p. 14.   16 M. O'Sullivan, *Brendan Behan: A Life* (1997), p. 115.   17 H. A. Kenny, *Literary Dublin: A History* (1974), p. 239. 18 D. Kiberd, *Inventing Ireland: The Literature of the Modern Nation* (1995), p. 522.   19 D. Cottom, *Ravishing Tradition: Cultural Forces and Literary History* (1996), p. 26.   20 T.S. Eliot, 'Tradition and the Individual Talent', *Selected Prose*, ed. J. Hayward (1953), p. 23.

novelist.'[21] In describing his circumstances thus, Behan was defining the condition which he and indeed his contemporaries inherited – a literature living in the shadow of the dead, or, as Neil Corcoran has argued, 'a literature having to come to terms with belatedness or subsequence.'[22]

Behan's shadows

In Behan's case, the condition of belatedness was experienced in a variety of forms. As a Republican in his early youth, he was surrounded by, and sought to emulate, the imagery and iconography of cultural nationalism, in which masculinity was defined and measured by the willingness to participate in armed struggle. From an early age, Behan could recite the whole of Robert Emmet's speech from the dock, delivered at his trial in 1803 for organising an insurrection against British rule in Ireland. Emmet's speech is characteristic in celebrating martyrdom as the sacred duty of Irish men devoted to their suppressed nation, while announcing that the memory of such martyrs could only be honoured by the perpetuation of sacrifice and the achievement of national liberation. More immediate than the canon of Irish heroes and martyrs was the Republican legacy of his own family, however, which had contributed both to the armed struggle and the cultural work of the revival. Stephen Behan was in a Free State jail when his son was born, while Brendan's uncle, Peadar Kearney, was the author of the Irish national anthem, 'The Soldier's Song.' Behan's juvenile writings were, not surprisingly, imitations of militant Republican verse:

> My children yet shall drive the foe before them–
> Whether clad in khaki coat or coat of green–
> And mercenaries will flee in droves ere vengeance
> O'ertakes them for the insults to their Queen.
> My flag shall fly o'er all my many counties–
> From Antrim's hills to Kerry's mountains blue–
> And my sons shall place the bright gold crown of Freedom
> On the dear dark head of deathless Róisín Dubh.[23]

As Colbert Kearney argues, Behan's ventures into patriotic verse in his teenage years 'invariably lapsed into banner-waving and sycophant-bashing.'[24] His

---

21 B. Behan, 'Letter to Sindbad Vail', June 1951, in Mikhail (ed.), *The Letters of Brendan Behan* (1992), p. 45. The letter was published as an 'open letter' in the Paris-based journal, *Points* (no.15, 1951), which Vail edited, and which published a number of Behan's stories.   22 N. Corcoran, *After Yeats and Joyce: Reading Modern Irish Literature* (1997), p. vii.   23 Quoted in Colbert Kearney, *The Writings of Brendan Behan*, p. 22.   24 Ibid., p. 23.

poems figured Ireland as mother, Queen or beautiful lover, seeking salvation by calling to arms her valiant men. The poems were published in Republican newspapers and magazines such as the *Wolfe Tone Weekly* and *Fianna: The Voice of Young Ireland*, where they conformed to the editors' expectations of political verse. Behan's juvenile poetry borrowed extensively from the language and ideology of the nineteenth century, but perhaps found difficulty adapting to the new political realities of post-independence Ireland. In his 'Róisín Dubh' poem, he attempted to address the transformation from colony to Free State:

> 'Eire' – O God! Why do they mock me
> With paper 'freedom' – under England's Crown?
> Even while they forge another link to bind me,
> Another traitor's chain to drag me down.[25]

The message was that nothing had changed, that the struggle was still the same as the one for which Pearse, Emmet and Tone had fought and died. Behan's immersion in the imagery of sacrifice and armed insurrection was frustrated only when Behan was imprisoned in England in 1939 for conspiring to cause explosion in Liverpool. In prison and borstal, ironically, Behan found an England and an Englishness for which his intensive tutelage in Republican prison narratives had not prepared him. By learning to love English boys, and discovering the hybridity of his own cultural identity, composed as much of industrialised working-class English culture as it was of Irish nationalism, Behan found the nationalist justification of war and sacrifice wanting. Prison afforded Behan the isolation in which he could discover through reading his cross-cultural inheritance, and afforded him the social interaction in which he could discern the mechanics of his urban working-class sensibility.

In contrast to Cronin's notion of Behan as the unlettered genius searching in frustration for a form in which he might articulate his visions of life, Behan had an extensive literary education within his family and further afield. His father, Stephen Behan, a house-painter who had once trained as a priest, read to his children from Lever, Shaw, Yeats, Maupassant, Synge, Pepys, O'Casey, Zola, Galsworthy, Doestoevsky, Boccaccio, Fielding, Kickham, even Marcus Aurelius, and, most frequently, from Dickens. Dickens' *Pickwick Papers*, in particular, was a favourite, from which Stephen performed all the parts in the manner of a 'seanchai.' Brendan's half-brothers, who subscribed to left-wing book clubs, brought books by Clifford Odets, Pushkin, Eugene O'Neill, George Orwell, Ernest Hemingway, Scott Fitzgerald, Graham Greene, Samuel Butler and J.B. Priestley into the house. Behan's mother, Kathleen Behan, who

25 Ibid., p. 22.

had once been housemaid to Maud Gonne, taught him the ballads and songs of the nationalist tradition, which he later claimed bred in him her hatred of the English. In the streets and pubs of his youth, Behan was also introduced to the songs and stories of ex-British army culture, so that 'Spion Kop' and 'Ladysmith' were names as familiar to him as 'Vinegar Hill' or the 'GPO.' In borstal in England, his engagement with literature continued, as Behan read Mrs Gaskell, Thomas Hardy, James Joyce, D.H. Lawrence, Somerset Maugham, as well as O'Casey, Wilde and Shaw, and the essays of Robert Lynd in the *New Statesman*. In Mountjoy in Dublin, Behan began to write the stories and plays which would become *The Quare Fellow* and *Borstal Boy*, and attracted the attention of Sean O'Faolain, who visited him in prison on several occasions to advise and teach him about writing. In Mountjoy, too, Behan learned Gaelic, and read Merriman, O'Conaire, Hyde, O'Cadhain, and Eoghan Ruadh O'Suilleabhain in their original language.[26] Behan was far from the 'instinctive, untutored, uninfluenced' writer which George Wellworth describes, and which Cronin suggests, then, for the Behan household was unusually intellectual for a tenement dwelling, and Behan's prison experiences unusually entailed intimate encounters with writers, poets, teachers, and, through them, an extensive literary education.[27]

To sketch such an account of Behan's literary education is not, however, to delineate a literary genealogy for Behan's writings, nor to identify sources which have a causal effect on Behan's techniques, but is merely to suggest that Behan's cultural contacts and horizons were wider than the narrow-gauge nationalism evident in his early writings. Thus, when Behan writes in the vein of a nationalist balladeer of the heroic struggle against the British imperialist, he elects to insert himself into a tradition of nationalist writing of which the conventions of imagery and form are his most apparent, but not his only, inheritance. As Raphael Falco argues, writers tender the work of their literary forebears within their own writings only 'in order to present themselves as progeny.'[28] The image of Behan as a nationalist writer, whose writing, in the words of a Republican newspaper mourning his death, 'was part of his political life as a Republican,'[29] was an image Behan repeatedly elected and proffered, par-

---

26 The account of Behan's literary knowledge and education given above is indebted to the following sources: Mikhail (ed.), *Letters* (1992), T. E. Boyle, *Brendan Behan* (1969), C. Kearney, *The Writings of Brendan Behan* (1977), U. O'Connor, *Brendan Behan* (1993), M. O'Sullivan, *Brendan Behan: A Life* (1997), Mikhail (ed.), *Brendan Behan: Interviews and Recollections* (1982), and Brian Behan, with A. Dillon-Malone, *The Brothers Behan* (1998). **27** G. Wellworth, *The Theatre of Protest and Paradox: Developments in the Avant-Garde Drama* (1965), p. 258. **28** R. Falco, *Conceived Presences: Literary Genealogy in Renaissance England* (1994), p. 12. See also Earl Miner's introduction to *Literary Transmission and Authority: Dryden and Other Writers* (1993) and G. Hermeren, *Influence in Art and Literature* (1975), both of whom make similar arguments about the importance of 'choice' in determining the significance of influence upon an author's work. **29** 'In Defence of B. Behan',

ticularly in the early stages of his writing career, but which fails to account for much of what he wrote. It does not explain, for example, his love affair with the English urban working-class, which manifested itself in *Borstal Boy* in his intimate friendship with Charlie Millwall, in *The Hostage*, in which he makes an English working-class soldier the hero of a play about Irish nationalism, and in *The Quare Fellow* (and, to some extent, *The Landlady*), where Dubliners slip comfortably and obliviously into Cockney slang. Nor does it explain the vituperative attacks on both state and fugitive nationalism which Behan made in *The Hostage*, which, in the words of the reviewer, Milton Shulman, did 'more to destroy Ireland's fondest legend than ever the Black and Tans did.'[30]

Thanks to Joyce

Behan's conversion from Republican bomber to revisionist writer took place while he was in prison. 'Someone else better start handing on the torch,' he wrote to an IRA comrade, 'Me hands are burnt.'[31] At the same time, Behan was inquiring about the rudiments of literary form and technique from his cousin, Seamus de Burca, reading Gaelic texts under the tutelage of the schoolmaster Seán Ó Briain, and sending early drafts of his play, *The Landlady*, to the Abbey theatre in Dublin and the Group theatre in Belfast, neither of which expressed interest in his work. When Behan was released from prison in 1946 under general amnesty, he proved incapable of extricating himself fully from the attractions of playing the Republican hero, participating in a disastrous jailbreak in Manchester in 1947 which perhaps offered too tempting an opportunity for Behan to mimic the heroics of the Manchester Martyrs, who were an important component in his personal iconography of martyrdom. But he began to social-ise in more bohemian circles, forming a kind of loose coterie with Anthony Cronin, John Ryan, Flann O'Brien, Alan Simpson, Carolyn Swift, Sean O'Sullivan and (briefly, before they quarrelled) Patrick Kavanagh, in the emerging literary pubs of Dublin. Here he made his first literary contacts – Ryan published Behan's poetry in his influential journal, *Envoy*, while Simpson and Swift gave *The Quare Fellow* its first production at the Pike Theatre, when the Abbey's Ernest Blythe refused it. Behan also attended the home of his mentor, Sean O'Faolain, who entertained scholars and writers every Sunday evening, regaling them with stories of European writers whom he had known and discussing current events.[32] But the tone of such encounters and coterie gatherings was coloured greatly by the complacency of the Dublin literary

Irish Democrat (May 1964), pp 4–5.   **30** M. Shulman, *Evening Standard*, 15 October 1958, p. 13. **31** B. Behan, 'Letter to Thomas Doran, 15th April 1943', in Mikhail (ed.), *Letters*, p. 19.   **32** M. Harmon, *S. O'Faolain: A Life* (1994), p. 188.

establishment, in which the successes of the revival period overshadowed the cultural endeavours of the living.

Joyce's exhaustive treatment of Dublin, in particular, appeared to leave little room for creative endeavour in the city thereafter. Behan's circle participated in the first 'Bloomsday' celebrations,[33] frequently drank in the pubs described in *Ulysses*, imitated his characters, and quoted his lines. As Brian Fallon argues, Joyce left a kind of 'cultural monotheism' in his wake, a cult of the genius author who had anticipated and exhausted every possible utterance, who had parodied that which had not yet been expressed.[34] Flann O'Brien satirised this state of cultural exhaustion in *At Swim-Two-Birds*, in which the narrator advises young novelists:

> The entire corpus of existing literature should be regarded as a limbo from which discerning authors could draw their characters as required, creating only when they failed to find a suitable existing puppet. The modern novel should be largely a work of reference.[35]

O'Brien's satirical novel, largely regarded now as an early metafictional or postmodern text, was in part responding to the closeted intellectual climate of post-independence Ireland. The seemingly interminable revival of Irish mythology and folklore, and the self-reflexive obsession with nationalism, had bred a new generation of writers desperate to be rid of the conventions of Irish literary tradition. There were sure signs of that desperation among Behan's contemporaries. Terence Brown suggests, indeed, that Behan, Kavanagh and Flann O'Brien were the 'tragic generation of modern Irish letters,' enduring 'years of public indifference or misunderstanding':

> The only future that seemed open to the Irish writer in the late 1940s and early fifties was penury in his own country or an appeal to the wider public gallery through eccentricity, showmanship and bravado, that would distract both public and writer from the serious business of his art.[36]

Literary censorship and cultural provincialism were only the most apparent symptoms of the intellectual stagnation of Ireland in the forties and fifties, leaving Behan's generation of writers little hope of success or inspiration. Kate O'Brien had warned Behan of the bitter consequences of this stagnancy in Irish intellectual circles. 'Dublin is a jealous city,' she told him, 'It's hard to find a writer who's prepared to admit that a fellow-writer can put two words togeth-

33 Behan, however, was excluded from the 'Bloomsday' celebrations, partly because of his antagonism towards Patrick Kavanagh, partly also because of his excessive drinking.   34 B. Fallon, *An Age of Innocence: Irish Culture, 1930–1960* (1999), p. 59.   35 F. O'Brien, *At Swim-Two-Birds* (1967), p. 25.   36 T. Brown, *Ireland: A Social and Cultural History, 1922–1985* (1985), p. 237.

er.'[37] O'Brien had several of her own books banned by the Censorship Board, and stood as a model of personal integrity for the ways in which she continued to weave subtly subversive portraits of the social and cultural values underpinning modern Ireland. But, like Joyce, she represented as inevitable the equation of a critical distaste for the puritan nationalism of modern Ireland with the estrangement of exile. Anthony Cronin cried out against this stifled atmosphere surrounding Dublin intellectuals when he wrote in *The Bell* in 1953: 'We must look outward again or die, if only of boredom.'[38]

For Behan, the legacy of Joyce and the revival writers was ambivalent, for as much as it provoked in him an intense anxiety of influence, it had also thrust upon Dublin a sense of cultural power and literary authority. Behan paid homage to this power, which he found pliable and transposable, in his poem 'Buiochas le Joyce' (Gratitude to Joyce):

> Here in the rue St André des Arts,
> Plastered in an Arab tavern,
> I explain you to an eager Frenchman,
> Ex-G.I.'s and a drunken Russian,
> Of all you wrote I explain each part,
> Drinking Pernod in France because of your art.
> As a writer we're proud of you –
> And thanks for the Calvados we gain through you.[39]

This was written when Behan was in Paris in the late forties, but even after Behan became successful, he wooed his American audiences with talks on Joyce. In 'Buiochas le Joyce,' Behan reveals his anxiety about his parasitical relationship to Joyce, living (or in this case, drinking) off the stories that he can tell to foreign audiences eager to hear about the great Irish author. Behan is describing the sterile function which he performs, reduced to glorifying the works of the dead in return for the anaesthetic rewards of drunkenness. Kavanagh had warned of the dangers of this culture of indebtedness, and its stultifying effects on contemporary writing, in the very first issue of *Envoy* in late 1949: 'We must beware of looking for another Yeats. The enemies, or the fools, of art, always want another of the same thing. They worship yesterday's Phoenix.'[40] Kavanagh's agonistic wrangle was with Yeats more than Joyce, but still Kavanagh denounced the parasitical culture spawned in Joyce's wake in his

---

37 Quoted in B. Behan, *My Life with Brendan* (1973), p. 26.   **38** Quoted in T. Brown, *Ireland: A Social and Cultural History*, p. 227.   **39** Breandhán Ó Beacháin (B. Behan), 'Buiochas le Joyce' (Gratitude to Joyce), trans U. O'Connor, in *An Crann Faoi Blath: The Flowering Tree*, ed. D. Kiberd and G. Fitzmaurice (1991), pp 106–7.   **40** P. Kavanagh, 'Diary', *Envoy*, 1, no. 1 (December 1949), p. 90.

poem, 'Who Killed James Joyce?'[41] The problem for Behan and his contemporaries was not simply that the Irish literary revival and its exiles were becoming enshrined in national myth in the forties and fifties, but that writers such as Yeats and Joyce remained such powerful *presences* in Irish culture.

As Behan suggests in 'Buiochas le Joyce,' however, there was a considerable degree of cultural power conferred upon the emerging generation of Irish writers because of the achievements of Yeats and Joyce. The 'impact' of literary tradition on Behan is thus not entirely concomitant with notions of influence or inheritance, since Behan becomes in the scenario he depicts in the poem the mediator of Joyce's legacy, and thus has the responsibility of explaining and interpreting Joyce to his listeners. Behan is not, in other words, the passive recipient of Joyce's legacy, but in some respects, Joyce's presence or power depends upon the ways in which he is mediated by contemporary writers. Behan implies this mellifluous traffic of power in the second stanza of 'Buiochas le Joyce':

> If I were you
> And you were me,
> Coming from Les Halles
> Roaring, with a load of Cognac,
> Belly full, on the tipple,
> A verse or two in my honour you'd scribble.[42]

In contrast to the image of the parasitical heir of Joyce's literary authority which begins Behan's poem, in the second stanza Behan proposes reciprocity between the two. Behan imagines himself the equal of Joyce, capable equally of having parented Joyce's works as Joyce has parented Behan's. But what is perhaps surprising about Behan's poem of gratitude to Joyce is the absence of any form of Joycean influence in it. It was written in Gaelic, contains no recognisable Joycean traits or themes, and alludes to nothing specific in the Joycean oeuvre. Joyce simply stands as a named forebear, while Behan identifies himself as grateful, but commensurate, progeny. Implicit in Behan's progenic role is his power to represent, indeed to re-invent, Joyce.

'Every writer *creates* his own precursors,' Borges writes in his essay on Kafka. 'His work modifies our conception of the past.'[43] In paying homage to Joyce, and to O'Casey, Yeats and others, Behan is not only claiming their authority for his own work, but also proposing a genealogical tradition of which his work is the latest manifestation. When Behan describes *Ulysses* as a 'gag-book' therefore,

---

41 P. Kavanagh, 'Who Killed James Joyce?', *Envoy*, 5, no. 17 (April 1951), p. 12.   **42** Ó Beacháin, 'Buiochas le Joyce', in *An Crann Faoi Blath*, pp 106–7.   **43** J. L. Borges, *Labyrinths: Selected Stories and Other Writings* (1970), p. 236.

which he says is 'the way it should be read,'[44] he is inventing it primarily as a compendium of jokes because this is the image of *Ulysses* which would establish it as an antecedent of Behan's own writings. Behan used *Ulysses* simply as a source for 'gags,' which he repeated within his own plays, particularly in *The Hostage*. He used Joyce as a compendium of songs, too, emphasising Joyce's debt to popular culture, as well as his own. So too, when the characters of Behan's stories in the *Irish Press* talk of Yeats, they comically misattribute every song and poem they hear to the pen of 'Yeets,' who, in their eyes is a prolific songwriter and a poet of popular verse:

> 'If we only knew,
> What she was going to do,
> Did she but reach a decision
> And end our surmission.'

quoted Crippen, adding: 'Them lines is be Yeets.' He turned to me ... 'I was going to ask Behing here, this honorary journalist, whether he was familiar with that poem be Yeets that begins "O, to have a little house".'[45]

Yeats and Joyce appear in Behan's stories as household names, tripping off the tongues of working-class Dubliners. Mr Crippen, indeed, invents verses which he then attributes to the pen of Yeats, indicating that Behan's Dubliners know the value and cultural power of the names, and the authority which is derived through quotation and cultural reference. Yeats and Joyce, Behan suggests, belong as much to the street argot and popular music-hall culture of Mr Crippen, Mrs Brennan and Maria Concepta as to the scholarly heights of European modernism or what Behan decries, with reference to Yeats, as 'the present attempt to drag Irish writers who happened to be Protestant after the fox-hunt and the Royalist inanity,' as if, he continues, 'the most rapacious rack-renting class in Europe were really lamps of culture in a bog of darkness, doing good by stealth and shoving copies of *Horizon* under the half-doors of the peasantry after dark and making wedding presents to the cottagers of Ganymed [*sic*] Press productions of Gaugin.'[46] It is perhaps evident from this critique of the mythology surrounding the Anglo-Irish literary tradition that Behan was as much a student of Shavian wit as he was of Joyce's appropriation of popular culture. Shaw's 'Preface' to *John Bull's Other Island* was a favourite recital of his youth, and informed his class perspectives on Anglo-Irish relations throughout his work.

44 *Brendan Behan on Joyce*, Folkways Records FL9826. [Behan's lecture to the James Joyce Society in New York, 1960]   **45** B. Behan, 'Our Budding Genius Here', *Hold Your Hour And Have Another* (1965), p. 47.   **46** B. Behan, 'Letter to Sindbad Vail', in E.H. Mikhail (ed.), *The Letters of Brendan Behan*, p. 54.

Behan creates through allusion and quotation his own distinctive canon or tradition of Irish writers, from which he claims descent, and from which he derives his sense of cultural authority. There is, therefore, a considerable process of empowerment and legitimation taking place in Behan's use of other writers and texts, particularly when such 'parent' texts already possess a degree of cultural power. For the most part, this process performs a conservative function in the sense that Behan reiterates and consolidates the notion of a genealogical evolution of a distinctive and national Irish literary tradition, into which he inserts himself, and which he represents within the terms of cultural nationalism. But to observe Behan's appropriation of Joyce as a gag-writer or Yeats as a street-corner versifier is to recognise a process of transformation and subversion, whereby Behan subsumes the canonical figures of modern Irish literature within a diffuse, popular folk tradition. Behan's model of 'tradition' is the quotidian scattering of literary and poetical enunciation across the vibrant exchanges of the urban working class, so that the excerpted puns of Joyce or the abbreviated and muddled verses of Yeats circulate in fluid exchange with the folk proverbs and stories of popular culture. Put into such circulation, the cultural authority and creative originality of Behan's literary precursors are also undermined, since the free-flowing traffic between literary 'giants' and folk culture subverts the notion of 'tradition' as a selective, elitist canon which transmits the authority and originality of one generation to the next, along the lines of aristocratic genealogy. Behan's representation of 'tradition' is of the incessant recirculation of the same stories, gags, witticisms and songs, in which literary and cultural enunciations are no more than deft moves in a conversational game, and in which authority is derived through quotation rather than invention.

Quotation, parody and authority

Quotation is just one of the modes of derivation featured and deployed in Behan's writings. It was a device familiar to him at an early age from the conventions of Republican oratory, in which to learn and recite the words of canonical nationalist heroes such as Emmet or Tone was to invoke their authority and their approval. It is a device which he also incorporated into his works in various forms, in the speech of his characters, as well as in the intertextual exchanges between his writings and the 'parent' texts to which they allude and with which they converse. Even his comic representations of Joyce's writings as compendia of gags, puns and observations, and of Yeats as a song-writer and popular versifier, are derived from a book which he read voraciously and performed enthusiastically to Anthony Cronin, Frank Swinnerton's *The Georgian Literary Scene*. Cronin describes how Behan would regale him every morning with his imitations and parodies of the Georgian writers Swinnerton discusses, so that 'an encounter with Hilaire Belloc or a conversation with Arnold Bennett would become a theme of fantasy.'[47] Neither Cronin nor Behan could fail to have noticed Swinnerton's characterisations of Joyce and Yeats, in particular. Swinnerton saw Yeats essentially as a singer, his poems meant to be sung or chanted, rather than pondered over studiously,[48] while Joyce he regarded as one of those writers who 'notice and remember for ever headlines and solecisms in newspapers, the clichés of barmaids, slips made by common, genteel and ridiculous persons, smells, lingerie, betrayals of vulgarity, scandals about well-known persons, and the *faux pas* of ingénues.'[49] For Swinnerton, Joyce was close to hackery, his gift as a writer the result of a keen ear and a voluminous memory rather than a capacity for creative endeavour. This was, undoubtedly, a popular means to devalue Joyce as a writer prior to his elevation by Ellmann and others into a modernist icon. But for Behan, the intimacy which Swinnerton suggests Yeats and Joyce shared with popular culture could only elevate them in his eyes.

In his sketches for the *Irish Press*, Behan parodied the relationship between the 'great' writer and the popular cultural forms which Swinnerton lists. There Behan, described as 'a pudding cheenyuss' (budding genius) by Maria Concepta, appears mingling with the hacks, curates and street traders, exchanging stories and anecdotes with them. Behan's sketches pick up on the quick dialogue and its dependence on derivative forms and phrases:

> A VOICE (hoarse, relentless): 'Where were you in 'sixteen?'
> 'I wasn't born till 'twenty-three.'
> A.V.: 'Excuses ... always excuses.'
> ('You borrowed that from *Living with Lynch*.' 'I stole it, sir. An artist never borrows.')[50]

In this sketch, 'Dialogue on Literature,' published in January 1956, the pub conversations overheard by the narrator are marked by the casual quotation of well-known quips and comic exchanges, so much so that even when one of the speakers is accused of quotation he replies with another quotation. This endless recirculation of familiar jokes and phrases may appear to be a symptom of cultural exhaustion, but for the gusto with which these conversations are conducted. In the ensuing lines, Behan is accused by 'the Rasher' Cambel of attacking in print 'a real writer': 'one whose name will not be found on the flyleaf of thick volumes, but whose more delicate moods ... whose happiest

---

47 A. Cronin, *Dead as Doornails*, p. 26.   **48** F. Swinnerton, *The Georgian Literary Scene: A Panorama* (1935), p. 271.   **49** Ibid., p. 433.   **50** B. Behan, 'Dialogue on Literature', *Hold Your Hour and Have Another*, p. 43.

sentiments may be found ...' to which Crippen adds the familiar phrase, 'In the slim sheaf of verse ... [r]edolent of the faintest faery feylike feeling.'[51] Crippen's interjection reveals that the Rasher's poetic celebration of the 'real writer,' and his accusation of Behan, has been rehearsed and repeated before. Behan and the Rasher accuse each other of hackery, the same accusation which Behan has levelled at the Rasher's writer friend, but Crippen exposes the dialogue between the two 'hacks' as a rehearsed, comic routine. Both Crippen and the Rasher engage in a parodic stylisation of the intellectual language in which poetry and hackery are opposite poles in the cultural spectrum. Parody in this instance, in keeping with the subversive potential of mimicry in general, serves to under-mine the pretensions of this distinction. The Rasher's acclamation of the 'delicate moods' of the poet is, it turns out, an affectation performed for amusement, while the 'budding genius' himself, Behan, is the butt of the humour which resolves the dialogue:

> 'Never mind poor Brending Behing,' said Crippen, 'he doesn't know what he writes.'
> 'How so?' asked the Rasher.
> 'Sad case,' said Crippen, looking at me with commiseration. 'Only went to school half the time, when they were teaching the writing – can't read.'[52]

In his sketches for the *Irish Press*, Behan created a cast of characters who were earthy and blunt, yet whose conversations were sprinkled with literary anec-dotes and witticisms. His characters circulate on the fringes of a pseudo-literary culture or coterie, and serve to bring the 'real' writers down to earth, hence Crippen's well-worn joke at Behan's expense suggesting illiteracy. So too, when Maria Concepta refers to Behan as 'pudding cheenyuss,' she adds sarcastically, 'you've the shape of wan, anyway,' a quip which circumvents the idiolectic spelling of 'budding' to allude to Behan's 'pudding' shape.[53] Self-deprecation and parody is a consistent feature of Behan's representation of himself as narrator in the sketches, and much of the humour revolves around deflating the pretensions and pomp of being a 'real' writer.

The deflated role of the writer in Behan's sketches is characteristic of his representations of authorship in general. On the opening night of *The Quare Fellow*, Behan declared 'I did not write this play – the lags wrote it.'[54] Behan puts this disclaimer into the mouths of the characters in *The Hostage*, when Pat ponders in Act Two if the play has an author, and the hostage and the IRA officer proceed to mock the author for his irreverence. He also informed his audiences

51 Ibid., p. 45.   52 Ibid., p. 46.   53 Ibid., p. 47.   54 Quoted in 'Theatre Workshop', *The Times*, May 25th 1956, p. 3.

in London that *The Hostage* was written by himself, his uncle [P.J. Bourke] and 'Trad.,' an attribution which is as generous in its debt to his playwright and theatre-manager uncle, as it is elusive in its invocation of tradition.[55] By no stretch of the imagination could it be argued that Behan avoided the cult of the personality which accompanied success and renown as an author, but the function of the author as creative source is repudiated, or at the very least resisted, in his writings. Behan's attribution of *The Quare Fellow* to 'the lags' is not just an acknowledgement of a very real debt – he did borrow the keynote song of the play, 'The Old Triangle,' from a fellow inmate of Mountjoy prison, and adapted the story of a real case of a murderer's execution, Bernard Kirwan. It is also an admission of the significance of the folk culture, speech and song in which Behan was immersed. This admission is implicit in Behan's sketches, for if he represents his characters as endlessly recycling the same songs, puns and anecdotes, then he represents his own role as author as an extension of this process. The stories and comic routines of his subjects are his stock-in-trade, and he rarely adds comment, irony or explanation to their offerings.

Behan's deflation of the role of the author in his sketches, and his attribution of authorship to various sources in his plays, might seem to some to anticipate the ways in which Behan would later relinquish authority in collaborations with Alan Simpson, Carolyn Swift and Joan Littlewood. Simpson described Behan as 'an extremely co-operative author ... [who] permitted my wife [Carolyn Swift] to cut and arrange various parts of the dialogue, and me to change the title.'[56] Simpson and Swift produced *The Quare Fellow* at the Pike Theatre in Dublin in 1954, but not before they had persuaded Behan (without much effort, it seems) to change the title from *The Twisting of Another Rope* (an allusion to Douglas Hyde's *Casadh an tSugáin* (*The Twisting of the Rope*), and tidied his script into a more amenable dramatic structure. Behan's tendencies to allow his producers and editors to adjust and alter his manuscripts became the stuff of legend, however, when he worked with Joan Littlewood's Theatre Workshop in London. According to Wolf Mankowitz, Behan spent most of his time 'pissed out of his mind,' while Littlewood and her cast improvised and rewrote the script of *The Hostage*:

> Joan took a play to pieces and she put it back together again with actor inserts, ad libs and catch phrases. Sometimes it worked, sometimes it didn't. Often in rewriting, the original idea was lost. I had to fight her for the survival of script. It was still only fifty-fifty in the end. Brendan didn't care. He was pissed out of his mind anyway when half the changes were made.[57]

55 Quoted in Kenneth Tynan, 'New Amalgam', *The Observer*, October 19th 1958, p. 19. 56 A. Simpson, *Beckett and Behan and a Theatre in Dublin* (1962), pp 40–41. 57 Quoted in U. O'Connor,

Mankowitz believed that Behan's play suffered from Littlewood's influence, and Ulick O'Connor quotes a number of Theatre Workshop playwrights voicing their resentment of the changes which Littlewood encouraged her actors to make. In the case of *The Hostage*, Littlewood pleads a case of necessity, since Behan spent so much time and energy getting drunk that he left Theatre Workshop without a script until days before the opening night. Littlewood records that her partner, Gerry Raffles, grew so exasperated at Behan that he threatened Behan with a large pistol: 'See that? If you don't finish that *******
play, I'll kill you.'[58] Littlewood's account of the process by which *The Hostage* emerged in the shape it did records no sense of resentment on Behan's part at the co-operative process which Theatre Workshop employed. Brendan's brother, Brian, however, recalled that Brendan was unhappy with Littlewood's production. 'Fuck Joan Littlewood,' said Brendan to his brother on the opening night in Stratford East:

> I was surprised and I looked at him closely. He looked suddenly as if he knew he had been 'taken for a ride,' that he had been adopted as a broth of a boy, that they had played a three card trick on him.[59]

If Brian Behan interpreted Brendan's looks correctly, it seems that the author was glimpsing the dangers of ceding authority, aghast at what he had allowed others to make out of his play. In Littlewood's hands, according to Declan Kiberd, *The Hostage* became a play 'calculated to appeal to Princess Margaret and the fashionable, *avant-garde* first-night audience.'[60] The conversion of Behan's Gaelic play, *An Giall*, into the music-hall variety show which Littlewood produced in London represents for a number of critics Behan's capacity for betraying his authorial responsibility and integrity in order to win fame and success. Richard Wall makes this argument from a close inspection of both *An Giall* and *The Hostage*,[61] while others, such as Ulick O'Connor and Declan Kiberd, make this point more generally in relation to Behan's oeuvre.

It is difficult to contest the argument that Behan ceded authorial control of his play, but that this was in some ways treacherous or irresponsible is to add a moral dimension to the question of authorial originality. The author who credited variously 'the lags,' his uncle, and 'Trad.,' with responsibility for his plays, and who represented authorship in his sketches as the passive recircula-tion of folk stories and comic routines which have been continually recycled already, was also the author who shared and learned from Littlewood's

---

Brendan Behan, p. 208.   **58** J. Littlewood, *Joan's Book: Joan Littlewood's Peculiar History As She Tells It* (1995), p. 529.   **59** Quoted in U. O'Connor, *Brendan Behan*, p. 220.   **60** D. Kiberd, *Inventing Ireland: The Literature of the Modern Nation* (1995), p. 520.   **61** See R. Wall's introduction to B. Behan, *An Giall/The Hostage* (1987), pp 1–21.

insistence on co-operative authorship of plays. 'Joan Littlewood ... suited my requirements exactly,' wrote Behan, preferring Littlewood's aspiration towards the theatre of music hall to the 'Abbey Theatre naturalism' which guided the director of Behan's *An Giall*, Frank Dermody.[62] Behan participated in Little-wood's workshops in the same spirit of ad-libbing and improvisation as she encouraged in her cast, giving no indication that he felt himself in any way above the cast as artistic creator. According to both Littlewood and Behan's wife, Beatrice, who accompanied him while he was in London preparing his play, Brendan welcomed and encouraged the collaborative assembly of the scenes, songs, dialogue and jokes which made up *The Hostage*.[63]

In his later years, when he grew increasingly incapable physically of writing and editing his own manuscripts, Behan would record his anecdotes and thoughts on tape, and his editors gave his final publications their shape and structure. This was the case in *Brendan Behan's Island*, *Brendan Behan's New York*, and *Confessions of an Irish Rebel*. Behan anticipated the accusations that his recordings were unliterary, and the product of laziness on his part: 'If the Mycenaean Greek Poets could do it; then so can I.'[64] Although the idea of tape recordings tapping into an ancient oral tradition of storytelling undoubtedly had its appeal to Behan, his defensiveness revealed a frustrated desire to continue being a writer. As his biographers have charted, his declining health due to a dangerous combination of diabetes and alcoholism meant that he was incapable of sustaining the stamina required to write a book. Consequently his editors became the unacknowledged co-authors of his final works, a trend of collaborative authorship which can be traced to varying degrees throughout his writing career.

'If this thing has an author ...'

Sean Burke argues that theories of authorship 'cannot withstand the practice of reading, for there is not an absolute *cogito* of which individual authors are the subalternant manifestations.'[65] Consequently, the model of literary authorship varies not only from writer to writer, but also within one writer's oeuvre, and indeed from reading to reading. Nevertheless, we can discern in Behan's writings in general a distinctive, socialised notion of authorship, from his early imitations of patriotic verse to his later tape recordings. The socialised author is one whose textual productions are manifestly the result of collaborations, whether actual collaborations of authors, editors and theatre companies, or the

---

62 B. Behan, *Brendan Behan's Island* (1965), p. 17.   **63** B. Behan, *My Life with Brendan*, p. 84.   **64** Quoted in U. O'Connor, *Brendan Behan*, p. 249.   **65** S. Burke, *The Death and Return of the Author: Criticism and Subjectivity in Barthes, Foucault and Derrida* (1992), p. 173.

less palpable kinds of collaboration which can be discerned in the relationship between texts and their precursors or contemporaries. As Jack Stillinger argues, 'literature has been produced in response to a range of extrinsically exerted requests, demands and pressures, many of which in effect become intrinsic elements in the process of creation.'[66] Behan's responses to the work of other writers and texts, through imitation and parody, for example, are thus acknowledging the dialogic element in literary creativity, and resisting the concept of monologic literary authority. The idea of the socialised author refuses the modernist (particularly Eliotic) model of authorial invisibility, just as it refuses the interpenetration of art and biography in Yeats. Behan is ever present in his own work, not least because he interrupted performances of his own plays, introduced himself as a character into his sketches, and made himself the central character and narrator of his autobiographical novel, *Borstal Boy*. The historical author is thus impossible to evade, but he is nonetheless a decentred author in the sense that his texts constantly reveal through quotation, mimicry and parody the extent to which he is merely a mediator between text and 'tradition.'

There are a number of intertextual mediations which figure prominently in the relationship between Behan's writings and those of his perceived forebears, and indeed his contemporaries, and which highlight both the derivative nature of much of Behan's work and the adaptive capacity of Behan as a writer. Such exchanges vary from perceived plagiarism to loosely comparable structures or themes. Perhaps most famously, Behan was accused of plagiarising Frank O'Connor's story, 'Guests of the Nation,' in his play, *The Hostage*. O'Connor recorded on the occasion of Behan's death that Behan had once admitted plagiarism to him: 'Ah, sure, of course I stole the ******* thing.'[67] He borrowed in more detail from Joyce's *Ulysses*, *A Portrait of the Artist as a Young Man*, and *Dubliners*. Behan borrowed the song 'The Old Triangle' which is used as a structuring device in *The Quare Fellow* from a fellow prisoner in Mountjoy, whom he is reputed later to have acknowledged both verbally and financially.[68] Many of his songs, jokes and stories, in fact, are borrowed from oral sources, and this is perhaps inevitable and even laudable in a writer for whom orality and colloquialism were important dimensions in bridging the divide between popular and high culture, and in preserving the music-hall roots of his art. In terms of Behan's intertextual exchanges on thematic or structural bases, his short stories tend to be modelled on Joyce's *Dubliners*, while his stories and anecdotes in the *Irish Press* partly derived from the style and character of Myles

66 J. Stillinger, *Multiple Authorship and the Myth of Solitary Genius* (1991), p. 182.   67 F. O'Connor, 'He was so much larger than life', *Sunday Independent*, 22 March 1964, p. 7.   68 M. Ó hAodha, 'Breandán Ó Beacháin – The Behan I Knew', in V. Uíbh Eachach and D. Ó Faoláin (eds), *Féile Zozimus: Volume 2 – Brendan Behan: The Man, The Myth, The Genius* (1993), p. 25.

na Gopaleen's column for the *Irish Times*, and partly also from J.B. Morton's columns in the *Daily Express* and Robert Lynd's essays in the *New Statesman*. *Borstal Boy* imitates the conventions of Republican prison narratives up to a certain point, particularly John Mitchel's *Jail Journal* and Thomas Clarke's *Glimpses of an Irish Felon's Prison Life*. *The Quare Fellow* models itself on the structure and themes of Wilde's *The Ballad of Reading Gaol*, as well as exercising a significant adaptation of Synge's *The Playboy of the Western World*. *The Hostage* borrows from the conventions of popular nationalist melodramas by Dion Boucicault, J.W. Whitbread and Henry Connell Mangan. Some of these inter-textual exchanges are the self-conscious projections and inventions of the author – Behan's figuring of himself as the heir of specific literary and cultural traditions – while others are exemplary of the inadvertent repetition of conventional forms, devices or stories circulating within a particular discursive field.

In defining intertextuality, John Frow argues that texts are 'shaped by the repetition and the transformation of other textual structures.'[69] In Behan's case, it is not only other literary texts and conventions which are repeated and integrated in his writings, but also a wider field of oral and colloquial traces. In order to produce in a study of Behan's writings what Frow calls 'an account of the work performed upon intertextual material and its functional integration in the later text,'[70] one would have to analyse, for example, the recirculation of music-hall jokes and folk proverbs, as well as the interactions with the literary canon. Behan's writings, in this sense, are composite structures, comprising the heteroglossic repetition and adaptation of pre-existing oral and textual materials. *The Hostage*, for example, while it borrows the conventions of plot and tragic resolution of the political melodrama, also uses those conventions as a frame on which to hang a series of jokes, puns, proverbs, songs, and imitations. The first act of the play alone contains two wild dances and eleven songs, some of which are comic, others political, while the characters weave into their dialogue nine proverbs and no less than thirty-seven jokes or witticisms. 'The tone of the opening of *The Hostage* is that of a stage-Irish interlude,' writes Richard Wall, 'and such interludes interrupt the play with monotonous regularity.'[71] Wall clearly implies his distaste for the music-hall elements of *The Hostage*, but even in the more conventional play, *An Giall*, which Wall prefers, the plot is frequently suspended or drawn out to allow for the regular incursion of songs, dances, proverbs and jokes. Such ingredients are not there in either play to compel the drama forward, but to infuse the theatre with the quotidian comic utterances and common folk songs of urban working-class culture. According to Joan Littlewood, these ingredients were added to *The Hostage* by

69 J. Frow, 'Intertextuality and Ontology', in M. Worton and J. Still (eds), *Intertextuality: Theories and Practices* (1990), p. 44.   70 Ibid., p. 45.   71 R. Wall, 'Introduction' to B. Behan, *An Giall/The Hostage*, p. 13.

a process of accretion, in which Behan phoned from pubs or scribbled notes with additional jokes, songs, or character idiosyncrasies while Littlewood and her cast ad-libbed and improvised other additions to the play.[72] 'The most difficult part,' Littlewood adds, 'was holding on to the theme and sustaining the tension behind the jokes and the laughter as the threatened execution of the hostage drew near.'[73] Beatrice Behan also records how Behan overheard songs and jokes in pubs in Blackheath, and integrated them into the play:

> Brendan was ready to embrace Rose, the barmaid at The Dragon. 'I don't care what they do, Brendan,' Rose had said, 'as long as they don't muck about with the moon.'
>
> There was a chorus of agreement among the regulars. The Russians had sent their satellite around the earth, and Rose was worried. Brendan reached across the bar and kissed her. 'Rose, daughter, you've given me the title for a song.'[74]

Miss Gilchrist sings this song in *The Hostage*, complete with references to Macmillan 'that multi-racial coon,' 'empire lamb,' and Kruschev.[75] As Pat ponders in the second act of the play on whether 'this *thing*' has an author, and indeed as Anthony Cronin suggests in his description of Behan's search for a form which would contain his particular gifts as comic, parodic imitator and storyteller, Behan's *The Hostage* evolved in amorphous, frivolous directions, becoming the cabaret form to which it was indebted. In assembling his play for production, Behan embraced the role of socialised author, collecting and testing his songs, stories and jokes in the pubs of Dublin and London. The pub cultures of both cities were the scenes of his gradual decline into alcoholic illness, but they were also the collaborative laboratories in which he could gather and play out the materials of his art.

Tradition and transgression

'Ireland is a figment of the Anglo-Saxon imagination,' Behan once wrote. The ease with which Behan found fame and notoriety in England, and drew the materials for his plays and writings from the urban folk cultures of London as much as Dublin, inspires many of Behan's critics as well as his biographers to attribute Behan's downfall to what Ulick O'Connor calls 'the fatal formula ... of how to play Paddy to the Saxon.'[76] Behan played up to that 'figment of the Anglo-Saxon imagination,' and gave his English public the raucous, drunken, gabby stereotype which they had paid to see. At least this is how the myth of

72 J. Littlewood, *Joan's Book*, pp pp 527–29. 73 Ibid., p. 529. 74 Beatrice Behan, *My Life with Brendan*, p. 137. 75 B. Behan, *An Giall/The Hostage*, p. 157. 76 U. O'Connor, *Brendan Behan*, p. 63.

Behan's transgression of the mores of Irish cultural nationalism accounts for the roaring success of Behan in England and the United States. Behan's undoing was his transgression of the ideological parameters of post-independence cultural nationalism. He abandoned the fledgling attempts to promote a modern literature in Gaelic (supposedly the official language of the Irish Republic), writing in complaint of his inclusion by Daniel Corkery in a list of promising young Gaelic writers: 'I don't know the half of these geezers and am in no way responsible for having my name stuck in among theirs.'[77] He also sold the rights (and, according to Richard Wall, the integrity) of his plays in English to the more imperious domain of Joan Littlewood's theatre in London's East End, and subsequently to the West End. The neo-colonial terms with which English reviewers greeted Behan's plays, and the seemingly imperialist methods which Littlewood deployed in her revision of *The Hostage* for the London stage, all appeared to confirm the worst nationalist fears for the fate of an Irish writer appropriated to the cause of English theatre. If, as W.J. McCormack has observed, 'no discernible effort was made by major Irish writers to respond to the new cultural objectives of the state' in the post-independence period,[78] Behan bucked the nationalist trend still further by appearing to some to return the Irish writer to the eighteenth-century tradition of the servile stage-Irish buffoon. Such a myth of Behan's transgression is, however, to confuse the sordid details of Behan's personal descent into alcohol abuse and attention-seeking, with the effective revisionism and critical incision of his writings.

Behan's writings refuse the puritan nationalism of the post-independence state, for even in his Gaelic writings, for example, he celebrates Bacchanalian drunkenness and Wildean bisexuality, and denounces the Irish-Ireland 'foolishness':

> Civil Servants from Corchauguiney
> Other eejits from Donegal foreshore,
> Clodhoppers from Galway to make my head sore.
> Dublin Gaels afflicted with fáinnes
> Puerile pioneers, pansified and punctured,
> Vacant virgins, vehement and vulgar.
> All dedicated to prudence and piety.[79]

---

77 For the list of promising young Gaelic writers, see Daniel Corkery, 'The Hidden Force in Irish Revival', *The Sunday Press*, 4 May 1952. Behan had had some of his Gaelic poems published in *Nuabhearsaiocht* (1950), which became an important anthology of contemporary Gaelic poets in the fifties. Corkery's list was ridiculed in 'The Old Foolishness' column of *Kavanagh's Weekly* in 1952, and Behan's response came in the form of a letter to the editor, published in *Kavanagh's Weekly*, 1, no. 6 (May 1952), p. 5. 78 W.J. McCormack, *From Burke to Beckett: Ascendancy Tradition and Betrayal in Literary History* (1994), p. 376. 79 B. Behan, 'Guidhe an Rannaire'/ 'The Versemaker's

For Behan, the resurgent attempts in the post-independence period to revive the use of the Gaelic language, and to 'purify' Ireland of its colonial legacy, were ridiculous in their underlying assumption of the mutual exclusivity of all things Irish and English. Consequently, he caricatured the figures of Gaelic revival in both his Irish and English language writings. Monsewer and the IRA Officer of *An Giall* and *The Hostage* extend Behan's scorn of the 'Puerile pioneers' and 'Vacant virgins' satirised in 'Guidhe an Rannaire' above. As Beatrice Behan records in her account of her marriage, Brendan Behan was accepted in the Gaeltachts of Connemara and the Aran islands, finding there a bawdy, unbridled culture similar to his own inner-city people, and antithetical to the Irish-Ireland of de Valera's reactionary ideologues. Behan's construction of the relationship between English and Irish cultures defied the mutual exclusivity posited in the worst excesses of cultural nationalist ideology. In place of the assumption of exclusivity, Behan mischievously offered a vision of the hybrid popular culture which was the common inheritance of Britain and Ireland:

> Such differences as exist between Britain and Ireland nowadays are due more to economics and to social environment than to racial characteristics. The two nations are inextricably mixed up and little in the way of national characteristics divide them. If you go into a pub in Manchester, Belfast, Dublin, Liverpool or London, you will hear people sing one song which might almost be their National Anthem: *I've got a lovely bunch of coconuts*, and their second favourite is *Nellie Dean*.[80]

Such a revisionist demolition of the notion of a distinctive national Irish identity and culture might well startle those expecting Behan to retain at least the ideological assumptions of his early Republicanism. It reveals instead the extent to which Behan was capable of proclaiming mature reflections even on those less palatable consequences of colonial culture, that modern Irish culture was largely indistinct from modern Anglophone culture in general, that there was little basis for a discrete Irish literature, or culture, or even nation.

'Ireland ... is not a piece of America, nor yet a piece of England,' wrote Behan, 'It's a different place.'[81] Despite this assertion of the residual difference between Ireland and the Anglophone world, Behan was drawn towards those anecdotes and myths of Ireland which revealed its cultural hybridity. In *Brendan Behan's Island*, his tape-recorded travelogue of Irish life, he celebrated Belfast, 'that Manchester-like city,' as 'the heart of proletarian Ireland.'[82] So too, in commenting upon the symbolic core of Celtic revival 'Irishness,' the Aran islands, Behan recalled approvingly Liam O'Flaherty's claim that the Aran

Wish', trans. U. O'Connor, *Life Styles* (1973), p. 32. **80** B. Behan, *Brendan Behan's Island*, p. 75. **81** Ibid., p. 191. **82** Ibid., p. 172.

islanders were descendents of Cromwell's army, and that the islanders still spoke in their native Gaelic with Cockney accents.[83] In *The Hostage*, Behan's characters referred to Ireland in the same breath as other colonial trouble-spots – Cyprus, Kenya and Suez – implying the incontrovertible colonial history which Ireland shared with India, Kenya or the West Indies. But Behan was also attracted to the notion of Ireland as a prototypical metropolitan colony, at one and the same time the victim and the collaborator in England's empire. Behan's Ireland struggled for the prestige and dignity of independence, while at the same time profoundly ambivalent about its shared cultural inheritance with England. If Behan in his early writings remained immersed in the narrative tradition of divinely-sanctioned revolutionary violence against England, in his later writings he reveals a more subtle critical nationalism, which as much as it retains in its sights the dreadful legacy of colonialism, recognises also the inextricable cultural and social bonds which crossed the Irish sea.

In common with many of his contemporaries, Behan's critical nationalism was a reaction against what Benedict Kiely called the 'grocer's republic,'[84] the economically-backward, culturally-insulated, priest-ridden Ireland of the thirties and forties. Behan's fondness for recalling instances and situations of cultural hybridity was, in many senses, a response to the abortive attempts in the early decades of the twentieth century to reconstruct Irish language, culture and identity *ab origine*, as if undisturbed by the course of colonial history. In an article in the *Irish Press* he denounced the attempt by the Irish-Ireland movement of the revival to impose a phoney, Gaelic league-sanctioned culture in place of the folk-culture of working-class Dubliners, which it attempted to obliterate as nothing more than neo-colonial propaganda.[85] It was part of his role as the socialised author mediating between the oral and folk traditions of his working-class upbringing and the literary cultures of mid-century Dublin and London to recall in song and dialogue what he called, with ironic reference to Corkery, 'the hidden Ireland of the slums.'

Behan was one of the principal revisionist writers of his generation, following in the footsteps of Joyce, O'Casey and O'Faolain in calling to attention the cultural oversights and myopia of the new dispensation in Irish cultural nationalism. He represented himself as the progeny of Irish nationalist literary tradition, partly in order to borrow the authority and force of tradition, but also in order to revise and subvert its precepts. 'One must have tradition in oneself, to hate it properly,' wrote Theodor Adorno,[86] which, in Behan's case, applies not to the Eurocentric modernity of which Adorno was speaking, but to the

83 Ibid., p. 131.   84 Quoted in Augustine Martin, 'Inherited Dissent: The Dilemma of the Irish Writer', *Bearing Witness: Essays on Anglo-Irish Literature*, ed. Anthony Roche (1996), p. 87.   85 B. Behan, 'Up the Ballad Singers', *Hold Your Hour and Have Another*, pp 31–34.   86 Theodor W. Adorno, *Minima Moralia: Reflections from Damaged Life*, trans. E.F.N. Jephcott (1978), p. 52.

'Irish-Ireland' nationalism which had ensconced itself in the early decades of the twentieth century. To hate tradition properly, in Adorno's terms, was not to reject it, but rather to commit oneself to its thorough critique and revision. Behan required the idea of a distinctly 'Irish' tradition in order to establish his own credentials as its heir and progeny, but in his writings it was subject to his constant, corrective attempts to 'hate tradition properly.'[87]

87 See N. Lazarus, *Nationalism and Cultural Practice in the Postcolonial World* (1999), who uses Adorno's call to 'hate tradition properly' as an appropriate description of the position of post-colonial intellectuals in relation to Eurocentric modernity. See in particular Lazarus' introduction, pp 1–15.

2 / Early writings: language, style and politics

The storyteller

'The storyteller takes what he tells from experience – his own or that reported by others. And he in turn makes it the experience of those who are listening to his tale.'[1] Walter Benjamin argues that the figure of the storyteller embodies the social rituals of legitimation and conferral, drawing authority from his capacity to relate stories to others, while simultaneously passing on the power of narrative to his listeners. Accordingly, as Ross Chambers has pointed out, the storyteller cedes his authority even as he exercises it, for in the act of disclosing his narrative 'secret' or germ, he ceases to possess and control its dissemination.[2] The storyteller is, thus, in classic Barthesian terms, the author of his own disappearance, which Benjamin acknowledges in the conclusion to his essay when he writes that the storyteller 'is the man who could let the wick of his life be consumed completely by the gentle flame of his story.'[3]

The basis both for the social significance of the storyteller and of his dissolution in the act of telling is the infinite iterability of the story. 'Storytelling,' Benjamin writes, 'is always the art of repeating stories.'[4] As such, it is at once both conservative and transitory, evoking the notion of a tradition in which stories are authorised and reproduced, and of their momentary value and consumption, usually for the purposes either of entertainment or education. For Benjamin, storytelling was an artisan craft of direct communication, in which the teller fashioned the 'raw material of experience' into something 'solid, useful.'[5] In contrast to the totalising speculation of the novel, stories were the vehicles of a kind of folk wisdom, and storytellers were akin to 'teachers and sages,' with 'counsel' to offer the many.[6] The authority of the storyteller is thus derived from the form itself, conferred upon the storyteller by his listeners in anticipation of a useful or gratifying narrative of experience or wisdom, the narrative itself in turn extending the compass of the listeners' own repertoire of stories.

The act of storytelling which Benjamin describes acquired considerable symbolic significance in the Irish revival of the late nineteenth and early

---

1 W. Benjamin, *Illuminations*, trans. Harry Zohn (1992), p. 87.   2 R. Chambers, *Story and Situation: Narrative Seduction and the Power of Fiction* (1984), pp 50–51.   3 Benjamin, *Illuminations*, p. 107.   4 Ibid., p. 90.   5 Ibid., p. 107.   6 Ibid., p. 107.

twentieth centuries, in both oral and written forms. It served as a model form of continuity and authority in which nationalist myths of tradition and legitimacy were both mirrored and disseminated. In the nationalist imagination of the late nineteenth century, storytelling figured both the intimacy of the national community and the endurance of dissident popular cultural forms. The movement to preserve, collect, revise, and popularise Irish folk tales in written form led in turn to the emergence of storytelling as a powerful trope of authority and conferral in literary nationalism. The recurrent nationalist motifs of popular folk tales, which functioned to delineate and define distinguishing characteristics of Irish culture, found a new form in the development of the Irish short story.

Benjamin argues that the short story is a reductive manifestation of the oral story form, 'which no longer permits that slow piling one on top of the other of thin, transparent layers which constitutes the most appropriate picture of the way in which the perfect narrative is revealed through the layers of a variety of retellings.'[7] Irish short story writers in the early twentieth century did not, in Benjamin's words, 'remove themselves from oral tradition,' however, but adopted the tropes and styles of oral fiction within the conventions of the written form. Thus writers such as Daniel Corkery, Liam O'Flaherty, Seamus O'Kelly, Frank O'Connor and Sean O'Faolain, although they departed from the folk and mythological themes of the oral storyteller, retained the narrative styles and addressive devices of the storyteller, and, it could be argued, appropriated the symbolic power of storytelling into the emergent genre of Irish short story writing. Such an act of appropriation was not unremarked, and indeed was parodied and satirised in the fictions of James Joyce, Samuel Beckett and, especially, Flann O'Brien.

The short fictions written by Brendan Behan between 1941 and 1953, however, maintain to a large extent the narrative conventions of oral storytelling, at least in the same form as practised by Behan's post-revival precursors, Corkery, O'Faolain and O'Connor. The argument of this section of the chapter is that Behan's stories reflect the thematic concerns and stylistic tendencies of nationalist short story writing, but that increasingly Behan's stories become stories about storytelling, about the formal exercise of narrative authority.[8] Read in this way, as considerations of the power and performance of narrative, Behan's stories reveal themselves to be more than thinly-masked autobiographical sketches, but also multi-layered reflexive narratives, more interested in style than plot. Before he abandoned the short story form, Behan used the form to reflect on the persuasive and, more specifically, seductive power of

---

7 Ibid., p. 92.   8 The exception to this is the story Behan published in various forms in the fifties, 'A Woman of No Standing', which explores themes of morality and shame within a realist setting.

narrative, and thus began to consider the properties which rendered narrative such a potent tool of political and cultural nationalism.

Behan thematises the ritual conferral and dissemination of narrative authority in his first piece of published writing, a short story entitled 'A Tantalising Tale,' which he published in a Republican journal, *Fianna*, in June 1936, when he was just thirteen years old. The title refers to the tale which is told within the story by an experienced narrator to his four younger guests, in a manner reminiscent of H.G. Wells' *The Time Machine*. Experience is foregrounded from the beginning as the necessary predicate of narrative disclosure. '"You ought to have some story worth relating," said the young Kerry O/C as we sat in my library after the Fianna Ard Fheis.'[9] The opening line establishes the narrator as a figure of authority, empowered to impart a story of 'worth' to his interested listeners. The narrator quickly establishes his credentials for speaking:

> I was out, you see, in the '67 Rising and had to clear the country, like many a better man. But the long years in the States had not changed my outlook and views, and I had been heart and soul with the men of '16 and '22. I had always had a great admiration for the young lads of Na Fianna Éireann... I supported them morally and financially – a surprising thing, you will, maybe, say in one who is almost a millionaire![10]

Behan ventriloquises the voice of a man who is mature, rich, powerful, and a veteran supporter of the nationalist cause. In a magazine devoted to the youth wing of the IRA the credentials of Behan's narrator could hardly have been much more impressive. Behan's story from the beginning equates the power to speak, to narrate, with the social and political credibility of the speaker, the authority which the narrator commands in his listeners.

The tale itself, as Ted Boyle recognises, 'is not much better than what one would expect from an intelligent thirteen-year-old,'[11] concerning a mysterious ring acquired by the narrator on his travels which involves him in all sorts of trouble and causes inexplicable intrigue wherever he goes. It concludes by returning to the scene in which the narrator is relating his tale to his listeners: 'they looked at each other and grinned. It was certainly, they agreed, a tantalising tale.'[12] Although the 'tantalising tale' itself is unremarkable, the use of frameworks in which the act of storytelling is itself fictionalised advertises a certain reflexivity in Behan's techniques. Behan's first story represents a scene of oral communication within the written form, and maintains the immediacy of speech which Benjamin celebrates in 'The Storyteller.'[13] Thus, Behan contrives

9 B. O Beachain, 'A Tantalising Tale', *Fianna* (June 1936), p. 30. 10 Ibid., p. 30. 11 Ted Boyle, *Brendan Behan* (1969), p. 49. 12 O Beachain, 'A Tantalising Tale', p. 30. 13 Benjamin, *Illuminations*, p. 84. Benjamin writes that 'Experience which is passed on from mouth to mouth is

to effect the illusion of vocal presence, and to draw the authority of the socially symbolic act of storytelling into the narrative frameworks of his fiction.

The effect of vocal presence is a consistent feature of all of Behan's short stories, which are modelled upon the intimacy and performance of storytelling, and which derive their narrative interest from the categorical authority of 'experience.' Two of Behan's stories, 'The Execution' and 'I Become a Borstal Boy,' draw upon the veneration of nationalist narratives of struggle and adventure for their narrative compulsion. 'I Become a Borstal Boy' is narrated by a sixteen-year-old remand prisoner on the day he is to be sentenced for an unspecified crime, who reports dispassionately on the concurrent hanging of two Republican prisoners in Birmingham, and on a fellow inmate who is sentenced to death in the same court. What happens to the narrator himself is of little significance – he is given a mandatory sentence of three years borstal detention for a crime which he records but does not explain or consider. The narrator's authority derives not from the interest of his own court experiences, but instead from his proximity to sensational events – amidst Republican prisoners when they react to the hangings, and in the cell next door to a condemned man. Here, the storyteller capitalises on his situation, on his contiguity to a 'story worth relating.'

'I Become a Borstal Boy' was published in *The Bell* in June 1942, and marked Behan's literary debut, since it was encouraged and accepted by Sean O'Faolain and Peadar O'Donnell, both highly respected in the world of Irish fiction. As an apparently autobiographical account of Behan's experiences as a captured IRA volunteer in Walton jail in Liverpool, the story conformed to the generic conventions of narratives of militant nationalism, such as Dan Breen's *My Fight for Irish Freedom* (1924), Ernie O'Malley's *On Another Man's Wound* (1936), and Tom Barry's *Guerrilla Days in Ireland* (1949). The aftermath of Irish independence witnessed an upsurge in autobiographical accounts of the actions and adventures of Republican heroes, each account staking its authority on the personal experiences and endeavours of its teller. Perhaps more important for Behan, however, was the fact that the literary careers of the most celebrated 'men of letters' in the Irish Free State – Sean O'Faolain and Frank O'Connor – were built on collections of short stories representing the struggle for independence. O'Connor published his collection, *Guests of the Nation* in 1931, followed by O'Faolain who published *Midsummer Night Madness and Other Stories* in the following year.

Both 'I Become a Borstal Boy' and 'The Execution' are, to appropriate Althusser's term, 'interpellated' through nationalist fictions and iconography, situating the subjectivity of the narrator within the bounds of post-independence, Catholic nationalist Ireland. Like the fictions of O'Connor and O'Faolain, Behan's stories reflect self-consciously on the experiences of insurrectionary activity and imprisonment, and hold in tension the moral imperatives of 'faith' with the political demands of the 'cause.' In 'I Become a Borstal Boy,' Catholicism is the medium through which the Irish prisoners in Walton jail are brought together, and it is through their ritual celebration of their religious faith that Behan and his fellow nationalist inmates renew their devotion to insurrection. They mourn the death of two Irishmen hanged in Birmingham jail with a military call to attention followed swiftly by the mass recital of the *De Profundis*, a Catholic prayer for mercy and forgiveness.[14] Similar ceremonies take place both in O'Faolain's 'The Bombshop' and O'Connor's 'Guests of the Nation,' and serve to identify nationalism with the symbolic codes and rituals of Catholicism.[15] In Behan's story, nationalism is almost homologous with the practice of the Catholic faith, in cultural if not in theological terms. The religious faith of the Irish prisoners functions to distinguish them morally and culturally from their fellow inmates, a distinction illustrated in the quotation from Patrick Pearse which the narrator inscribes on the wall of his remand cell: 'We cannot be beaten because the cause we serve enshrines the soul of Ireland.'[16]

Behan's story would evolve over time into *Borstal Boy*, in which the scenes represented in 'I Become a Borstal Boy' take on a very different form. In the story, Behan the narrator is the product of Pearsean ideologies of the spiritual and ethical justice of the nationalist cause, whose defiance of the English prison regime is inspired by the notion of himself as a modest but diligent crusader for the sanctity of the nationalist cause. In *Borstal Boy*, Behan's actions and opinions are decidedly more lukewarm about the cause, even to the extent that he cowers from the call to commemorate the men hanged in Birmingham. The evolution of this story, then, remarks not just in biographical terms on Behan's emotional and intellectual transformation from an assiduous nationalist devotee into the bawdy, irreverent narrator of *Borstal Boy*. It also situates Behan's writing at this time (1941–42) within an ideological framework entirely concomitant with the governing doctrines of Irish cultural nationalism.

There is, then, a certain mimetic compliance of Behan's earliest stories to the fictional and cultural mores of his literary precursors, O'Faolain and O'Connor. Like them, Behan sought to foreground the interplay of 'religious conscious-ness' with the political ideologies of nationalism, which Corkery suggested would define the emergent trends in Irish literature.[17] This is particularly evident in 'The Execution,' which draws heavily upon the theme and treatment

---

the source from which all storytellers have drawn. And among those who have written down the tales, it is the great ones whose written version differs least from the speech of the many nameless storytellers'. **14** B. Behan, 'I Become a Borstal Boy', *After the Wake*, ed. P. Fallon (1981), p. 25. **15** See S. O'Faolain, 'The Bombshop', *Midsummer Night Madness: Collected Short Stories, 1* (1982), pp 102–23; and F. O'Connor, 'Guests of the Nation', *Guests of the Nation* (1985), pp 5–18. **16** Behan, 'I Become a Borstal Boy', p. 28. **17** D. Corkery, *Synge and Anglo-Irish Literature* (1966), p. 19.

of O'Connor's 'Guests of the Nation' in its depiction of an IRA operation, and the moral qualms which each of the 'executioners' must face. 'The Execution' was written in 1942 while Behan was in Mountjoy jail, but was not published until after Behan's death. The narrator describes the actions and behaviour of an IRA unit detailed to execute an informer called Ellis who they had held captive. As in O'Connor's story, Behan's characters find it hard to distance themselves emotionally from the man they are to execute, attempt to conceal their intentions from him, and struggle with guilt and anxiety as they near the completion of their deed. By the side of a grave Ellis and the gunmen kneel together to recite the 'Act of Contrition,' the gunmen asking for forgiveness for a sin they have not yet committed. The narrator finds the irony too much for him: 'I tried to pray for his soul. I couldn't. It seemed awful to think of souls just then.'[18]

Here, Behan intimates the conflict between religious faith and nationalist discipline in men who conduct their orders effectively, even if with moral repugnance. 'The Execution' articulates the ideological contradictions inherent in a nationalism motivated by religious imagery and iconography, through the dispassionate observations of its first-person narrator. This is made particularly poignant in the concluding lines of the story:

> We put him in the grave. He felt quite warm. I told the lads to be careful not to get bloodstains on their clothes. We began to shovel in earth. I moved a big stone off my shovel – it might smash in his face.[19]

The concluding image of the story suggests the paradoxical humanity of the narrator and his fellow executioners, who wish Ellis no harm, and yet have just killed him. Colbert Kearney argues that the story shows that 'the young lad dies not because anybody desires his death but because the system demands it.'[20] There is an element of desire in the behaviour of the gunmen, however, who are exceptionally characterised in Behan's story by the guns they carry. 'You can sometimes judge a fellow by his taste in skits,' the narrator tells us. 'Gerry dearly loved automatics, especially ones with queer names,' while Kit, 'a wild lad', had 'a *grá* for the Colt.' The narrator, guileless and blunt, carries a 'nice small skit,' a police revolver, as practical and efficient as his short, economic prose.[21] The gun fetish of Behan's characters in 'The Execution' suggests that they desire the disciplinary power of nationalist ideology as much as they are its products.

18 B. Behan, 'The Execution', *After the Wake*, p. 34. The editor of this collection, Peter Fallon, has altered the syntax of the story slightly, and tidied up Behan's lavish use of commas and capitals, but other than this the story is as it exists in manuscript form at University College Cork Library. 19 Ibid., p. 35. 20 C. Kearney, *The Writings of Brendan Behan* (1977), p. 29. 21 Behan, 'The Execution', p. 32. 22 R. English, *Ernie O'Malley: IRA Intellectual* (1998), pp 116–117.

This is one of the principal differences between 'The Execution' and O'Connor's 'Guests of the Nation.' O'Connor's gunmen carry out their duty reluctantly, even with some difficulty, and dream of a humanism which would transcend and make obsolete the factional political causes to which they are enslaved. Behan's gunmen are shown to fetishise the tools of the political discourse which they serve, even when they regard its duties with some degree of moral disdain. O'Connor teases the reader with the possibility that the soldiers to be executed might be saved, or let free, but in Behan's story the execution is inevitable from the beginning, and the narrator knows that his victim will not run away even if he is given the opportunity. 'The Execution' depicts political violence as the inevitable product of historical and ideological forces, which determines and shapes the subjectivities of its agents.

To a large extent, the ideological differences between the two stories are the result of different formal and linguistic techniques. O'Connor's story is heavily indebted to romanticism, positing the notion of a transcendent space of judgement and moral values 'outside' of nationalism, in which an abstract notion of moral and political 'freedom' is the mark against which Bonaparte and Noble are measured. As Richard English has argued, many intellectuals of the nationalist movement were deeply indebted in their writing and thinking to the ideals of English Romanticism, including Frank Ryan, Peadar O'Donnell, Ernie O'Malley, as well as O'Connor and O'Faolain.[22] O'Connor himself identified significant overlaps between Irish nationalism and, in particular, Shelleyan Romanticism in *An Only Child* (1961), the first volume of his autobiography,[23] while O'Faolain has one of his characters in 'The Bombshop' defending his nationalism with recourse to Shelley's notions of the artistic beauty of 'freedom.'[24]

In contrast to this persistent strain in the cultural nationalism of Behan's precursors and patrons, Behan's stories are heavily resistant to romanticist ideas and techniques, and nowhere is this more evident than in the literary styles of his fiction.[25] 'The Execution' resembles the pared-down prose of Hemingway: 'He knelt down and began to pray. We knelt down with him.'[26] Behan's sentences avoid adjectives and metaphors as much as possible, reflecting the consciousness of a narrator who professes his dislike of euphemistic speech: '"Let him have it," "plugging him," "knocking him off". It's small wonder people are shy of describing the deed properly. We were going to kill him.'[27]

23 F. O'Connor, *An Only Child* (1961), pp 253–54.   24 O'Faolain, 'The Bombshop', p. 116.   25 The anti-romantic strain in Behan's writings could be usefully discussed in relation to the rejection of neo-romanticism in British poetry and fiction in the 1950s, as well as to Kavanagh's ambivalent reactions to Yeats, and the post-revival scepticism which characterised Flann O'Brien's parodies of revival romanticism in *At Swim-Two-Birds* and *The Third Policeman*.   26 Behan, 'The Execution', p. 34.   27 Ibid., p. 33.

The characters are described in minimalist terms by the guns they carry and the drinks they prefer, while there is little or no physical description, other than to suggest the emptiness of the place where Ellis is finally executed. Behan also makes use of a technique familiar from Hemingway and Joyce of the 'proper word,' the repetition of the same words in close proximity to insist on a particular visual (as well as aural) effect: 'I raised my revolver close to his head, not too close. If I put it against his head maybe the muzzle would get blood on it, blood and hair, hair with Brillantine on it.'[28] Here the repetition of the words 'close,' 'head,' 'blood' and 'hair' forcibly conveys the grotesque image of the executioner before his victim. Dialogue is sparse, unlike much of Behan's prose, and there is hardly any deviation from the plot. Perhaps more significantly, there are no indications of the beliefs or motivations of any of the characters involved, merely the sense of inevitability suggested by the narrator. The story refuses to do any more than its duty. Without frills or digressions, it fulfils its function in disclosing the event which its title promises, and so resembles the singular conviction and cold exercise of orders which characterises Behan's gunmen. 'The Execution' is a story in which the narrative form itself contributes to the impression of historical determination, allowing no extraneous factors or superfluous anecdotes to interrupt the 'duty' of the storyteller in telling his story of the tragic, predictable exercise of 'duty.'

The equivalence between the narrative itself and the event represented in that narrative does imply, therefore, the association of monologic narration with the fundamentalist reasoning of political nationalism. This suggests the power of narrative itself, that narrative authority and compulsion may be culpable for the execution described in the story. The execution of Ellis is justified and sanctioned within the narrative of the story, which excludes the 'counter-narratives' which might dissolve and question the logic of political violence. As Homi Bhabha argues, the 'political unity of the nation consists in a continual displacement of its irredeemably plural modern space,' a process which Bhabha correlates with language in its dependence on practices of exclusion and alienation.[29] Even, or perhaps especially, the curious lack of dialogue in this story indicates the degree to which one voice is permitted to dominate the narrative, for as Bakhtin has shown, character dialogue is one of the principle ways in which narrative becomes 'dialogic,'[30] and hence refuses the singular narratives of inevitability and preordination which dominate the discourses of political nationalism.

'The Execution,' then, represents the correlation of the exercise of narrative authority with the exercise of political authority (and quite literally, in the sense

28 Ibid., p. 35.   29 H. Bhabha, 'DissemiNation ...' (1990), p. 300.   30 M.M. Bakhtin, *The Dialogic Imagination: Four Essays*, ed. M. Holquist, trans. C. Emerson and M. Holquist (1981). See in particular 'Heteroglossia in the Novel', pp 301–31.

that the man who gives the order and pulls the trigger is the man who tells the story). 'To tell a story is to exercise power,' writes Ross Chambers, although he also argues that such power 'is not absolute ... [but] relational, the result of an act of authorization on the part of those subject to the power, and hence something to be earned.'[31] Behan's narrators in other short stories earn their narratorial power by acting as conduits for anecdotes and yarns from Behan's childhood in working-class Dublin, and hence traffic in what Benjamin characterises as the stock-in-trade of the storyteller, autobiographical experience. This is the case in 'The Confirmation Suit' and 'The Last of Mrs Murphy,' in both of which the narrator returns reflectively to his childhood, to confess remorse for his behaviour in one story, to celebrate the virtues of eccentric characters and community spirit in the other story. In 'After the Wake,' however, the issue of narrative authority and power reappears, but departs from the mimetic authority of the narrator which characterised 'The Execution' and Behan's autobiographical stories.

'After the Wake' was published in Sindbad Vail's Paris-based magazine, *Points*, in December 1950. It was published anonymously, and at least one critic has suggested that it may be the 'pornography' to which Behan referred later in life when he said that 'hunger makes pornographers of us all.'[32] 'After the Wake' is not properly pornographic, however, since it represents sexual desire, but not the sexual act itself. The story concludes only with the implication that the narrator's endeavours to seduce his male friend have succeeded. Behan's reluctance to publish the story in his own name was not because the story was sexually explicit, but because it took as its theme the ease with which same-sex friendship could become erotic. This theme departs radically from the conservative nationalism of 'I Become a Borstal Boy' and 'The Execution' (although it threatens to subvert the tropes of masculine bonding which occur in both stories), and it owes little to the anecdotal folk culture evoked in Behan's other stories. If Behan's short fiction focuses mainly on debates and situations familiar from the cultural nationalism of mid-twentieth century Ireland, 'After the Wake' is the exception, for its theme was routinely censored in literary representations, as it was indeed proscribed and policed intensively in Irish society generally.

The narrator of 'After the Wake' is constructed as a libertine seducer, who narrates the story of his stealthy efforts to draw his male friend into sexual relations after his friend's wife has died. Homosexuality is implied from the beginning of the story when the narrator recalls his friend's wife saying that 'a woman can always tell them – you kind of smell it on a man – like knowing

31 Chambers, *Story and Situation*, p. 50.   32 P. Fallon, 'Introduction', in Behan, *After the Wake*, p. 13.

when a cat is in a room.'[33] Her observation is made ironic, of course, by the fact that she has not recognised the narrator's sexual intentions, and even comes to believe, when the narrator 'tangle[s] her scents' that he is attracted to her, not her husband. The narrative *dénouement* is constructed around the gradual success of the narrator's campaign of seduction, as he orchestrates conversations and encounters with the couple, and with his friend alone, which bring him closer to his purpose. The narrator is cultured and articulate, quoting lines from Marlowe and citing cultural and historical anecdotes which subtly support his 'campaign' of seduction. His narrative accounts of conversations with the couple depict him as amiable and thoughtful, but the subtext of his sexual desires reveal a more cynical and secretive character, who is single-minded and tenacious in pursuing sex. He is, in some respects, according to Baudrillard's conception, the vulgar or impure seducer, who employs subterfuge to achieve his desires.[34]

The narrative is not just about seduction, however, but is seductive in itself, assuming sympathy with the narrator's desired object, and drawing us towards its implied homoerotic resolution. 'After the Wake' connects the process of seduction with the persuasive power of narrative:

> From that night forward, I opened the campaign in jovial earnest.
>
> The first step – to make him think it manly, ordinary to manly men, the British Navy, "Porthole Duff", "Navy Cake", stories of the Hitler Youth in captivity, told me by Irish soldiers on leave from guarding them; to remove the taint of "cissiness", effeminacy, how the German Army had encouraged it in Cadet Schools, to harden the boy-officers, making their love a muscular clasp of friendship, independent of women, the British Public Schools, young Boxers I'd known (most of it about the Boxers was true), that Lord Alfred Douglas was son to the Marquess of Queensbury and a good man to use his dukes himself, Oscar Wilde throwing 'Q' down the stairs and after him his Ballyboy attendant.
>
> On the other front, appealing to that hope of culture – Socrates, Shakespeare, Marlow – lies, truth and half-truth.[35]

The narrator tells his friend stories and anecdotes – 'lies, truth and half-truth' – in an attempt to seduce him. Seduction is here depicted as a strategic appeal to specific images and identifications, a concerted attempt to manoeuvre the seducee towards particular sexual desires. The narrator's 'campaign' is organised around tropes and images which he knows his friend will find

---

33 Behan, 'After the Wake', *After the Wake*, p. 46.   34 J. Baudrillard, *Seduction*, trans. B. Singer (1990), p. 176.   35 Behan, 'After the Wake', p. 48.

conducive, and thus the act of seduction performed in the passage cited above entails the performance of mimicry. The seducer must appear in the guise of what the seducee already desires, and must make the sexual desire he describes conform to the seducee's own desires and expectations. As Baudrillard argues, seduction 'proceeds by absence; or better it invents a kind of curved space, where the signs are deflected from their trajectory and returned to their source.'[36] The seducer desires nothing more than to be seduced, and so we find in Behan's story that the narrator's campaign concludes when his friend calls him into bed:

> I first loosened his collar to relieve the flush on his smooth cheeks, took off his shoes and socks and pants and shirt, from the supply muscled thighs, the stomach flat as an altar boy's, and noted the golden smoothness of the blond hair on every part of his firm white flesh. I went to the front room and sat by the fire till he called me.[37]

The narrator succeeds as a seducer by inviting an act of seduction, by maneouvring his friend not simply into desire, but into becoming a seducer himself. In a variation on the narrative performances of Scheherazade, Behan's story presents seduction as a form of circular narrative which must tie each seduction on to the next, and in which the ultimate gratification of desire is infinitely deferred. 'After the Wake' thematises the relationship between narrative and seduction, and proffers the notion that there can be no seduction without narrative, no narrative without seduction.

The significance of this notion in Behan's work concerns the relationship between identity and narration. In each of his stories, Behan's narrators perform the masks of specific personae – gunman, seducer, prisoner, observer – each assuming the authority of the storyteller to deliver his fragment of autobiographical memory. What sets 'After the Wake' apart from Behan's other stories, however, is that it begins to represent the swerving motion of narrative itself, the capacity of narrative to divert desire in the course of its trajectory. Narrative in 'After the Wake' becomes the site of conversion as much as it is the site of conservation, where there is, as Ross Chambers argues of oppositional narratives in particular, 'the kind of room for maneuver that is capable of producing change out of the discourse of power through the deflection of desire.'[38] If in the early stories, Behan derives his narrative authority by mimesis, by conforming to the thematic and tropological conventions of his precursors, in his later stories he moves steadily towards this principle of narrative deflection or 'swerving.'[39] The

---

36 Baudrillard, *Seduction*, p. 108.   **37** Behan, 'After the Wake', p. 52.   **38** R. Chambers, *Room for Maneuver: Reading the Oppositional in Narrative* (1991), p. 245.   **39** S. Greenblatt uses this term, 'swerving' to describe the movement of *Twelfth Night* towards the 'spectacle of homoerotic desire'

narrator of 'After the Wake' is no longer the conduit for conferring the power of tradition and memory on to his listeners, but represents instead the potential for conversion within narrative, and the function of seduction as a narrative mode.

'Genres,' Fredric Jameson argues, 'are essentially literary *institutions*, or social contracts between a writer and a specific public, whose function is to specify the proper use of a particular cultural artifact.'[40] In both its oral and written forms, storytelling functioned in early twentieth-century Ireland to legitimate and ground nationalist ideologies and identities. The story unit thus serves in Irish cultural nationalism as an *ideologeme*, to adopt Jameson's term, which signals in its thematic concerns and stylistic devices its conformity to a system of national-ist values and identifications. Behan's early short stories belong to this genre, for, aside from the anti-romanticism which marks his style apart from O'Connor and O'Faolain, Behan's stories repeat the tropes and themes of nationalist storytelling. 'After the Wake' departs decisively from these generic conventions, however, not just in thematising the subversive shift in sexual identities, but also in its reflexive consideration of the trope of seduction within narrative. If in Behan's early stories, and those of his precursors, we encounter narrative as a process of assuming and conferring legitimacy on a predetermined system of values and identities, in 'After the Wake' Behan reveals the seductive power within narrative to shift or deflect desire.

To show the capacity within narrative for seduction, for change, is thus to foreground the process by which narrative makes and shapes identity, rather than simply disseminating preexistent identities. 'After the Wake' anticipates the manner in which Behan's later writings would highlight the subversive play of sexual and national identities, in the farcical form which this took in *The Hostage*, for example, but also in the subtle seductions and conversions which recur throughout *Borstal Boy*. That Behan published his story anonymously in Paris, and possibly referred to it as a piece of hack 'pornography' indicates his anxiety about its likely reception in mid-century Ireland. He would never republish it in his lifetime, or return to its themes in such an explicit manner, but its attention to the potential for subversion and change within conservative literary forms, and its articulation of dissident identities and desires would find expression throughout his most successful writings.

before returning back to the propriety of heterosexual relations, thus serving as a metaphor for his argument that literature represents subversive acts or potential only in order to contain subversion more effectively. My use of the term differs from this, in that the 'swerve' which occurs in 'After the Wake' is a movement away from the conventional heterosexual trajectory towards the deviant narrative of homoerotic desire. There is no subsequent 'comfortable' containment of dangerous sexual desire in Behan's story. See Stephen Greenblatt, *Shakespearean Negotiations: The Circulation of Social Energy in Renaissance England* (1988), pp 66–93. **40** F. Jameson, *The Political Unconscious: Narrative as a Socially Symbolic Act* (1981), p. 106.

Behan and the Irish language

'Go to the Aran Islands,' Yeats advised Synge in 1896. 'Live there as if you were one of the people themselves; express a life that has never found expression.'[41] Yeats is frequently given credit for directing Synge towards the Gaelic-speaking culture of western Ireland, but, as Declan Kiberd argues, Synge's predilection for Gaelic language and culture was already well established.[42] He had been educated in Gaelic at Trinity College in Dublin, and had read Gaelic literature extensively, although, as Kiberd points out, he had much to learn from the experience of living on the Aran islands, which he did each summer from 1898 to 1902. His education on Inishmaan, the middle island in which Gaelic was the first language of most inhabitants, involved not just elements of linguistic translation, but cultural and stylistic translation too.

'Is not style born out of the shock of new material?' he wrote to Yeats, suggesting, as indeed Yeats does in his lecture to the Royal Academy of Sweden, that the style of Synge's plays derived from his 'shocking' immersion in the language and culture of the Aran islands.[43] 'There is hardly an hour I am with them,' Synge writes, 'that I do not feel the shock of some inconceivable idea, and then again the shock of some vague emotion that is familiar to them and to me.'[44] Synge likened the life of the islanders to that of artists, steeped in familiar, apparently timeless traditions of storytelling and poetry, compelled by the rigours of their environment into dramatic shifts in mood and sentiment, as well as contemplating 'some of the emotions that are thought peculiar to men who have lived with the arts.'[45] The 'shock' which Synge records, then, alludes not just to the discovery of the alterity of the islanders, but to the shock of common identifications, and, more specifically, of the hybrid cultural formations which he witnesses in a community he believes remote from the mainstream of modern European life. When he hears a local version of a story familiar from Shakespeare, he writes that 'it gave me a strange feeling of wonder to hear this illiterate native of a wet rock in the Atlantic telling a story that is so full of European associations.'[46] Synge's affection for the Aran islands, and his adoption of its myths and idiolects for his plays, grew from his recognition that the islands were a model not of cultural otherness but of wondrous cultural hybridity. Whilst one legacy of revival writers such as Synge, Yeats and Lady Gregory was to have re-energised the tropological distinction between the insular cultural purity of the Gaelic West and the corrupted cosmopolitanism of the Anglicised East of Ireland, a careful reading of Synge's work reveals that

---

41 W.B. Yeats, 'Preface to the First Edition of *The Well of the Saints*', *Essays and Introductions* (1961), p. 299. 42 D. Kiberd, *Synge and the Irish Language* (1979), pp 19–53. 43 W.B. Yeats, *Autobiographies* (1955), p. 531; pp 568–69. 44 J.M. Synge, *The Aran Islands* (1979), p. 83. 45 Ibid., p. 37; p.106. 46 Ibid., p. 23.

the Aran islands are figured as a successful model of cultural fusion and inter-section. The islanders move easily between Gaelic and English, recite stories and verses which derive from many different cultures, and conjoin the rudi-ments of Irish social customs with the liberal attitudes towards morality, law and sexuality which Synge associates with the unconventional liberal élites of New York or Paris.[47]

Synge was a crucial role model for Behan in negotiating between Gaelic and Anglophone culture, not least in the ways in which Synge figured the West in terms of cultural hybridity, for in doing so Synge made the Gaelic West analo-gous to the cultural experiences of a working-class Dubliner. Behan's academic education in Gaelic was of similar intensity if somewhat different in circum-stances to Synge's. While Behan was imprisoned in the Curragh camp between 1943 and 1946 he was tutored by the schoolmaster Seán Ó Briain, who recalled that Behan studied Gaelic language and literature devotedly, and achieved some dexterity in articulating vernacular Gaelic.[48] Behan was also encouraged and guided in his studies by the novelist and short story writer Máirtín Ó Cadhain, who was interned in the Curragh with Behan, and whose modernist, anti-pastoral novel, *Cré na Cille* was published in 1942. Ó Cadhain was one of a new generation of Gaelic writers who departed from the conservatism of the revival, and whose work in Gaelic mirrors Joycean techniques in English. Behan became under their tutelage not just a good conversationalist, however, for he also took to translating Merriman's classic eighteenth-century satire, *Cúirt an Mheáin Oíche* (*The Midnight Court*) into English, as well as translating some poems of Marlowe into Gaelic (He also made the incredible offer to Ernest Blythe 'for a hundred pounds, I could translate *Finnegans Wake* into Irish'[49]). The manuscript of Behan's translation of Merriman has since disappeared, but his biographer Ulick O'Connor records at least one occasion on which Behan recited his translation for an audience, in McDaid's pub in 1952, and a small fragment of his translation survives in *Borstal Boy*.[50] Behan's translations indicate his proficiency in reading Gaelic literary language, and, like Synge, were his first steps in putting his command of the language to creative use. Synge was much more scholarly in his translations than Behan, of course, but for both writers the mechanics of linguistic translation exemplified early concerns for issues of cultural translation which pervaded their writing careers.

Seán Ó Briain encouraged Behan to immerse himself in the language and culture of the Blasket islands, as well as Ballyferriter, Dun Chaoin, and Sliabh

---

47 There are many examples of this liberalism in *The Aran Islands*, but see also his remarks on women and morality in Synge, *Prose*, ed. Alan Price (1968), p. 143. **48** S. Ó Briain, 'Brendan Behan', the *Irish Press*, 21 May 1964, p. 8. **49** B. Behan, 'Letter to Ernest Blythe, 6–VI-46', in Mikhail (ed.), *The Letters of Brendan Behan* (1992), p. 32. **50** U. O'Connor, *Brendan Behan* (1993), pp 128–29. For the fragment of Behan's translation, see *Borstal Boy* (1961), p. 319.

Luachra. This was no Yeatsian invitation to 'express a life that has never found expression,' for indeed Behan had already become acquainted with the writings of the Blasket islanders, Peig Sayers, Tomas O'Crohan, and Maurice O'Sullivan, as well as the classic Gaelic poetry which emerged from Ó Briain's Kerry homelands, the poetry of Eoghan Rua Ó Súilleabháin, Aogán Ó Rathaille, and Piaras Feiritéar. Behan read widely in the Gaelic of this region, and indeed of Ó Cadhain's Connemara, and shortly after his release from prison in 1946 he visited the Blaskets and Ballyferriter. He returned several times before the last Blasket islanders were moved to the mainland in 1953.

The experience produced a shock of recognition which manifested itself in his poem, 'Jackeen ag Caoineadh na mBlascaod' ('Jackeen Crying for the Blaskets'), which he translated in *Brendan Behan's Island*:

> The great sea under the sun will lie like a mirror,
> Not a boat sailing, not a living sign from a sinner,
> The golden eagle aloft in the distance the last
> Vestige of life by the ruined abandoned Blaskets.
>
> The sun will be gone, the shadow of night spreading
> As the moon, rising, through a cloud coldly stretches
> Its ghostly fingers over the silent earth
> Where, wracked, the shells of the houses stand deserted
>
> – Silent save for the birds all homeward flying
> Glad to be back, their heads on their breasts lying,
> And the wind soughing, softly a half-door swinging
> By cold wet hearths, their fires forever extinguished.[51]

Behan replicated in this poem the elegiac tone which characterised the way in which the islanders themselves represented the decline of the Blaskets as a living community. According to Brendan O'Hehir, 'the Blasket book,' an amazing sub-genre of autobiographical narratives of island life, was typified by its 'nostalgic maunderings,' and posed a threat to the development of modern Irish literature in its association of the Gaelic language with dying ways of life.[52] Behan might be accused of contributing to this mournful tone in mid-century Gaelic writing, in this poem at least, by presenting the death of the Blasket islands as a process of inevitable, natural change. The poem represents the Blaskets through a series of images of emptiness, loneliness and desertion,

51 B. Behan, *Brendan Behan's Island* (1965), p. 70. For the Gaelic, see B. Behan, *Poems and a Play in Irish* (1981), p. 17.   **52** B. O'Hehir, 'Re-Grafting a Severed Tongue: The Pains and Politics of Reviving Irish', *World Literature Today*, vol. 54, no.2 (Spring 1980), p. 215.

culminating in the unhomely vision of 'cold wet hearths,' signifying the death of a symbolic as much as a literal home.

In Behan's time, the decline of the Blaskets came to symbolise the paradoxical fate of the surviving traces of Gaelic communities under an Irish government. Deserted houses and cold hearths were the stock images of Irish poetry commemorating the tragedies of the Great Irish Famine. For Behan to return to them in a poem lamenting the depopulation of Gaeltacht areas under an Irish government suggests an ironic commentary on the claims and ambitions of political nationalism. The poem is an expression of solidarity or commiseration, as indicated in its title, which situates the poet as an outsider. 'Jackeen' is a term used by country people to refer to a Dubliner or town person innocent of country matters, a reference to the foreignness of the urban person. Behan positions the speaker, 'Jackeen,' in relation to a boundary, 'the last vestige of life' (or, a more accurate translation of Behan's original would be 'the edge of the world'), a boundary which serves to illustrate the symbolic significance of the Blaskets as a peripheral and antithetical space. The Blaskets, like the Aran islands, served in popular nationalist mythology to define the differences between vestigial, pre-colonial Irishness against the reign of Anglophone culture. The desertion of the Blaskets thus illustrated the continuing process of Ireland's absorption into the Anglophone world, even after independence, hence the exaggerated (and possibly even ironic) apocalyptic metaphors which Behan employs in the second verse.

Behan's decision to immerse himself in Gaelic culture, and to write in Gaelic (as he did for much of this formative phase of his writing career), was not inspired by his adherence to the 'separatist ideal of the Republican cause,' as Ulick O'Connor has argued.[53] What motivated Behan more directly was his identification of the bawdy, liberal culture of the Gaeltacht with the working-class culture of Dublin, which had also been eroded by the social and cultural programmes of post-independence governments. In particular, the slum clearances of the 1930s struck Behan for their casual destruction of working-class cultures and communities in exchange for what his brother Brian called 'a little old dog box of a house and a shilling's worth of "free beef".'[54] Behan expresses his sense of despair in 'Jackeen ag Caoineadh na mBlascaod' for the fate of the culture of the islanders, certainly, but the poem is also a refraction of his lament for the life of working-class communities in inner-city Dublin, articulated through the eyes of a 'Jackeen' poised to watch the dissolution of another community. Thus, the fate of the Blasket islanders signifies and refracts the subalternity of the Jackeen.

53 O'Connor, *Brendan Behan*, p. 125.   54 B. Behan, with A. Dillon-Malone, *The Brothers Behan* (1998), p. 7.

That he chose to express this lament for urban communities through an imitation of a language and style which belonged to the culture of a remote island in the Atlantic indicates persistent features of his Gaelic poetry – imitation and refraction. 'Guí an Rannaire' follows the satirical wit and rhythmic style of Dáibhí Ó Bruadair in attacking the pretensions of Gaelic revival purists. 'L'Existentialisme' borrows from the parodic style of Pope and Swift, by imitating closely the rhetorical and philosophical conventions of the movement he mocks, French existentialism. 'Do Bhev,' as Colbert Kearney suggests, parodies the *aisling* form, popular in Gaelic poetry of the eighteenth century, in depicting a young woman who symbolises Ireland, but who, in Behan's twist, prefers materialist values to spiritual ones: '"True love my arse", said she to me sweetly, "I'd sooner my old man, my wardrobe and style".'[55] 'Teacht an Earraigh' mirrors the asceticism and sensuality associated with the monastic poems of eighth and ninth-century Gaelic literature. As O'Connor notes in his biography, 'when Brendan began to write poetry in Gaelic, he wrote it after different schools, as an English poet might experiment with an Elizabethan, Augustan or Georgian style before finally forming his own.'[56] The one problem with this analogy is that Behan never seems to have finally formed his own style. All of his Gaelic poems which have survived are imitations of other styles and forms. His innovation lies in turning these styles to new materials and themes – the bisexuality of Oscar Wilde ('Oscar Wilde'), the spiritual vacuum in modern commercial Dublin ('Sraid Grafton'), or the prevailing philosophies of the European continent ('L'Existentialisme').

Behan used his poetic writings in Gaelic as a space in which to experiment with the relationship between style and contemporary themes, between the apparent solidity of traditional forms and the 'shocking' or disorientating effects of new experiences and material. 'Uaigneas' ('Loneliness'), for example, imitates the fashion for Haiku-type verse in modern imagist poetry to articulate three figures of loneliness:

> The tang of blackberries
> wet with rain
> on the hilltop.
>
> In the silence of the prison
> the clear whistle of the train.
>
> The happy whisperings of lovers
> to the lonely one.[57]

---

55 The translation is quoted in C. Kearney, *The Writings of Brendan Behan* (1977), pp 55–56. 56 O'Connor, *Brendan Behan*, p. 125. 57 Behan, 'Uaigneas' and 'Loneliness', *Poems and a Play in Irish*, p. 22.

Of course, 'Uaigneas' does not have the regular metre of Haiku, nor quite the objective purity of imagism, but it attempts to imitate the style of both forms. It also echoes the short line styles and simple imagery of early Gaelic poetry, suggesting again the fusion of traditional and modern styles and images which recurs in almost all of Behan's poems. It is a bleak, sensual poem, which offers three instances of loneliness in separate verses which may themselves be read in isolation, or in relation to each other. The perspective of the poet is unclear, so that he may be lonely in prison contemplating the taste of blackberries, or, conversely, he may be on the hilltop remembering the loneliness of prison. Accordingly, the thought of sweet blackberries may either relieve or darken the tone of the poem, depending on the positional perspective of the poet. The first verse may stress that the blackberries may be sweet, but if there is no one to enjoy their taste, the pleasure they have to offer is lost, and thus may suggest that the same goes for the prisoner and the lonely one. Alternatively, thoughts of the tang of blackberries, the feeling of rain, the movement of the train, and the happiness of lovers, may serve either to nourish the imagination and mood of the prisoner, or emphasise the conditions of his deprivation and confinement.

'Uaigneas,' then, places the existentialist themes of loneliness and estrangement at the centre of a poem which echoes a mixture of traditionalist and modernist styles. Its paucity of expression and irregular verse and syntax shape the impressions of loneliness articulated in the poem, and so, as in his other poems, the style appears to be chosen for its pertinence to the theme. In some cases, the marriage of style and theme is effective but predictable. 'Filleadh Mhic Eachaidh,' Behan's poem commemorating the death of IRA leader, Sean McCaughey, uses the conventional form of the nationalist ballad to express its conventional sentiments of glory and martyrdom. In both this poem and Behan's commemoration of Jim Larkin, Colbert Kearney argues, the loose imitation of traditional expressions of remembrance and mourning indicate that 'Behan felt obliged to mark the occasion but the command performance lacks depth.'[58] Where Behan succeeds brilliantly is in turning the very traditions of Gaelic literature against the Gaelic traditionalists of his own time, by using the sharp satire of Ó Bruadair against the 'Dublin Gaels afflicted with fáinnes... All dedicated to prudence and piety' in 'Guí an Rannaire,'[59] or indeed adopting the *aisling* form against the objectification of women as spiritual symbols of Irish nationalism in 'Do Bhev.' Here, Behan exhibits not only his talent for imitation, but for irony too.

Behan's persistent experimentation with style in Gaelic poetry between 1946 and 1951 was an attempt to resolve his early concerns with the relationship

---

58 Kearney, *The Writings of Brendan Behan*, p. 50.   59 B. Behan, 'Guidhe an Rannaire'/ 'The Versemaker's Wish', trans. U. O'Connor, *Life Styles* (1973), p. 32.

between conservative formal structures and modern themes. It was also, however, an indication of Behan's search for a role in the Irish literary scene. At the same time as he was composing poems in Gaelic, he was experimenting in English with short stories, anecdotes, historical narratives, and short plays, many of which involved his experiences as a member of the IRA. In his Gaelic poetry, however, there is such a variety of imitated styles and forms that Behan appears to be searching for a mode of expression which would mould his experiences into artistic shape. Like Synge, he discovered in Gaelic literature the forms through which he could express the hybridity and subalternity of his own position, but he also found it increasingly difficult to wrestle free of the conservative connotations of the traditional forms he imitated and adapted. Behan ceased to write poetry in Gaelic shortly after he achieved widespread recognition of his talents in this medium. He was the youngest contributor to Seán Ó Tuama's influential collection of new Gaelic poetry, *Nuabhéarsaíocht*, published in 1950, and was hailed as one of the most promising young writers in the language by Daniel Corkery. The following year he published 'Uaigneas' in the English language journal, *Envoy*, the first time he published one of his poems with an English translation, and thereafter he never returned to the poetic form, in either language. Perhaps he realised then that the Gaelic literary culture of mid-century Ireland was too close to his own satirical portrait of it in 'Guí an Rannaire,' or perhaps like Synge, he felt the need to return the shocking recognition of his own cultural subalternity to the language and culture in which he had been raised.

The urban raconteur

'I am a city rat,' Behan wrote in 1951.[60] It marked the beginning of his interest in representing the city in fictional and particularly anecdotal form over the next five years of his career. He styled himself as the urban raconteur (or, in his brother Brian's hyperbolic phrase, 'the Poet Laureate of the proletariat'[61]), first when he made a series of broadcasts for Radio Éireann on Dublin folk stories and songs between 1951 and 1952, and then when he began to write serial features for the *Irish Times* and the *Irish Press* between 1953 and 1956. The anecdote was the basic formal unit in which Behan worked during this time, so that even his serialised novel, *The Scarperer*, which appeared in thirty parts in the *Irish Times* in 1953, contains almost as many digressive anecdotes and sketches as it pursues its own plot of criminal intrigue and misadventure. It was

---

60 B. Behan, 'Letter to Sindbad Vail, June 1951', in Mikhail (ed.), *The Letters of Brendan Behan* (1992), p. 45. The letter was published by Vail in *Points*, no.15 (Winter 1951). **61** B. Behan, with A. Dillon-Malone, *The Brothers Behan* (1998), p. 13.

also the form in which Behan was given the chance to experiment and develop, in his weekly column for the *Irish Press*, between 1954 and 1956, at the same time as his more acclaimed friend, Flann O'Brien, was then writing his column, 'Cruiskeen Lawn' (as Myles na Gopaleen, of course), for the *Irish Times*.

Behan's first radio broadcast, 'On the Northside,' was recorded at the request of Michael Ó hAodha on 11 September 1951 and broadcast on 29 December of the same year. It drew upon his memories of life in the tenement dwellings of northside Dublin, and packed into thirty minutes a virtuoso performance of storytelling, singing, wit, impersonation, and commentary. He would record other programmes for radio, most notably his regular appearances as a contributor and singer on the *Ballad Maker's Saturday Night* in 1952. But his first broadcast collected together a number of diverse anecdotes and songs in which Behan began to define and characterise the culture of working-class Dublin. It was a culture marked by poverty, petty class distinctions, hunger, war, and unemployment, but Behan represented it principally in terms of vibrancy and presence. It had its own sense of cultural confidence, its own distinctive dialect and modes of expression, which could see itself through the eyes of Joyce and O'Casey, and yet also recognise its own sense of cultural disinheritance and marginalisation:

> If we wanted to imitate a policeman, it was always a country accent we would use. We had never met a civic guard, or a teacher, or a doctor in the hospital that spoke like ourselves. We accepted that as a natural law... When we talked about the rest of Ireland, we never divided it north and south. It was all 'the country', outside and around. In ways, 'the bog' was an enchanted land, and we weren't jeering it, we were very respectful about it.[62]

Dublin was the centre against which the rest of Ireland was simply defined as 'the country,' yet the figures of civic authority within Dublin society were drawn from the provinces. Behan captures here the constitutive paradox of postcolonial Dublin, a city which was the administrative and political centre of the country, yet in its modernity and urbanity ran counter to the prevailing celebration of rural cultures and lifestyles which defined the cultural nationalism of the time. As Fintan O'Toole argues, the opposition between rural idyll and urban corruption was 'vital to the maintenance of a conservative political culture in the country.'[63] If 'the bog' appears in such a culture as 'an enchanted land,' the city streets are defined by chronic absence and mundanity.

---

62 B. Behan, 'On the Northside', *Radio Éireann*, 11 September 1951.   63 F. O'Toole, 'Going West: the Country versus the City in Irish Writing', *The Crane Bag*, 9, no. 2 (1985), p. 111.

Behan's response to the persistent representation of Dublin as the corrupt, destitute metropolis varied in its intensity and its tenor. In some anecdotes, he simply inverted the cultural hierarchy – for example, in his story of the old country woman whose dying regret was that she had never seen Dublin, in which the city is cast as the object of rural desires and dreams.[64] De Valera's 'comely maidens' dancing at the crossroads were, it seems, merely rehearsing for the joys of metropolitan society. A more humorous, and more frivolous, example of cultural inversion is present in Behan's story of the Japanese submarine commander who arrives in Cork, and 'the only difficulty he and the crew had was in distinguishing one Corkman from another.'[65] By playing on racial stereotypes of the Japanese, and turning them against Cork, which Behan includes in his depiction of the 'country' as an antithesis to Dublin's metropolitan identity, Behan highlights the sense of playful provincial rivalry underlying the debates about cultural and national identity in mid-century Ireland. 'The Dubliner is the victim of his own prejudices,' Behan writes, and goes on to suggest that the prejudices are not strictly 'his own,' but that of state ideology, which he then proceeds to satirise, stating that he has been 'conditioned all the days of my life to the belief that people from the three other provinces, Cork, the North and the Country, could build nests in your ear, mind mice at a crossroads, and generally stand where thousands fell.'[66] The exaggeration, both of Dubliners' naïveté and the dexterity of country people, betrays an ironic touch, but the general assertion remains of the Dubliner as victim, as outsider.

Behan was not alone, of course, in countering the nostalgic discourse of rural pastoral, in which, as Declan Kiberd has argued, 'the urbanized descendants of country people ... helped to create the myth of a rural nation.'[67] Patrick Kavanagh, Flann O'Brien, and Máirtín Ó Cadhain were the most prominent writers of an emerging anti-pastoral trend, who either exposed the rural idyll as fallacy, or satirised the urban mythologies which gave rise to such nostalgia in the first place. Behan responded with nostalgia of his own, for the folk culture of the northside streets in 'Up the Ballad-Singers,' for example, or the communal spaces of the tenements in 'On the Northside.' 'Up the Ballad-Singers,' one of his contributions to the *Irish Press*, articulated Behan's lament for the 'old songs of the Northside and the Liberties' which were denigrated and mocked out of existence by the cultural prescriptions of post-independence nationalism.[68] Similarly, in the slum clearances of the thirties, Behan sensed the loss of

64 B. Behan, 'To die without seeing Dublin', *Hold Your Hour and Have Another* (1965), p. 175. 65 Behan, 'I help with the sheep', *Hold Your Hour and Have Another*, p. 53. 66 Behan, 'The Road to Lyons – the poet Yeats disliked parsnips', *The Dubbalin Man* (1997), p. 36. 67 D. Kiberd, *Inventing Ireland* (1995), p. 481. 68 Behan, 'Up the Ballad-Singers', *Hold Your Hour and Have Another*, p. 32.

a sense of urban community, epitomised for him in the space of a tenement hallway: 'The hall was used as a public thoroughfare. Fellows played cards there, couples courted, kids had a concert of a wet night with a mouth organ and a papered comb, and on winter nights ran through it chased by a runner or playing relievio.'[69] It was also where the homeless, dubbed 'lobby-watchers' in Behan's vernacular, could find a dry space in which to spend the night. It was this community which Behan attempted to capture in his writings, although the tone was more frequently lively and contemporary than it was nostalgic.

As Gerry Smyth argues, most modern fictional representations of Dublin, 'whether pastoral or counter-pastoral, have tended to operate unproblem-atically within this received tradition, condemning or celebrating the city for qualities that it never possessed, and implicitly measuring it against a lost organic society that never existed in fact.'[70] Behan's celebration of the culture of Dublin's tenement dwellers at a time when the city was changing and expanding rapidly situates him within the terms of this 'received tradition,' evoking an ideal of community spirit and survival even as he charted its disappearance. In *The Scarperer*, in particular, Behan casts the city as a theatrical space, a series of stages filled with ebullient characters and lively verbal interplay.[71] It is far from urban pastoral, however, as the city is a playground for villains and vagabonds, conspiring and hiding out in its dark cellar bars and dockside pubs. Behan moves his characters by devious routes between Dublin and Paris, and depicts both cities as labyrinthine dens in which vice runs rampant and the police are the alienated outsiders struggling to contain the lawlessness of the city.

In part, Behan's depiction of Dublin in these terms is the product of the generic conventions which he sought to replicate. The crime novel, in its modern American and French apparition, abounded in black humour and gritty realism. *The Scarperer* mirrors these conventions, and thus represents Dublin as a visceral, anarchic city, analogous with New York or Paris. Yet, at the same time, the novel fails to achieve the full flavour of *noir* writing, precisely because its characters are so ebullient. Nancy Hand continually breaks into song, Dunlavin and Tralee Trembles are more comic than tragic, and the plot turns more by farcical accident than by fateful encounter. The fatal end of the two villains of the novel, Pierre and the Scarperer occurs by chance, undermining the illusion sustained throughout the narrative that they have control over their environments. They are mistaken for horse-murderers by a woman who works for an animal welfare organisation, who sets the police on their trail. This bizarre intervention of chance in a story otherwise tightly controlled might

69 Behan, 'On the Northside', *Radio Éireann*.   **70** G. Smyth, 'The Right to the City: Re-presentations of Dublin in Contemporary Irish Fiction', in L. Harte and M. Parker (eds), *Contemporary Irish Fiction: Themes, Tropes, Theories* (2000), p. 20.   **71** B. Behan, *The Scarperer* (1964). It was originally published in the *Irish Times* in serial form, beginning on 19 October 1953.

indicate a lack of narrative continuity on Behan's part, but it also suggests a further implication of the anarchic underworld which Behan's villains frequent, that the city is itself an indeterminate, contingent space.

The Scarperer presents Dublin within the terms of counter-pastoral discourse, a city rampant with vice and beyond rational control, but it equally refrains from pushing home the moral implications of this representation. Gus Martin argues that it is the technical challenge of modern urban novelists to present the city in its vibrancy and multifariousness without succumbing to the nineteenth-century tendency to charge it with moral significance, a challenge which he finds answered in Joyce.[72] In Behan's writings, the city is never a neutral space, but neither is it fully comprehensible as the antithesis to rural paradise, nor as urban pastoral. The labyrinthine metropolis which the characters of *The Scarperer* inhabit is not a site of loss, but is instead a productive space of interconnection. Dunlavin can cross between bohemia and the criminal fraternity, for example, or, in a more bizarre instance, Tralee Trembles sees the devil drinking in some of the city's dens, believing that the city is the ligature between the earthly and the supernatural. The city thus returns to its symbolic roots, a place of symbiotic exchange and interaction, which operates according to a relational rather than identical logic.

The Scarperer has failed to impress Behan's critics as a novel because it tends towards the digressionary fragment rather than teleological narration. Although the plot itself is tightly controlled, the episodes in Behan's serialisation frequently veer off towards songs, puns, farcical accidents, amusing dialogue, or eccentric characters, 'compounding' in Desmond MacNamara's words 'a mixture of recollections, lags' lore and fantasy'.[73] The two central villains of the novel are muted and crowded out by the riotous assembly of minor but more interesting characters whose idiosyncrasies take centre stage, and, perhaps more importantly, the cities of Dublin and Paris, particularly their pubs and cafes, command the narrative foreground themselves. Each episode of the novel, as it appeared in the *Irish Times*, functioned almost ideogrammatically, to be read for its incident, character, dialogue or witticism either in or out of teleological sequence. Like the novel which Behan's father read to him as a child, Dickens' *The Pickwick Papers*, Behan's novel was too concerned with its cast of minor characters and the delight of frivolous conversation to follow the demands of sequential narrative rigidly. But this is what makes *The Scarperer* an exemplary experiment in the attempt to render the city in fictional form. In aspiring towards the condition of the episode or anecdote, Behan's novel tried to harness

72 A. Martin, 'Novelist and City: The Technical Challenge', in Maurice Harmon (ed.), *The Irish Writer and the City* (1984), pp 37–51. A shorter version of this essay is collected in *Bearing Witness: Essays on Anglo-Irish Literature*, ed. A. Roche (1996), pp 67–77. 73 D. MacNamara, 'Early and Late', *New Statesman*, 72 (18 November 1966), p. 750.

the popular cultural forms which were already central to the representational modes of urban society.

The fragment or anecdote is peculiarly suited to representing the dominant tropes of metropolitan experience as Henri Lefebvre describes them: 'assembly, simultaneity, encounter.'[74] These are, after all, the defining tropes not just of the metropolis, but of the modern forms of communication – the radio and the newspaper – in which Behan was working. Stephen Young argues that Flann O'Brien had attempted already to mimic the representational codes of the newspaper in his 'Cruiskeen Lawn' column, embracing the digressiveness and polylogism central to journalism so that O'Brien's column becomes 'a news-paper in itself.'[75] Such a form, Young argues, is necessarily bound to the current of modernity, for while 'the novelist may go afishing in time's river, the journalist must swim in it.' This is not to argue that Behan's, or indeed Flann O'Brien's, newspaper columns are relentlessly topical. Behan's writings for the *Irish Press* serve variably within the newspaper as fictional interludes, mnemonic aids, travel memoirs, and nostalgic reveries, as parodies, sketches, satires, com-mentaries, or, indeed as archives of songs, stories and puns. Although they have their distinctive qualities and recurrent themes, the columns mimic week after week the digressive and amorphous properties of the newspaper form, and by extension mimic the modes of metropolitan experience. In this sense, although it was associated with folk tales and the pastoral vision of the rural storyteller, the anecdote in Behan's hands, as in Flann O'Brien's, was a thoroughly modernist form. It was a form which embodied the contingency and transience of metropolitan living, and hence, as Walter Benjamin recognised, the exem-plary form in which to express the flux of events and cacophony of voices which defined the city.

Stephen Greenblatt argues, in a study of the literary and cultural forms used to register the disorienting experiences of travel and colonial encounter, that the anecdote is peculiarly suited to the representational difficulties of modernity:

> Anecdotes ... are among the principal products of a culture's represen-tational technology, mediators between the undifferentiated succession of local moments and a larger strategy toward which they can only gesture. They are seized in passing from the swirl of experiences and given some shape, a shape whose provisionality still marks them as con-tingent ... but also makes them available for telling and retelling.[76]

---

74 Quoted in G. Smyth, 'The Right to the City', p. 18.   **75** S. Young, 'Fact/Fiction: Cruiskeen Lawn, 1945–66', in A. Clune and T. Hurson (eds), *Conjuring Complexities: Essays on Flann O'Brien* (1997), p. 117.   **76** S. Greenblatt, *Marvelous Possessions: The Wonder of the New World* (1991), p. 3.

Greenblatt describes here the avant-garde properties of the anecdotal form, which he argues is distinct from the characteristics of sustained narrative and teleological design. The function of the anecdotalist is to sweep into provisional artistic shape 'the undifferentiated succession of local moments' which he encounters merely 'in passing.' The anecdote is thus situated at the 'here and now' of modernity, defined by its proximity or simultaneity to the flux of time, and its capacity to assemble and present for retelling the snippets of songs, puns, myths, jokes, conversations, proverbs and stories which gather around the narrator. Behan effects the impression in his column in the *Irish Press* of talking to the reader, of passing on a joke or song, of recalling a shared memory, of alluding to characters (wholly made up) who are the common acquaintances of the narrator and reader.

Behan anecdotes function, in other words, to effect the impression of com-munity. He repeats a stock of proverbs and sayings – some of curious meaning, such as 'Carry on with the coffin, the corpse will walk,' which occurs most frequently – which form the illusion of a distinctive set of idiolectic conver-sational styles and conventions to which both narrator and reader subscribe. He also shifts the subjects of his anecdotes according to the whims of his imagined readers. 'I'm fed up and brassed off ... with the Continong,' Behan's character Crippen tells him, 'I'm gone blue melanconnolly from reading about it. Why can't you write about something natural?'[77] Crippen's criticism followed a series of weeks in which Behan had written of his travels in France and Switzerland, and thus retained the illusion that Crippen, Maria Concepta, and Mrs Brennan, the three comic characters to which he repeatedly returned in his column, were also his readers. The device allows Behan to present an imagined community of eccentric Dublin 'characters' within his columns, defined by their humour, conversational styles, and cultural expressions, and serving to emblematise the distinct cultural identity of a working-class Dubliner in the minds of Behan's readers.

The anecdote functions in one sense as an archival technology, a device for collecting and re-presenting the cultural expressions of the 'here and now,' but it is also, in Behan's hands, similar to the newspaper in its capacity both to represent and to invent the community which it serves. Benedict Kiely complained in 1950 that the rapid transformations being effected in Dublin were passing unnoticed in the pages of modern Irish literature. 'The Irish novel,' in particular, he argues, 'has failed to keep up with the development of modern Dublin ... Dublin as it appears in contemporary Irish fiction is almost always Dublin of the past.'[78] As Gus Martin notes, as Kiely wrote those words

77 Behan, 'We Fell into the Waxies' Dargle', *Hold Your Hour and Have Another*, p. 130. 78 B. Kiely, *Modern Irish Fiction: A Critique* (1950), pp 47–48.

James Plunkett had already begun to represent the emergence of this new Dublin, with its housing estates and suburban satellites, in the stories which he collected in 1955 as *The Trusting and the Maimed*.[79] In similar terms, Behan's column attempted to reproduce Dublin as a 'knowable community,' marked by its distinctive dialectal style and conversational rhythms, even as it registered the dissolution of that community. In recalling the jovial rivalry between old Dublin communities ('Monto' and the 'Coombe'), for example, Behan is compelled to remark on the changes: 'we're all that mixed up in the last twenty years of new housing that, as the woman said in the Flats, "You never know what kind you're going to have beside you".'[80]

Behan's anecdotes chronicle the expansion of Dublin into what he called 'the new breathing spaces of the Dublin people – Cabra, Crumlin, Kimmage and Ballyfermot,'[81] debating the merits of nostalgia and modernity throughout. His fund of stories and songs are drawn mainly from the confines of his northside childhood, and thus celebrate the old Dublin for its culture and community, but equally in 'What are they at with the Rotunda?,' which includes an untypical rant about modern restoration ideas, Behan counters the nostalgic language of heritage with the more compelling arguments for social welfare. 'God knows life is short enough without people wearing themselves out hauling prams round lobbies so that we can know what Hardwicke street looked like in 1790,' he writes, after his Pearsean call to 'let Ireland, building for its own people, do the best that modern technique can do for them.'[82] Behan gives us a rare glimpse here beyond the casual and comic styles of the raconteur into the urban crusader striving to get out.

Dublin, in Behan's anecdotes, was a living, vibrant expression of a diverse people brought together by the accidents of geography and time, but it was also a theatre of memory and an imagined community. It was a community in transition, which was becoming more dependent on mass modes of communication for its sense of communal identity and coherence. Behan created in his anecdotes, for radio and newspaper, the impression of a knowable, organic community of the past which was in the process of being dismantled and reconfigured into a modern, designer city. His responses to the process of urban redevelopment were ambivalent and contradictory, but his writings participate in the cultural formation of the new Dublin. They functioned as a site of definition, recollection, debate and comparison, in which he identified Dublin with the metropolitan street cultures of Paris, New York and London, with the postwar drive for urban regeneration which was sweeping changes across Europe,

79 Martin, 'Novelist and City: The Technical Challenge', p. 50.   80 Behan, 'Let's go on a pupil's tour of the nation, via the Tolka', *The Dubbalin Man*, p. 64.   81 Behan, 'Spring – it brings back memories of Dublin, London and Paris in the hopeful days of May', *The Dubbalin Man*, p. 1.   82 Behan, 'What are they at with the Rotunda?', *Hold Your Hour and Have Another*, p. 134.

and with the potent legacy of the cultural and political revival which had transformed Ireland in the early decades of the twentieth century. Behan recalled for his readers that Dublin was the city of Joyce, Yeats, and O'Casey, as well as Pearse and Connolly. But it was not all recollection, for what he was also proclaiming, in adopting the style and mask of the urban raconteur, was that Dublin was also the city of Behan.

3 / *The Quare Fellow:* cultural nationalism and the law

Ireland at the bar

In 'Ireland at the Bar' (1907) James Joyce wrote of his namesake, Myles Joyce, a seventy-year-old 'patriarch of a miserable tribe' accused of murder in Maamtrasna in 1882, who was tried by a court in English, a language he did not understand, and sentenced to death for the crime many believed he did not commit. 'The story was told,' Joyce wrote, 'that the executioner, unable to make the victim understand him, kicked at the miserable man's head in anger to shove it into the noose.'[1] Joyce chose this story of his condemned kinsman, executed in the year of Joyce's birth, to illustrate for his Italian readers the injustice of the colonial system imposed in Ireland. 'The figure of this dumbfounded old man, a remnant of a civilization not ours, deaf and dumb before his judge,' Joyce argued, 'is a symbol of the Irish nation at the bar of public opinion.'[2] The injustice in this case is not merely, or even principally, the hanging, however, but that Myles Joyce becomes subject to a series of tragic (if not indeed tragi-comic) misrepresentations, first by an interpreter who fails to convey his protestations to the court, and second by the subsequent descriptions of his trial and execution in English newspapers. Joyce's point in 'Ireland at the Bar,' as John Nash has argued, is to stress the 'great ethical and representational difficulty' of reporting such clashes between the English legal and political system and 'a civilization not ours.'[3] Representation is necessarily fraught in colonial contexts. Myles Joyce is not simply excluded or alienated from the legal process, but is misrepresented *within* it, for, as Nash rightly points out, 'British law did *not* exile him but colonized his voice.'[4] For James Joyce, this 'dumbfounded old man' symbolises the catastrophic fate of Ireland within colonial discourse, his voice appropriated and perverted, even his frustration and protest mutated into the 'excessively ceremonious' misrepresentations of an interpreter.

Such an emblem of the incommensurable breach between English law and Irish subjects serves to reinforce the ideological bases for the rise of Irish cultural nationalism, justifying the search for a language, form, even a law,

1 J. Joyce, 'Ireland at the Bar', in *The Critical Writings of James Joyce*, ed. E. Mason and R. Ellmann (1989), p. 197. **2** Ibid., p. 198. **3** J. Nash, 'Counterparts before the Law: Mimicry and Exclusion', in J. Brannigan, G. Ward and J. Wolfreys (eds), *Re: Joyce – Text, Culture, Politics* (1997), p. 8. **4** Ibid., p. 11.

which might enable the Myles Joyces of Ireland to be represented fully and authentically. If English law and English journalism could fail so utterly to represent the Irish, then by extension English literature, culture, government and economics were indicted also. Joyce in 'Ireland at the Bar' is, therefore, merely articulating the assumptions and presuppositions of the diverse efforts of Douglas Hyde, D.P. Moran, and, later, Daniel Corkery, in identifying the failures endemic to the clash of two indefatigably divergent civilisations. The revival entailed not just the struggle to define a national culture, but to present the *authentic* voice of the Irish. Thus we find literary critics and poets such as Thomas MacDonagh and W.B. Yeats sifting through the archives of Irish literature to distinguish between the authentic and the inauthentic note in Irish literature. In *Literature in Ireland* (1916), MacDonagh dismisses the writings of the English-speaking Pale, even those who sound the patriotic note, since 'the patriotism of the Pale [is] a very different thing from the national feeling of real Irish people.'[5] The Irish people, he writes, 'are agricultural people, fresh from the natural home of man, the fields and the country, busy with the oldest and simplest things of life, people who have not grown up in the streets of towns among the artificialities of civilisation.'[6]

The reigning tendency of revival intellectuals was to distinguish between the artificial (read anglicised), urban culture of the eastern seaboard and the authentic, rural culture of the West. By the late nineteenth century, Ireland was predominantly English-speaking, and, with the exception of a powerful strand of thought advocated principally by Douglas Hyde and Patrick Pearse that the Irish should return to speaking Gaelic *en masse*, the problem for most Irish intellectuals was to identify the *cultural* traits which would mark the originality of a people who, for the most part, spoke and wrote in the language of their colonisers. The problem of representing the colonised subject, in law as in literature, was essentially a mimetic problem, of discovering the native forms of expression in which Ireland could, finally, be represented authentically.

We can discern in the fascination of revival writers with the mythology and iconography of Irish nationalism the familiar quest to find the racial and cultural origins which would in turn give rise to the beginning of cultural authenticity in Ireland, for it is only in the production of a mythic radical difference between colonised and coloniser that the historical basis for separation can be grounded and inscribed. Literature became the primary vehicle in which the fiction of radical difference could be disseminated, but, as both Homi Bhabha and David Lloyd argue, the prescriptivism of nationalist criticism requires a literature whose rationale is monologic. As Bhabha puts it, 'nationalist criticism ... re-presents the problem of difference and discrimination as the

5 T. MacDonagh, *Literature in Ireland: Studies Irish and Anglo-Irish* (1996), p. 17.   6 Ibid., p. 15.

problem of image and its distortion.'[7] It is a problem which reverberates through Irish texts of the period: when Synge attempts to present in English the authentic rhythms and speech patterns of the Gaelic peasant, when Mac-Donagh dismisses the 'spasmodic and fragmentary' Anglophone ballads of the Pale, when Molly Ivors in Joyce's 'The Dead' entreats Gabriel Conway to shed his sham West Britonism in return for his true Irish identity. What is presented in each case is the inversion of a violent colonial hierarchy, privileging as pure and authentic what had been subordinated, tailoring by an assiduous process of exclusion the image of an homogenous Irish nation.

In 'Ireland at the Bar' Joyce chose the example of a man condemned under English law because of his own alienation from English language and culture, but as Hyde and Yeats recognised in the early 1890s, the problem for Irish nationalism was not an insurmountable chasm between Irish and English cultures. Rather, the constitutive anxiety of modern Irish nationalism, in Hyde's words, is that 'in Anglicising ourselves wholesale we have thrown away with a light heart the best claim which we have upon the world's recognition of us as a separate nationality.'[8] Hyde recognises that the task of Irish nationalists is to drive the people back into inventing the cultural basis for the political claim to separatism. Ironically, the rise of cultural and political nationalism in the nineteenth century coincided with, and was in many respects produced as a result of, the increasing Anglicisation and Anglo-centralisation of Irish society. Ireland was consequently caught in an anomalous state of cultural suspension, 'ceasing to be Irish without becoming English.'[9] For Hyde, the enemy of cultural nationalism is not English culture, or language, or law, *per se*, but the aporetic space of cultural hybridity engendered in Ireland in the mid to late nineteenth century.

Hybridity, Hyde argues, is no basis for the construction of a national culture. 'The Irish race is at present in a most anomalous position,' he writes, 'imitating England and yet apparently hating it. How can it produce anything good in literature, art, or institutions as long as it is actuated by motives so contradictory?'[10] Art flourishes, he implies, only in those conditions of national unity, in which the traces of foreign taste and influence have been filtered out, and the authentic forms of native expression are reinvigorated. Hyde was more modest in his arguments even than his Irish-Ireland followers, D.P. Moran and Daniel Corkery, however, who institutionalised the correlation of Irish culture with the political developments of nationalism. Corkery, indeed, prescribed the ingredients which would define and validate an authentic Irish literary tradition within the monologic terms of cultural nationalism: '(1) The Religious Con-

7 H. Bhabha, 'Representation and the Colonial Text', in F. Gloversmith (ed.), *The Theory of Reading* (1984), pp 105–6 (pp 93–122); see also D. Lloyd, *Anomalous States: Irish Writing and the Post-Colonial Moment* (1993), p. 90.   8 D. Hyde, 'The Necessity of De-Anglicising Ireland', in S. Deane (ed.), *The Field Day Anthology of Irish Writing*, 2 (1991), p. 527.   9 Ibid., p. 527.   10 Ibid., p. 528.

sciousness of the People; (2) Irish Nationalism; and (3) The Land.'[11] These were to form the basis not merely for the prescriptive forms of Irish literature which would be legitimised and celebrated in the cultural institutions of the Irish Free State (not least by the Censorship Board), but were its central social and political values too. Thus, the reigning cultural prescriptions of nationalist intellectuals in the revival period became the orthodox values of the post-colonial state, rooted, as Colin Graham has argued, in the potent claims to authenticity which underpinned the anti-colonial ideologies of Irish nationalism.[12]

The twisting of another rope

Hyde's considerable contribution to the national struggle for cultural authenticity consisted largely of his re-presentation and translation of collected Irish myths, folk-tales and songs, and his popular one-act play, *Casadh an tSúgáin* (*The Twisting of the Rope*). Behan mistakenly believed that Hyde's play was the first Irish language drama to be produced in Dublin, and when he first conceived of writing a play, called it *Casadh Súgáin Eile* (*The Twisting of Another Rope*).[13] 'The title was a homage to Douglas Hyde,' writes Behan's biographer, Michael O'Sullivan, 'Behan admired Hyde, and believed any Irish play bearing a title similar to that of Hyde's would stand a chance of winning favour with Ernest Blythe, Director of the Abbey Theatre.'[14] O'Sullivan suggests that Behan's motives in alluding to Hyde's play were partly deferential, but partly also mercenary, in seeking to win favour with the notoriously narrow-gauge Irish-Ireland agenda of Ernest Blythe via a deliberate reference to the founder of the Gaelic League. This chapter will suggest that there was more at stake in Behan's allusion to Hyde, however, for Hyde's dramatic version of an Irish myth of banishment was transformed in the play which was eventually performed as *The Quare Fellow* into a stinging indictment of the practices of capital punishment endorsed by the Irish Republic, of which Hyde was President from 1938 to 1945. *The Quare Fellow* registered a growing sense of recalcitrance on the part of Irish intellectuals towards the dominant social, political and cultural trends sanctioned and policed in the Irish Republic, both as a powerful protest play against hanging, and as a satirical representation of the legacy of anti-colonial nationalism on the Dublin working class.

Behan's first full reference to the play appears in his letter of submission to Ernest Blythe in 1946, when he professes to have written the first act of *The Twisting of Another Rope*:

11 D. Corkery, *Synge and Anglo-Irish Literature* (1966), p. 19.   **12** C. Graham, '... maybe that's just Blarney: Irish Culture and the Persistence of Authenticity', in C. Graham and R. Kirkland (eds), *Ireland and Cultural Theory: The Mechanics of Authenticity* (1999), pp 7–28.   **13** M. O'Sullivan, *Brendan Behan: A Life* (1997), p. 176.   **14** Ibid., p. 176.

I have written one Act of another play. *The Twisting of Another Rope* I call it, because everything is shown in the black cell in some prison. Two men are condemned to death and waiting for the Rope – I would send it with this but better not scare the Department of Justice before we have anything done. There is nothing political in it, of course.[15]

When Behan sent the script of *Casadh Súgáin Eile* to Blythe, it was a one-act play written in Irish which Blythe reputedly rejected firmly and curtly. In the meantime, Behan had written a play called *Gretna Green* or *Ash Wednesday* in English for IRA sympathisers who wanted to commemorate the hangings of James Barnes and Peter McCormack for the bombing of Birmingham in 1940. Although the script is now lost, the play is reported to have been set outside an English prison on the eve of a double hanging, focusing on the reactions of four characters to the plight of the men inside.[16] *Gretna Green* thus enabled Behan to experiment with the central structural device of *The Quare Fellow*, which revolves around the reaction to a hanging which is itself absent from the stage.

In the early fifties, Behan completely revised *Casadh Súgáin Eile* by translating it into English and extending the drama to three acts. He sent it again to Blythe, and Blythe invited Behan to consult with his artistic director, Ria Mooney, on revisions which needed to be made to the play. What happened next is unclear. Seamus de Burca maintains that Behan refused to allow Ria Mooney to make any changes to the script, sat on the script for a month and then sent it to Blythe again without making any corrections, at which point Blythe 'threw the script at the author's head.'[17] Behan's problem, de Burca claims, was with a producer interfering in his play. But other accounts dispute this, particularly as Behan was so willing to allow other producers, such as Carolyn Swift and Joan Littlewood, to make substantial changes to his scripts. Carolyn Swift argues that Ernest Blythe claimed never to have received the three-act version of the play, and refuted the notion that he had rejected Behan's play.[18] Behan then sent the script to the Gate Theatre, but was rejected by Hilton Edwards, allegedly because the play had no lead role for Michael MacLiammoir.[19] MacLiammoir's niece, Sally Travers, noticed the script among the rejects at the Gate, and brought it to the attention of her friends, Carolyn Swift and Alan Simpson, who had opened a new small theatre, the Pike, in Herbert Lane. Both Swift and Simpson already knew Behan from McDaid's pub, from his column in the *Irish Press*, and from the poems and stories which he had published in John Ryan's magazine, *Envoy*.

15 B. Behan, 'Letter to Ernest Blythe, 18th May 1946', in Mikhail (ed.), *The Letters of Brendan Behan* (1992), p. 31. 16 See S. de Burca, *Brendan Behan: A Memoir* (1993), pp 19–20. 17 Ibid., p. 22. 18 C. Swift, *Stage by Stage* (1985), p. 138. 19 O'Sullivan, *Brendan Behan*, p. 178.

Swift acted as script editor on Behan's play, trimming his verbose sentences and paring the 'thick wedges of dialogue' which Behan had stuffed into his play.[20] The most significant change which Swift and Simpson suggested, however, was to change the title from *The Twisting of Another Rope* to *The Quare Fellow*. According to Swift, the change in title was made necessary by the shortage of funds available at the Pike for advertising. In order to keep advertising copy as brief, and therefore cheap, as possible, the title had to be shortened, and Simpson found Behan entirely receptive to the snappier title, which refers to the name the condemned man is called by the prisoners and warders in the play. *The Quare Fellow* opened at the Pike on 19 November 1954, heralded even in advance of its first performance by the *Evening Press*, which conjectured that 'Brendan Behan could well begin where Sean O'Casey left off.'[21]

The condemned man

Behan's characters in *The Quare Fellow* are drawn mostly from what he referred to as 'O'Casey's battalion,' the northside tenement dwellers of Dublin who scraped a living through petty crime and casual labour.[22] The play is set in a 'city prison,' based on Mountjoy jail in Dublin, and dramatises the reactions of warders and prisoners alike to the execution of one man, referred to as 'the quare fellow' throughout, and the reprieve of another, called 'silver-top' or 'lifer.' The device Behan used of keeping the condemned man absent may have been borrowed from Wilde's *The Ballad of Reading Gaol*, which extrapolates from a glimpse of the condemned man to encompass the dehumanising effects of hanging on the other prisoners: 'Something was dead in each of us, And what was dead was Hope.'[23] Wilde projects the image of the crucifixion of Christ on to the condemned man in Reading Gaol, and infers the guilt and shame of humanity for every man condemned and executed - 'every prison that men build/ Is built with bricks of shame,/ And bound with bars lest Christ should see/ How men their brothers maim.'[24]

Behan's depiction of the effects of hanging on the prisoners and warders is less solemn than in Wilde's poem. *The Quare Fellow* opens with a song, 'The Old Triangle,' and witty dialogue between some of the old 'lags,' and closes with a ribald verse of the same song. Even the execution itself is narrated through a comic parody of a radio racing commentary, evincing the gallows humour and cynical indifference which the play implies is the dehumanising

20 Swift, *Stage by Stage*, p. 139.   **21** Quoted from *Evening Press*, 16 November 1954, in Swift, *Stage by Stage*, p. 141.   **22** B. Behan, 'Letter to Bob Bradshaw, December 4th 1943', in Mikhail (ed.), *The Letters of Brendan Behan*, p. 27.   **23** O. Wilde [C.3.3.], *The Ballad of Reading Gaol* (1898), p. 17.   **24** Ibid., p. 26.

consequence of ritual, legalised murder. But despite the casual humour and cynicism of the prisoners – they squabble at the end of the play for possession of the condemned man's letters, so that they can sell them to the newspapers – the play is relentless in describing the grotesque spectacle of death by hanging. What will happen in the execution room is foretold in detail by the 'lags' early in Act One, previewed at the end of Act One with the attempt by 'silver-top' to hang himself (the only hanging which the audience do see), and anticipated with an ever greater degree of intensity and gruesome detail throughout the play.

By the time 'the quare fellow' is brought to the rope, the audience know how the hangman calculates the drop, what shameful vigils have been kept by warders and chaplains by the condemned man's side, what delicacies and privileges he has been offered in guilty penance by the prison authorities, and what horrific scenes might occur should the hanging go wrong. One prisoner imagines the hanged man 'wriggling to himself in the pit,' strangled slowly by the rope.[25] Another prisoner, 'Neighbour,' recalls being paid in stout by a warder to cut the hood from a hanged man: 'I cut the hood away; his head was all twisted and his face black, but the two eyes were the worst; like a rabbit's; it was fear that had done it' (60). A warder, Regan, also reminds the audience of the horror of hanging: 'You forget the times the fellow gets caught and has to be kicked off the edge of the trap hole. You never heard of the warders down below swinging on his legs the better to break his neck, or jumping on his back when the drop was too short' (114). Behan does not show the hanging to the audience, but never allows the gruesome spectacle of hanging to wander far from their thoughts.

Perhaps the most melodramatic device in effecting the anti-hanging message of the play occurs in Act Three, Scene One, in which the hangman's calculations for the length of rope needed for the weight and build of the condemned man is interspersed with the blithe singing of his assistant, who sings a Christian hymn about repentance and salvation. The point of this scene is not merely to illustrate the hypocritical morality of a Christian state, which calls for the salvation of sinners at the same time as it enforces their deaths, but to also mock and expose the delusional notions which underpin public perceptions of hanging. This is developed from an earlier encounter between Warder Regan and the visiting 'do-gooder,' 'Holy' Healey, in which they discuss the theological implications of hanging:

> HEALEY: Well. We have one consolation, Regan, the condemned man gets the priest and the sacraments, more than his victim got maybe. I

---

25 B. Behan, *The Quare Fellow*, in *The Complete Plays* (1978), p. 46. All subsequent references to *The Quare Fellow* appear in parenthesis and are taken from this source.

venture to suggest that some of them die holier deaths than if they had finished their natural span.

WARDER REGAN: We can't advertise "Commit a murder and die a happy death", sir. We'd have them all at it. They take religion very seriously in this country. (67)

Regan comments sardonically on the grim task of executing the men condemned by the judicial system as unfit to live. 'It's a soft job between hangings,' he tells Healey (71), but Regan increasingly becomes the discomforting voice of cynicism and doubt as the play progresses. More so even than the prisoners, Regan feels the burden of sympathy and guilt with the plight of 'the quare fellow,' and struggles to suppress his disdain for the hypocrisy of the governor, the chief and Holy Healey, while the prisoners savagely take bets on the hanging, and squabble for the hanged man's letters.

As a piece of anti-hanging propaganda, *The Quare Fellow* works by exposing the dehumanising effects of execution and imprisonment. It builds and sustains the atmosphere of hypocrisy and guilt among the prison authorities, and the callous indifference of the prisoners. The only indication that the prisoners share sympathy for the condemned man is when they cry out at the moment of execution a mocking parody of the warders: 'One off, one away, one off, one away' (121). This unanimous piece of disturbing mimicry by the prisoners clearly enrages the warders, by playing on their sense of guilt and shame. In this moment, the prisoners reveal the complex interplay of emotions and ideologies which underpins the relationship between captors and captives, and threatens to expose the contradictory situation of capital punishment within a nominally liberal society.

The Quare Fellow works not simply by a mimetic principle of exposition, but also by connecting the audience cathartically to the guilt of the warders, and thereby implicating the ethical and political values of the audience and wider society in the practice of capital punishment. Regan is again central to articulating the implications of capital punishment for the audience. He tells fellow warder, Crimmin, that the hangman is not to blame for the condemned man's hanging: 'Himself has no more to do with it than you or I or the people that pay us, and that's every man or woman that pays taxes or votes in elections. If they don't like it, they needn't have it' (103). Regan is more sardonic in a later comment on the ambivalence of public attitudes to hanging:

WARDER REGAN: [*almost shouts*] I think the whole show should be put on in Croke Park; after all, it's at the public expense and they let it go on. They should have something more for their money than a bit of paper stuck up on the gate. (114)

As Anthony Roche argues, such moments in Behan's play reveal a dramatic approach which is deliberately Brechtian: 'to acknowledge the spectacle as a theatrical event and penetrate through it to the motives which put it on, the social practices which authorise its continuance.'[26] *The Quare Fellow* appeals, perhaps naively, to the audience to recognise their political and ethical responsibility for the condemned, reminding them of their secret complicity in the grotesque act which the play refuses to show us. Regan's exasperation with public ambivalence about hanging recalls for the audience the onerous moral position in which the warders and hangman are placed at the volition of society. If it is the general will to twist a rope around 'the quare fellow's' neck, it is Regan's particular duty to assist in the dirty deed. Thus, Behan's play echoes, in very different circumstances, Pegeen's line in Synge's *The Playboy of the Western World*, that 'there's a great gap between a gallous story and a dirty deed.'[27]

The 'dirty deed' of hanging was not far from the minds of Behan's original audiences, both in Dublin in 1954 and London in 1956. Joan Littlewood's production of the play at the Theatre Royal in London was timed and marketed to chime in with contemporary anxieties about capital punishment. The theatre's producer, Gerry Raffles, invited the hangman Albert Pierrepoint to attend the opening night, while the House of Commons had recently debated the bill for the abolition of the death penalty.[28] But debates on capital punishment were not just coincidental to the play's production. Indeed, they played a more formative role. The play was based on Behan's own encounters with capital punishment under what Behan pointedly called 'Mister Eamon de Valera's Republican Government,' in Mountjoy prison from 1942 to 1943.[29]

'The quare fellow' himself was based on the convicted murderer, Bernard Kirwan, who had allegedly butchered his own brother with a knife and buried his body parts around the family farm. Behan is more circumspect in his description of Kirwan: 'as he is not here to defend himself, I'll say no more about him, except that he had a very gay personality.'[30] Kirwan's case preoccupied the public imagination in 1943, for while the details of his crime were horrific, his execution caused considerable consternation in a state which styled itself a moral, Catholic country. The *Irish Times* reported that on the morning of the execution 'about fifty people, several women among them, knelt and recited the Rosary outside Mountjoy Prison.'[31] Behan comments knowingly and sensationally on his final encounter with Kirwan in Mountjoy the day before he was hanged in *Confessions of an Irish Rebel*, but in many respects

26 A. Roche, *Contemporary Irish Drama: From Beckett to McGuinness* (1994), p. 52. 27 J.M. Synge, *The Playboy of the Western World*, in *Collected Works IV*, ed. A. Saddlemyer (1982), p. 169. 28 Debates on the bill had taken place roughly five days before, and in the middle of the first run of the play, in May 1956. 29 B. Behan, *Confessions of an Irish Rebel* (1985), p. 65. 30 Ibid., p. 55. 31 'Bernard Kirwan Executed', the *Irish Times*, 3 June, 1943, p. 2.

Kirwan's execution affected Behan less than the other infamous executions of the forties in Ireland, namely the executions of nine convicted IRA men, several of whom were hanged for the same offence as Behan.

Maurice O'Neill, a young IRA man from Kerry, was hanged by Pierrepoint in Mountjoy on 12 November 1942. He had fired shots at three policemen near Dublin in October 1942, and was sentenced by a military court a week before he was executed. In April of the same year, Behan had fired shots at two detectives, and appeared before the same court on the charge of attempted murder. He was sentenced to fourteen years penal servitude. 'The inscrutable ways of the Lord being what they are, [O'Neill] was thought to be more important than I was, and he was shot,' Behan wrote, attempting to explain the reasons why he was not sentenced to death. As Michael O'Sullivan argues, however, Behan's escape from the noose may also result from the fact that his father shared a prison cell with a minister in de Valera's government, Sean T. O'Kelly, to whom Stephen Behan appealed to ensure that his son was not shot on sight or executed for his crime. That Behan's family had connections with government ministers illustrates how contentious the convictions and executions of IRA men could become. De Valera and his government had been IRA outlaws just fifteen years prior to the execution of O'Neill, and in 1942 were executing as dangerous felons men who believed in the same cause as de Valera had fought for, and who shot at the same Free State authorities as de Valera had commanded rebels against in the 1920s. De Valera announced his punitive reactions to the renewed IRA campaign in a radio broadcast in 1940, when he described the IRA as 'the enemy within,' intimating a sense of betrayal as well as outrage.[32]

By 1944, there was growing unease about the executions of IRA men, partly because of the limited rights of defence or appeal available to the men charged, but partly also because the context in which de Valera had pursued the IRA, namely the grave threat to national security posed during World War Two, had diminished considerably. When Charles Kerins was executed on 9 September 1944, again for the same offence as Behan, police intimidated, arrested and beat a group of men and women who gathered outside the prison to recite the Rosary, provoking debates and strong criticisms of the government's actions in Dáil Eireann by scandalised TDs. Kerins' execution was reported in slightly more detail in the newspapers than preceding executions, partly because the severe press censorship in effect in the early forties, particularly on IRA matters, had relaxed a little by then, and partly also because the campaigns for the reprieve of condemned men gathered more public support.

Louis le Brocquy registered the public ambivalence and anxiety about capital punishment in 1945, when he exhibited his painting, *The Condemned Man*. Le

---

32 E. de Valera, 'Danger from Within, 8 May 1940', *Speeches and Statements, 1917–73*, ed. M. Moynihan (1980), pp 433–34.

Brocquy became concerned about institutionalised executions after learning about the hangings conducted in Ireland in the forties from a family friend, Dr Redmond, who had supervised at several of the hangings conducted by Albert Pierrepoint.[33] In *The Condemned Man*, he uses modernist techniques akin to those of Picasso to disorient the shapes and lines of the cell confining the condemned man, but the central figure of the painting is a man drawn in a style which more closely resembles the figurative art familiar from Celtic crosses. The subject is modern, with the cell illuminated by an electric light, and the man holding a small book in his hand, but the dress and appearance of the condemned man belong to early Irish representations of Christian monks. Le Brocquy thus returns a sense of the historical persecution of Irish monks, an early symbol of the suffering exacted in Ireland under colonial rule, to this modern image of the public banishment of the undesirable. The condemned man's face turns in distraction from the book, one side of his face illuminated and wide-eyed with fear, the other side cast in shadow and shown to be in remorse and anguish. In an influential essay in *Horizon* in 1946, Ernie O'Malley described this painting as 'a mental as distinct from a visual idea of a gaol ... [of] particular interest in a country where gaol was a natural place in which to meet friends or to say goodbye.'[34] The prison, for O'Malley as well as for Behan, was a place of considerable familiarity and symbolic power within the iconography of Irish nationalism, defined here as a threshold or liminal space.

O'Malley celebrated le Brocquy as an artist who had emerged with a distinctive style and artistic vision out of the economic and cultural insularity imposed on Ireland during the Second World War. Hence, le Brocquy had in common with Behan the same sense of turning inwards in the forties to discover the cultural resources and mental landscapes of Ireland which would lend themselves to artistic representation. Neither could register the same 'little-Ireland' vision represented in de Valera's famous St Patrick's Day Speech of 1943, when the Taoiseach celebrated the dream of 'a land whose countryside would be bright with cosy homesteads, whose fields and villages would be joyous with the sounds of industry, with the romping of sturdy children, the contests of athletic youths and the laughter of comely maidens.'[35] Instead, both le Brocquy and Behan chose as their subjects a symbol of what divided and festered beneath the apparent concord of Irish society in the forties, a symbol of the literal exile or banished of the Irish State under a Republican government. For both, representing 'the condemned man' entailed bringing into focus the spectacle of the unwanted, of the exiled other of hegemonic nationalism.

33 A. Madden Le Brocquy, *Seeing His Way: Louis Le Brocquy – A Painter* (1994), p. 65.   34 E. O. Malley, 'Louis Le Brocquy', *Horizon*, 14, no. 79 (July 1946), p. 35.   35 de Valera, 'The Ireland that we dreamed of, 17 March 1943', *Speeches and Statements, 1917–73*, p. 466.

Parables of exclusion

Behan's critical engagement with state nationalism shares much in common with the writers whom David Lloyd remarks are noted for being 'remarkably recalcitrant to the nationalist project.'[36] Samuel Beckett, Patrick Kavanagh, Flann O'Brien, Mary Lavin, John Montague, Kate O'Brien, to name just some of Behan's contemporaries, each in their own way articulated disdain for the institutionalised and sanitised nationalism of the post-independence period, while also departing from, if not actively mocking or parodying, the cultural nationalism of the revival. There is, of course, a certain aleatoric intertextuality to be traced between *The Quare Fellow* and the writings of some of Behan's contemporaries on the theme of cultural nationalism and its myopic visions of post-independence society, but Behan's play imposes itself more forcefully into the interpretive grid of the cultural nationalism of the revival. *The Quare Fellow* is a thoroughly 'post'-revival play, in the sense in which it replies to the cultural politics and allegorical codes of revival texts, and, in its original title and conception, reads itself belatedly into a dialogue with Hyde's *Casadh an tSúgáin*.

Hyde's play is set at a house dance in Munster around the year 1800, and pits jealous and superstitious local people against the passion and puissance of the 'wandering poet,' Hanrahan. Hanrahan charms a young woman, Una, who is engaged to be married to Seamus. Hanrahan compares her to Helen of Troy, makes verses in honour of her beauty, and they dance together, impatient of interruptions. The locals set out to banish Hanrahan from the house, but they fear his curses and his physical strength. They trick him into leaving, however, by getting him to make a rope by twisting hay, and, when he has twisted it outside the door of the house, they close the door and refuse to let him in. The twisting of the rope is explicitly associated with hanging on two occasions – by Una's mother, Maire, when she observes that Seamus would 'like to choke the vagabond,'[37] and by Hanrahan himself who scorns Munstermen for stealing their rope from the hangman.[38] It is also connected to exile, since the locals are not the first to evict Hanrahan from their homes – Maire tells us that 'he has neither place nor house nor anything, but he to be going the country.'[39] Hanrahan is the 'wandering' poet, the perpetual exile, whose imaginative powers and untrammeled wildness puts him in conflict with the 'settled' lifestyles of his contemporaries.

Hanrahan's expulsion from the house dance is compared by association, then, to other forms of expulsion – hanging and exile, the twin forms of banishment most familiar to nineteenth-century Irish nationalism. *Casadh an tSúgáin*

36 Lloyd, *Anomalous States*, p. 89.   37 D. Hyde, *Casadh an tSúgáin*, in *Selected Plays* (1991), p. 39.
38 Ibid., p. 51.   39 Ibid., p. 39.

recapitulates debates and anxieties within nationalism concerning the dynamics of national unity, and the corresponding necessity for forms of exclusion and banishment. For Hyde (as for Yeats, with whom Hyde shared an interest in the 'Red Hanrahan' stories and songs), the story of Hanrahan's expulsion from the house dance was an instance in the conflict between the material and the spiritual in Irish society, or, put another way, between the economic nationalism of the mercantile and agricultural middle classes and the cultural nationalism of the intellectual middle classes. Hanrahan tells Una early in the play that 'poetry is a wonderful gift from God; and as long as you have that, you are richer than the people of stock and store, the people of cows and cattle.'[40] Una is the symbolic currency in the conflict between Hanrahan's romantic vision of an Ireland raised to the classical mythological eminence of Greece and Seamus' more mundane vision of an Ireland of cosy homesteads.

Like Yeats' *Cathleen Ni Houlihan*, Hyde's play reproduces a recurrent dilemma of Irish nationalism, whether the Irish people are as respectably decent and normal as English people and deserve the same rights to property and self-government, or whether Irishness itself, racially or culturally determined, constitutes a profound challenge to the prevailing values and structures of Englishness, and demands cultural and political separatism. Hyde's *Casadh an tSúgáin* illustrates then the fractious, contentious nature of the formation and unfolding of cultural nationalism in the revival period and, in keeping with his arguments for the necessity of de-anglicisation, implies that nationalism progresses by exclusion, exile and selection.

It is as a parable of exclusion that *The Quare Fellow* engages productively with Hyde's play, and offers in virulent revisionist fashion a panacea to cultural nationalist utopianism. While Hyde offered his turn-of-the-century audiences a nationalist play which made humour from the provincial rivalries of Connacht and Munster, *The Quare Fellow* hardens those rivalries into political and class-based factions within a nationalist state. Political and religious élites coalesce to form a powerful, conservative orthodoxy, symbolised in *The Quare Fellow* by the men who talk of God 'so as you'd think God was in another department, but not long off the Bog' (63), men who attempt to conceal their failures through hypocrisy and neglect. The prison setting of the play is an obvious dystopian site, and, like the various representations of emigration and poverty in writings contemporaneous with *The Quare Fellow*, serves as a strong counter-point to the self-serving narrative of progress and contentment proffered in post-independence political discourse. *Casadh an tSúgáin* emphasised the divisions and debates within nationalism, while Behan's play belatedly reveals through heavy irony the tragi-comic incoherence of nationalist ideologies. Dunlavin tells us

40 Ibid., p. 37.

that 'the Free State didn't change anything more than the badge on the warder's caps,' despite his belief that when the Free State came into being the prisoners would get feather beds to replace their mattresses (59). The Free State is no feather bed, Behan implies, its prisons full of murderers, thieves and the corrupt politicians foolish enough to get caught. The most ardent defence of the state comes from a prisoner who, it turns out, is a politician imprisoned for embezzlement, whose powerful nationalist connections have enabled him to send his nephew to the British military academy at Sandhurst (94). Such ironies abound in *The Quare Fellow*, in which the inclusivist, cosy rhetoric of nationalist political discourse is undermined consistently by poignant reminders of failure, corruption and the routine acceptance of shameful practices established under English colonial rule.

Hyde was President of the Irish Republic when Behan began to write *The Quare Fellow*, or *Casadh Súgáin Eile*, as it was then called. Indeed, Hyde had signed the Emergency Powers Act, albeit with some hesitation, which gave de Valera's government such sweeping powers to intern, arrest, convict, and, if necessary, execute, Behan's IRA comrades. *The Quare Fellow* avoids any suggestion that its critique of the nationalist state reproduces the terms of civil war conflict, between the partitionist 'Staters,' and the Republican idealists. To have focused on the hanging of an IRA prisoner would have rendered Behan's revisionist critique necessarily and crudely partisan. Instead, *The Quare Fellow* features the more sensational hanging of a man who killed his brother with a 'meat-chopper'; a 'real bog-man act,' as Dunlavin tells us (42). To establish both continuity and dialogue with Hyde's own classic play, however, deftly shifted the grounds of Behan's critique into a re-consideration of the formative discourses and representations of cultural nationalism. Behan was attempting to appropriate the authority of Hyde's play for his dystopian vision of what Fanon called the 'sterile formalism' which would 'imprison national consciousness' in the post-independence state.[41]

Nicholas Grene argues, in a study of the cultural politics of Irish drama, that Behan, along with O'Casey and Johnston, was 'engaged in demythologising, de-dramatising revolution, denying it the miraculous transformatory powers which it claimed for itself in the light of the intractable, untransformed political realities it had left behind.'[42] This is evident not only in the farce he makes of the IRA in *The Hostage*, but also in the disillusionment and discontentment represented by prisoners and warders alike in *The Quare Fellow*. *The Quare Fellow* functions allegorically, by drawing forth its own parables of nationalist exclusivism and intolerance, and by mocking the political, cultural and religious

---

41 F. Fanon, *The Wretched of the Earth*, trans. Constance Farrington (1967), p. 165.   42 N. Grene, *The Politics of Irish Drama: Plays in Context from Boucicault to Friel* (1999), p. 137.

creeds of the state. The authorities of the prison, visible and invisible, are depicted as the efficient mimics of an older, Victorian order. It is no accident that the details of the 'quare fellow's' crime, and the caricatures of the English hangman and his assistant, resemble some sensationalist Victorian melodrama, for, just as in Joyce's representation of the sensational appeal of hanging in the 'Cyclops' chapter of *Ulysses*, the point is surely that Irish nationalism plays to the tune of the Victorian melodramatic form (a point I'll take up further in the chapter on *The Hostage*).[43] The inmates scavenge to feed the same needs as they always had, while the new visions of national self-sufficiency are parodied in the resourceful ways in which the prisoners smoke cigarettes made from mattress coir and pages from the bible, and steal methylated spirits from a warder administering medical therapy. So too, both warders and prisoners are quick to defend the prison as their own, when comparisons are suggested with English prisons:

> WARDER REGAN: There's the national inferiority complex for you. Our own Irish cat-o'-nine tails and the batons of the warders loaded with lead from Carrick mines aren't good enough for him. He has to go Dart-mooring and Parkhursting it. It's a wonder you didn't go further while you were at it, to Sing Song or Devil's Island. (98)

Regan caricatures a defensive response to the suggestion of national inferiority, ironically endorsing 'our own Irish' forms of oppression against their foreign rivals. The allegory of Behan's play functions comically as much as it makes pointed allusions to the political disillusionment of the state of post-independence nationalism. But such comedy is effective because it represents as typical the absurd and farcical situations and expressions of the characters. Characters such as Holy Healey, Warder Regan, Dunlavin and Neighbour are presented as indicative of either the pious authoritarianism or the flat cynicism of post-colonial Irish society, while the absent 'quare fellow' substitutes ominously for all that is ritually banished or outlawed.

In one of the more trite phrases of *The Wretched of the Earth*, Fanon argues that the national government, 'if it wants to be national, ought to govern by the people and for the people, for the outcasts and by the outcasts.'[44] Fanon dis-tinguishes between the nationalism of the bourgeois élite and the national consciousness which might encompass all sections and interests of the nation, including what he calls the 'outcasts' and which other post-colonial theorists have called 'the subaltern,' after Gramsci. What both Hyde and Behan show, in

---

43 J. Joyce, *Ulysses: Annotated Students' Edition* (1992), pp 376–449.　　**44** Fanon, *The Wretched of the Earth*, p. 165.

their respective dramatic versions of 'the twisting of the rope' theme, is that cultural nationalism suppresses as well as empowers, contains as well as liberates. Each play presents on stage the means of exclusion, and implies the destructive power of the bourgeois morality which dominates the centre ground of cultural nationalism. Hyde proffers an Ireland wrestling with the dilemma of an imaginative, spiritual future, steeped in poetry and learning, or a cosy, materialist future, built on economics and morality. In *The Quare Fellow*, the Ireland won from colonial rule is shown to be bankrupt, economically and poetically, and turning with ill temper on its citizens. Behan's vision of the post-colonial state chimes in with the land depicted in John Montague's 'Rhetorical Meditations in Times of Peace,' of empty politics, slum clearances, and incomprehensible emigration. 'At times in this island,' Montague wrote, 'dreaming all day/ In the sunlight and rain of attained revolutions,/ We are afraid, as the hints pile up, of disaster.'[45] The anxiety of the post-independence state was that after the revolution, there appeared to be no substance to the dream, that Ireland was condemned to nostalgic reveries of former glories, and incapable of effecting progress beyond post-colonial atrophy.

A people not so strange

One symptom of this sense of atrophy and stagnation, as argued in chapter one, was the widespread perception of cultural exhaustion in literary and intellectual circles, particularly the sense that the literary efforts of post-revival writers were overshadowed by the achievements of Yeats, Joyce and Synge. The critical revisionism of writers such as Behan, Kavanagh and Flann O'Brien does little to diminish this impression, since revisionism by definition is a belated engagement with the historical consciousness of the past. Revisionist writers are, therefore, especially concerned to revisit the dreams of 'attained revolutions,' out of a suspicious distrust and critical disillusionment with their own time. For Behan it was imperative to revisit the dramas of the cultural revival, and to trace the genealogical faultlines of contemporary cultural nationalism.

'There's an odd flush of Synge,' Behan observed of his play, *The Landlady*, when he was writing it in Mountjoy prison in 1943.[46] He acknowledged this debt in a letter to his cousin, Seamus de Burca, to whom he frequently turned around this time for advice on theatrical form and for criticism of his drafts. But it follows an observation, and in part, speculation by Behan, that Synge wanted to write and produce his last play, *Deirdre of the Sorrows*, in Dublin dialect. Thus,

45 J. Montague, 'Rhetorical Meditations in Time of Peace', in *Collected Poems* (1995), p. 201.   46 B. Behan, 'Letter to Seamus de Burca', 16 August 1943, in Mikhail (ed.), *The Letters of Brendan Behan*, p. 24.

for Behan, Synge might have corrected a persistent misrepresentation of Dublin in the Abbey theatre as the corrupted, anglicised metropolis, which had lost touch with its Gaelic, pre-colonial roots. That 'Deirdre' might have spoken in the dialect of O'Casey's tenement dwellers, but for the influence of Yeats and Lady Gregory, posed for Behan the problem of the revival's ambivalent legacy for the urban working-class of Dublin. In representing a mythic, remote 'West' as the home of Gaelic culture, the preserve of all that was truly, authentically Irish, Yeats and his followers left little room for Dubliners other than co-opted 'West Britons,' whose culture was deemed inauthentic because cosmopolitan. Behan argued in one of the few 'serious' essays which he wrote for the *Irish Press* that the Irish-Ireland movement of the revival had in fact attempted to obliterate the folk-culture of working-class Dubliners in order to replace it with a phoney, Gaelic league-sanctioned culture.[47] These 'Irish-Irelanders,' Behan argues, 'practically killed the old ballads of Dublin forty years ago with the rise of the Gaelic League':

> I often heard it regretted that most of the people in the country parts lost the language, in one generation removed from the older people of now, but surely it was some loss that the people of the period of 'sixteen and after were told that the old songs of the Northside and the Liberties were 'stage-Irish,' 'coarse,' 'made a show of the country,' and were made ashamed of the old songs to such an extent, that even the sad and lovely *Kevin Barry*, known and sung the two sides of the Irish Sea and the Atlantic, has been, all its life, an outlaw from any Dublin hooley.[48]

Behan counts the folk song on which both Hyde's play and his own are based, *Casadh an tSúgáin*, among those songs lost in the Gaelic League sanitisation of Dublin folk-culture, as well as those songs 'looted from the London musical shows.' Behan's point is to stress the cultural suppression of the 'authentic' folk life of the urban working class imposed in the formation of puritan cultural nationalism. As the peasant was exalted as the sacred repository of pre-colonial Gaelic Ireland, so the urban proletariat were condemned as the unwitting agents of colonial contamination. Behan's comparison of the loss of Dublin folk culture to the destruction of the Irish language is a powerful rhetorical parry to the discourse of Gaelic League nationalism. Thus, in reference to Corkery's famous study of the suppressed Gaelic poets of eighteenth-century Munster, Behan argued that there was a 'Hidden Ireland of the slums' yet to be recovered and represented.[49]

---

47 B. Behan, 'Up the Ballad Singers', *Hold Your Hour and Have Another*, pp 31–34.   48 Ibid., pp 31–32.   49 Ibid., p. 32.

Behan's engagement with Synge revolves around the notion of an alternative morality and social order distinct from, and antithetical to, the values of English colonial rule. Synge, apparently at the suggestion of Yeats, located this alternative morality in the peripheral regions of the west of Ireland in the belief that the society and culture of the Aran islands, for example, had survived untouched by colonialism, and therefore presented revival Ireland with a model of cultural difference descending uninterrupted from pre-colonial mythology. As Deborah Fleming argues, Synge and Yeats made a highly mythical characterisation of the Western peasant symbolically central to the revivification of Irish culture: 'The literary treatment of the peasant played a crucial and controversial role in the emerging sense of Irish national consciousness in the early twentieth century.'[50] Douglas Hyde, Lady Gregory and Padraic Colum produced dramatic versions of this peasant myth, too, which by Behan's time had become trite and caricatured. 'At home on the corner of the North Circular Road we used to make a jeer of that Abbey Theatre bogman talk. "Oh, woman of the roads, be not putting it on me now". "With your long arm, and your strong arm, be after pulling me a pint of porther".'[51] Harry Morrow, writing as Gerald MacNamara, satirised this tendency in revival drama in his play, *The Mist That Does Be on the Bog*, produced in 1909, which made humour at the expense of Synge's attempt to acquire the rhythms and cadences of peasant speech. To be fair to Synge, however, his own sketches and drafts show some awareness of the degree to which the formation of 'national drama' was in danger of becoming caricatured. In *National Drama: A Farce*, for example, Synge rehearses the debates of a committee convened to establish the forms and conventions of Irish national drama, and parodies the rhetoric of cultural nationalism:

> MURPHY: An Irish drama gentlemen is a drama that embodies in a finished form the pageant of Irish life, and shines throughout with the soft light of the ideal impulses of the Gaels, a drama in short which contains the manifold and fine qualities of the Irish race, their love for the land of their forefathers, and their poetic familiarity with the glittering and unseen forms of the visionary world.[52]

But Synge's reservations about the idealisation of the Gael in the literature of the revival were less noticeable in the plays produced at the Abbey, where Yeats in particular celebrated him for his ability to depict the lawless morality of the peasantry.[53] Synge's *The Playboy of the Western World* articulates the cultural

50 D. Fleming, '*A Man Who Does Not Exist*': The Irish Peasant in the Work of W.B. Yeats and J.M. Synge (1995), p. 1.   51 B. Behan, *Borstal Boy* (1961), p. 106.   52 J.M. Synge, *National Drama: A Farce*, in *Collected Works III*, ed. A. Saddlemyer (1982), p. 222.   53 See in particular W.B. Yeats, *Autobiographies* (1955), pp 567–9.

distinctiveness of this peripheral preserve of authentic pre-colonialism primarily through the attitudes of his characters to violence and murder. Both
Synge and Yeats recorded the story that when they arrived on the Aran islands,
an old man told them that if someone had committed a murder on the mainland
and came to the island the islanders would hide him from the authorities. This
prompted in Yeats and Synge the notion that the islanders preserved an
alternative set of moral values and priorities, and this is reflected in *The Playboy*
in the way that the locals idolise Christy Mahon as daring, brave and noble
when they believe that he has murdered his father.

In *The Quare Fellow*, however, Behan depicts the morality of working-class
Dubliners in a similar vein. When the prisoners consider the murder committed by 'Silver-top,' they explain this as a natural act. 'Killing your wife,'
Dunlavin says, 'is a natural class of a thing could happen to the best of us' (43).
While Dunlavin's sympathetic view of misogynist murder is also played for
comic effect, Behan is also indicating a view of the world in which a murderer
is higher on the moral scale than a prison warder or a judge. Even Regan, the
warder, is believed to hold this view by the prisoners, as one prisoner recalls
being told by Regan that the inmates 'were doing penance ... for the men who
took us up, especially the judges, they being mostly rich old men with great
opportunity for vice' (93). Implicit in Behan's depiction of this alternative
morality is the notion that the prisoners are being punished for their poverty,
and that such labels as 'murder,' 'robbery' or 'assault' are applicable only to
those who are disenfranchised from the apparatus of the state. The grotesque
detail in which the hanging of 'the quare fellow' is described, therefore, functions to draw attention to the ways in which 'murder' is committed legitimately
and, apparently, 'morally' by the state. In Behan's play, then, the antithesis
between the implied moral schema of working-class Dubliners and the 'official'
morality of the state replicates the antithesis posed between the alternative
morality of Synge's peasants and the corrupting influence of colonialism.
Violence is seen in both plays to occur naturally, even to have become the
measure of power and honour in each society, while the humour in both plays
belongs to black comedy.[54] So too, like Synge, Behan uses a modified, hiber-
nicised (although recognisably Dublin) dialect, suffused with song, proverb, and
slang, to indicate a distinct cultural identity – urban, working class, anarchic,
secular, and disenfranchised.

Behan exerts corrective pressure on Synge's play by figuring his peripheral,
pre-colonial, lawless peasants as the working-class outcasts punished by the laws
of the Irish Free State. *The Quare Fellow* might be read in these terms as a

---

54 Indeed, presumably not finding any playwright suitable, Kenneth Tynan, theatre critic with *The
Observer*, compared Behan to Ned Kelly for the quality of his gallows humour.

counter-text to the urban myopia of the literary revival, the ways in which the 'West,' in particular, was signified as the symbolic preserve of authentic Irishness, and Dublin's working class figured by implication as the corrupted legacy of colonialism. Behan's characters, in their dialogue, but also in their songs, articulate an urban sensibility which in its bawdiness, secularism and communality conflicts with the apparent rural bias not only of the literary revival but also of post-independence Irish politics and culture. Behan identified himself as a specifically urban writer in the wake of Joyce and O'Casey, and of popular urban cultures, in 1951. 'I prefer to drink over the northside where the people are not so strange to me,' wrote Behan in a revealing letter to Sindbad Vail in 1951, published in *Points* in Paris in the same year:

> Cultural activity in present-day Dublin is largely agricultural. They write mostly about their hungry bogs and the great scarcity of crumpet. I am a city rat. Joyce is dead and O'Casey is in Devon. The people writing here now have as much interest for me as an epic poet in Finnish or a Lapland novelist.[55]

Behan was only half-joking when he wrote this, and indeed, in consenting to have it published in *Points* was advertising a manifesto of sorts, antithetical to the peasant literature of the Irish revival and its mimics and parasites in post-revival Ireland. It is, of course, a thinly veiled attack on Kavanagh, but it was also referring to the Abbey theatre, which, as Michael O'Sullivan writes in his biography, Behan believed was producing 'dreary kitchen-cottage dirge,' which 'consisted mostly of The Abbey company of actors eating endless pans of fried rashers and sausages during a play.'[56]

Behan thus incorporated into his work what he perceived to be the neglected culture of working-class Dublin, continuing the legacy of Joyce and O'Casey in storing up a repository of popular cultural songs, anecdotes and witticisms which delineated a counter-culture antithetical to the crossroads mentality and puritan morality of the de Valera years. He even argued that de Valera's project of clearing the inner-city slums of Dublin, in which, of course, Behan had been brought up before the family were moved to the isolated outreaches of Crumlin, bore the smell of 'Irish-Ireland,' part of de Valera's puritan ruralism, bent on destroying the folk-life of the city.[57] Thus, Synge features in Behan's intertextual exchanges as an antithetical model of privileging the rural over the urban, and failing to recognise the authenticity of an urban folk-culture, a flaw in the revival notion of Ireland which Behan perceived to have been legitimated

55 B. Behan, 'Letter to Sindbad Vail' (June 1951), in Mikhail (ed.), *The Letters of Brendan Behan*, p. 45. 56 M. O'Sullivan, *Brendan Behan*, p. 177. 57 B. Behan, 'Letter to *The New Statesman and Nation*', (8 December 1956), in Mikhail (ed.), *The Letters of Brendan Behan*, p. 82.

in the policies and attitudes of the independent state. In this sense, the delineation of working class cultural forms and expressions in *The Quare Fellow* participates in what David Lloyd has described as 'post-colonial critiques,' 'which are aimed at freeing up the processes of decolonization from the inhibiting effects of nationalism invested in the state form.'[58]

Beyond the law

The Quare Fellow projects its postcolonial critique of state nationalism in terms of conflict between culture and the law, and specifically between the popular forms of cultural nationalism and the imperatives of the state to maintain its customs and systems of control through legal and juridical means. 'The Law,' Gramsci argues, 'is the repressive and negative aspect of the entire positive, civilising activity undertaken by the State.'[59] Thus for Gramsci the sites of legal and juridical application define and delimit the imaginative scope and civilising mission of the state. The courtroom, the prison, the police barracks and the execution cell, in telescoping the failures of political hegemony in the nation state, become the sites on which the cultural and political bases of the nation are tested and prescribed.

As de Valera articulated most strongly in a radio broadcast in May 1940, those breaking the law were identified as the 'enemies of the state,' the 'danger from within,' whose acts of lawlessness were interpreted as attacks on the nation.[60] In the eyes of the state, Paul Gilroy argues, 'law-breaking is seen as an active rejection of national civilization of which law is the most sacred expression':

> The subject of law is also the subject of the nation. Law is primarily a national institution, and adherence to its rule symbolizes the imagined community of the nation and expresses the fundamental unity and equality of its citizens.[61]

Gilroy makes these observations in advance of an analysis of the racialised discourses of law and order in Thatcherite Britain, but they pertain equally well to the intense infusion of legality with the cultural politics of state nationalism in Ireland in the 1930s and 1940s. De Valera's governments radically altered the constitutional status of the Irish Free State by making the law bear the weight of political prescriptions on social, cultural, gender, religious, sexual and moral

58 D. Lloyd, *Ireland After History* (1999), p. 41.   59 A. Gramsci, *Selections from Prison Notebooks*, ed. and trans. Q. Hoare and G. N. Smith (1971), p. 247.   60 De Valera, 'Danger from Within', in *Speeches and Statements*, pp 433–34.   61 P. Gilroy, *'There Ain't No Black in the Union Jack': The Cultural Politics of Race and Nation* (1987), pp 74–76.

politics, especially in *Bunreacht na hÉireann* (1937), which institutionalised a set of implicit assumptions familiar to cultural nationalists in the revival period on the relationship between the state and Catholicism, the Irish language, women, and Northern Ireland.

The Quare Fellow responds particularly to the notion that the applications of the law – imprisonment or hanging – are not primarily designed to reduce crime, but instead attempt to police and censure national and cultural identity. Thus, the prisoners rightly attempt to explain the reason why 'the quare fellow' is hanged and 'silver-top' reprieved in terms of class and culture, not strictly within the bounds of legal definitions of criminality. 'The quare fellow' is hanged, Dunlavin argues, because he committed a 'real bog-man act' with a 'meat-chopper,' while 'silver-top' is reprieved because, having dispatched his wife with his 'silver-topped cane that was a presentation to him from the Combined Staffs, Excess and Refunds branch of the late Great Southern Railways,' he is deemed to be 'a cut above meat-choppers whichever way you look at it' (43). For the prisoners in Behan's play penality is a means of censuring cultural differences, for, if crime is the issue, both men would either be reprieved together or hanged together. The specific transgression of 'the quare fellow' is not to commit murder, which the play shows in any case is both punished and prescribed by the law, but rather to commit a 'bog-man' act, which sins against the pastoral visions central to the cultural nationalism endorsed in the early twentieth century. The crime of 'the quare fellow' (and Bernard Kirwan, of course) is to have butchered his victim in one of de Valera's cosy homesteads, signifying that rural Ireland was the scene of slaughter and strife as much as it bore the symbolic weight of nationalist idealism.

Behan's play depicts the relationship between culture and the law in dialogic terms, however, attributing to the prisoners the capacity to circumvent and disrupt the power of the law. Certainly the state has the power to imprison and to execute, but *The Quare Fellow* does not end with the hanging. Instead, the prisoners have the last word, resolving the tension of the execution with more singing and banter borrowed straight from the music hall. Again, the alternative moral values and cultural codes of the prisoners are in evidence: one prisoner quips sardonically that 'a crook [is] only a businessman without a shop,' while the play concludes with an offstage voice singing the final verse of 'The Old Triangle':

> In the female prison
> There are seventy women
> I wish it was with them that I did dwell,
> Then that old triangle

Could jingle jangle
Along the banks of the Royal Canal. (124)

While the old triangle signified in previous verses the call to order within the prison, a sign of the demands of the Law, in this final verse it signifies something more playful and bawdy, becoming a euphemism for sexual desire. Anthony Roche argues that this final scene evokes 'the comedy of survival,' for both the prisoners and the audience: 'The grave has opened and closed, without claiming either the plays' characters or the audience.'[62] The function of this scene is not simply to lift the audience from the gloom of capital punishment with some light comic relief, however, but instead it re-emphasises a consistent feature of the relationship between the culture of the prisoners and the authority of the law: the capacity of the prisoners to find room for pleasure within the strictures of the penal system. This is present in the ways in which the prisoners adapt the bible into cigarette papers, find the means of looking out on to the women's prison, and swig methylated spirits belonging to an unwitting medical warder. In each case, the prisoners show the impossibility of absolute repression, and the leakage of forbidden practices and expressions even into the space of penal containment.

If, then, the law defines the limits of national culture, *The Quare Fellow* demonstrates the degree to which the hybridised popular culture of the prisoners exceeds the prescriptive desires of cultural nationalism. The prisoners speak as much in Cockney slang as they do in Dublin street argot, counter the puritan Catholicism of the visiting civil servants with their agnostic affirmation of pleasure over repentance, and adopt the wit and song of Anglophone music hall culture to articulate their disenfranchisement from the nationalist state. The Irish language is also used to undermine authority, when a warder and prisoner converse in Irish in intimate tones, free from the routine disciplinary discourse of their conversations in English. The culture of the prisoners is, to use MacNeice's phrase, 'incorrigibly plural,' impossible to confine and contain.[63]

In part, then, *The Quare Fellow* is a parable of cultural defiance, in common with the parables of cultural defiance and definition which prevailed in the literary revival, except that Behan's play shows the degree to which cultural nationalism mimicked the repressive and exclusivist structures of cultural imperialism. As David Lloyd argues, 'the critique of nationalism is inseparable from the critique of post-colonial domination,'[64] which is to say that there is no text of cultural nationalism which is not at the same time indebted to and inseparable from the texts of imperialism. In the revisionist critiques of cultural

---

62 Roche, *Contemporary Irish Drama*, p. 69.   **63** L. MacNeice, *Collected Poems* (1966), p. 30.   **64** Lloyd, *Anomalous States*, p. 115.

nationalism, in which Behan's plays participated, Ireland was, to return to James Joyce, still 'at the bar.' Just as the case of Myles Joyce symbolised the ethical and representational problem of Ireland within the British empire, the case of 'the quare fellow' conjoins this nationalist icon with the revisionist one of a victim of misrepresentation within the Irish nationalist state. And just as James Joyce attacks the representation of the hanging of Myles Joyce in the English press, Behan points too at the hypocritical, terse prose of the representation of hanging in the Irish state: 'Condemned man entered the hang-house at seven fifty-nine. At eight three the doctor pronounced life extinct' (45). Throughout *The Quare Fellow*, Behan exposes the ironic and insidious ways in which the continuation of colonial practices of political oppression and cultural containment is masked by the pseudo-objective discourses of state nationalism, as if the hanging of one of its citizens was the routine, unremarkable practice of a democratic, benevolent state, 'looking after its own.'[65] But it is indicative of the critical mode in Behan's plays that he allows one of the prisoners to answer this piece of state hypocrisy with an assured but curt dismissal: 'That's a lot of mullarkey' (45).

---

65 Behan comments on this contradiction between the continuation of capital punishment and de Valera's election slogans of 'your own looking after you', in *Confessions of an Irish Rebel*, pp 56–57.

4 / *The Hostage:* melodrama, music hall and cultural hybridity

The politics of form

'*An Giall* was, essentially, a naturalistic tragedy; *The Hostage* is a musical extra-vaganza.'[1] The formal distinction which Colbert Kearney makes between Behan's *An Giall* and its translation for the London stage, *The Hostage*, is central to the critical reception of the two plays. For Behan's sternest critics, *The Hostage* is the extravagant, hybrid corruption of its more innocent, earnest precursor. 'It is alleged,' Declan Kiberd writes, '[by such critics as Ulick O'Connor and Richard Wall] that *An Giall*, an austere and moving tragedy became something very different, *The Hostage*, a music-hall variety show complete with references to Profumo, Macmillan, and Jayne Mansfield.'[2] Kiberd suggests that such critic-isms tend to focus on translation and adaptation as corrupting processes, whereby the 'purity' of form in *An Giall* is debased to suit the requirements of Behan's more metropolitan audiences. *The Hostage* thus becomes the mark of inauthenticity and adulteration.

'The principal effects of the changes [between *An Giall* and *The Hostage*],' Richard Wall writes, 'are the destruction of the integrity of the original play.'[3] Likewise, Ulick O'Connor spurns the music-hall tones and 'high camp' of *The Hostage*: '*An Giall* had its roots in Ballyferriter, the Blaskets and the Atlantic; *The Hostage* in a commercial entertainment world Brendan had no real contact with.'[4] For both critics, however, there is a considerable degree of symbolic significance invested in notions of 'integrity,' 'authenticity,' and 'purity.' *An Giall* is associated with the austerity and integrity of the Gaelic West, in contrast to the West British follies of *The Hostage*. So too, the 'original' play bears the unmistakable stamp of the author's own experiences, whereas his translation contains allusions and stylistic devices supposedly unfamiliar to him. *An Giall* retains the conventional naturalism familiar in the institutionalised national theatre of the Abbey, while *The Hostage* seemed to be the hybrid product of several cultures, forms and styles, 'a blown-up hotch-potch compared to the original version,' according to O'Connor.[5] Wall acknowledges that these are not two different plays, as the contrasting terms which he and O'Connor use to

1 C. Kearney, *The Writings of Brendan Behan* (1977), p. 131.   2 D. Kiberd, 'Introduction', in B. Behan, *Poems and a Play in Irish* (1981), p. 10.   3 R. Wall, '*An Giall* and *The Hostage* Compared', *Modern Drama*, 18 (1975), p. 171.   4 U. O'Connor, *Brendan Behan* (1993), p. 219.   5 Ibid., p. 212.

describe them might suggest, but that the virtues of *An Giall* 'are almost buried under the avalanche of issues added for the amusement of an English audience.'[6]

There are recognisable features of larger cultural and political debates at work in these responses to Behan's translation and adaptation of *An Giall* into *The Hostage*. There is, to begin with, the problem of hybrid cultural forms within the monologic terms of Irish cultural nationalism. Wall and O'Connor imply their predilection for the conventional form of naturalist tragedy rather than the concoction of music hall and melodramatic farce served up in *The Hostage*. Moreover, *The Hostage* is understood within these terms as a betrayal of cultural nationalism (in addition to, and quite distinct from, the overt mockery of political nationalism evident in both plays). For O'Connor, *The Hostage* is the principal register of the depths to which Behan would sink in his capacity to 'play Paddy to the Saxon.'[7] Wall argues with equal conviction that *The Hostage* recapitulates the stage-Irish stereotype:

> A serious play about the age-old 'Irish question' stood little chance of notice in England in the late fifties, particularly in view of the fact that it contains no drinking except tea, no wild Irish jigs, no anti-English rebel songs and no mob scenes. By the random addition of such ingredients, *The Hostage* panders to popular conceptions of the Irish.[8]

Perhaps even crossing the Irish Sea, and crossing from the Gaelic to the English language, renders the critique and mockery of political nationalism found in *An Giall* as controversial a betrayal of nationalism as the production of *The Hostage* in London seems to represent to Wall and O'Connor. *The Hostage* appeared to ridicule the IRA, and make mockery out of Irish nationalism for the amusement of English audiences. Milton Shulman remarked, in his review of the play for the *Evening Standard*, that 'it is not going to be easy to take the IRA very seriously again.'[9] But Wall's criticism goes further than recognising the ways in which Behan makes the IRA resemble the 'Keystone Cops,' for it suggests that the adaptation of *An Giall* for the London stage was calculated to appeal to colonial discourses of stereotypy and discrimination.

Such criticism as cited from Wall and O'Connor above is unambiguous in situating *The Hostage* within the nefarious realm of stage-Irish drama, a belated addendum to the theatrical legacy of colonialism. The play's adoption of wild dancing and bawdy songs is treated as frivolous; its confounding of cultures, sexualities and styles deemed to be in the service of titillation rather than dramatic purpose. Even Shulman, who admired the play, cannot help but comment

---

6 Wall, '*An Giall* and *The Hostage* Compared', *Modern Drama*, p. 166. **7** O'Connor, *Brendan Behan*, p. 63. **8** Wall, '*An Giall* and *The Hostage* Compared', *Modern Drama*, p. 171. **9** M. Shulman, 'Mr Behan Makes Fun of the I.R.A.', *Evening Standard*, 15 October 1958, p. 13.

on its shifting shape and form: '[Behan] is constantly interrupting the action with irrelevant ballads and he would rather burst than sustain a mood.'[10] Shulman attributes this insistence on carnivalesque concoctions of song and dance with dialogue and action to Behan's immaturity as a dramatist ('Celtic primitive with sophisticated tendencies' was Shulman's telling description of Behan's qualities as a playwright). Both O'Connor and Wall, on the other hand, blame the Brechtian experiments of Theatre Workshop, with its 'random' addition of ingredients calculated either to appeal to or shock the audience.

The 'form' of *The Hostage*, especially in comparison to *An Giall*, is then the principal cause of controversy in its critical reception. The controversy surrounding *The Hostage* encompasses questions about the degree to which Behan authored it; the extent to which Behan betrayed in his play the cause of nationalism which he had once vowed to serve; the cultural authenticity of the play, the characters of which swerve between a variety of Irish and English dialects; and the adequacy of the play's 'substance,' whether the abundant addition of jokes, songs and dances in *The Hostage* detracts from the tragic core pertaining from *An Giall*. All of these issues revolve around the notion of the formal coherence and dramatic purpose of Behan's most successful play, and raise serious concerns about its value and function. All of these issues also take on acute political and ethical dimensions when situated within the cultural dynamics of post-colonial relations between Ireland and England, bringing into focus key issues of authenticity, hybridity, difference, marginality, and mimicry. Wall writes that '*The Hostage* frequently conveys the impression of being adrift somewhere between Dublin and London.'[11] It is my intention in this chapter to explore the politics of the hybrid form of *The Hostage*, and to argue that it is the play's cultural 'adriftness' which contributes to the formation of a post-colonial critique both of Irish nationalism and English imperialism.

An Giall *and* The Hostage *reconsidered*

The history of the genesis and production of Behan's *An Giall* and *The Hostage* is, in many respects, as important as the cultural politics of both plays. Behan had already achieved considerable box-office success and critical acclaim in London with *The Quare Fellow* by the time he wrote *An Giall* for a small, Gaelic language theatre in Dublin. In the summer of 1957, Behan was approached by the editor of the Irish journal *Comhar*, Riobárd MacGoráin, to write a play in Gaelic for a theatre in the Damer Hall, Dublin, founded and managed by Gael Linn, an organisation which promoted Irish language and culture. Behan had discovered after sending drafts of *The Quare Fellow* first in the Irish language

---

10 Ibid.   **11** R. Wall, 'Introduction', in B. Behan, *An Giall/The Hostage* (1987), p. 17.

and then in English that it was easier to find success in English. His return to writing in Gaelic has prompted his biographers and critics to question his motives. 'His decision to return to writing in Irish may seem curious,' writes his biographer, Michael O'Sullivan, 'He was now a highly successful writer in English – what did he have to gain by writing in an obscure language for a tiny theatre in Dublin? The truth is that he never really resolved for himself his reasons for his earlier abandonment of Irish as the vehicle for his writing.'[12] There is in such questions an implicit sense of vacillation about Behan's primary motivations as an author, whether he was perpetually predisposed to seek the limelight of fame and fortune, or, alternately, if he was interested, more altruistically, in the potential and pliability of different literary forms and media for themselves.

Declan Kiberd goes some way to making the latter case when he argues that Behan's decision to write in Irish after his commercial success in England with *The Quare Fellow* was driven by a desire for 'authentic' self-expression. The Irish language, Kiberd argues, 'was his truest medium, the language in which Behan expressed that part of himself which was incorruptible, which could not be bought.'[13] Whilst Kiberd overplays the argument that Gaelic was the means by which Behan could express himself most sincerely (Gaelic was an acquired language for Behan, which he began to write only when he learned the language in prison), the sense that Gaelic might have allowed Behan to express different things by different means from his writings in English is important. 'Irish is more direct than English, more bitter,' Behan remarked to a reporter, 'It's a muscular fine thing, the most expressive language in Europe.'[14]

It is no accident that Behan agreed to write *An Giall* after he returned from a long holiday in the Gaelic-speaking Connemara region, in which he tested his Gaelic and revelled in the company of people he believed similar in culture and circumstance to working-class people in inner-city Dublin. MacGoráin recalls that Behan was initially evasive about writing in Irish,[15] but when he returned from Connemara he seemed to be enthusiastic to begin. He had started to write *An Giall* by the end of September 1957, as he recorded in a letter to Iain Hamilton, the editor of *Borstal Boy* at Hutchinson publishers,[16] and, as Ted Boyle indicates, he probably wrote most of it while in Ibiza in the early months of 1958.[17] Although Behan told journalists that he had written the play in twelve days, this appears to have been his usual attempt to pass off his writing style as casual and instinctive. The play's director, Frank Dermody, recalled that Behan was continually revising the script of the play throughout the last weeks of May,

12 M. O'Sullivan, *Brendan Behan: A Life* (1997), p. 223.   13 D. Kiberd, 'Writers in Quarantine? The Case for Irish Studies', *Crane Bag*, 3 (1979), p. 19.   14 Quoted in O'Connor, *Brendan Behan*, p. 204.   15 S. McCann (ed.), *The World of Brendan Behan* (1965), p. 186.   16 R. Jeffs, *Brendan Behan: Man and Showman* (1968), p. 40.   17 T. Boyle, *Brendan Behan* (1969), p. 86.

sending in scraps of revisions and additions to the theatre 'on backs of cornflake bags.'[18]

The play opened on 16 June 1958 and ran for two weeks, which was the routine run for plays at the Damer Hall. Dermody had been a director at the Abbey theatre in the forties, and Behan associated him with the naturalist style for which the Abbey had become renowned by that time. There are slightly divergent accounts of Behan's reactions to the play. MacGoráin recalled that Behan 'thought [Dermody] was one of the best producers in these islands. He felt that he subdued the play more than he would have done, but later when he saw the audience's reaction he was delighted.'[19] Behan's retrospective opinion was more critical, however. '[Dermody's] idea of a play is not my idea of a play ... He's of the school of Abbey Theatre naturalism of which I'm not a pupil.'[20] Behan astutely retained the rights of translation for *An Giall*, and at the end of the run at the Damer Hall, Joan Littlewood contacted Behan to ask him if he would translate *An Giall* into English for Theatre Workshop.

Littlewood shows little awareness in her autobiography of the existence of *An Giall*, however, and narrates the account of the production of *The Hostage* as if it originated and evolved under her direction. According to Littlewood, Behan was in London to launch *Borstal Boy* when the idea for *The Hostage* was conceived. *Borstal Boy* was not published until 20 October 1958, one week after *The Hostage* had opened at Theatre Workshop's venue in Stratford East, so that Littlewood's account from the very beginning appears flawed. The primal scene of inspiration and conception, Littlewood tells us, came when she and Behan saw together the headlines splashed across a newspaper: 'British Soldier Found Dead in Nicosia ... Eighteen Years Old ... A Hostage.'[21] 'There's a play in it,' Littlewood remembers telling Behan, to which he replied, as if the idea of a play about a hostage struck him for the first time, 'I know nothing about Cyprus, but I do know about Ireland.' 'Write it,' Littlewood commanded Behan, and sent him off to work on the idea which they had apparently dreamt up together.[22] Needless to say her account is fanciful, and she misremembers her own role in the conception of *The Hostage* as more significant and indeed more dramatic than the actuality. She and Gerry Raffles, moreover, are represented rescuing the play from its author. Behan continually got drunk and failed to deliver the script of the play, phoning them with songs, jokes and anecdotes which might be included. Littlewood and Raffles pieced together the play as a collage from the titbits fed to them by their wayward author, with Act Three missing four days before the play was due to open. Littlewood records yet another dramatic, decisive scene, in which the exasperated Gerry Raffles threatened the erring

18 O'Connor, *Brendan Behan*, p. 204.   19 McCann, *The World of Brendan Behan*, p. 187.   20 B. Behan, *Brendan Behan's Island* (1965), p. 17.   21 J. Littlewood, *Joan's Book: Joan Littlewood's Peculiar History As She Tells It* (1995), p. 521.   22 Ibid., p. 522.

Behan with a gun, after which Behan began to write furiously.[23] As Nicholas Grene argues of Littlewood's account, 'what is significant is the way she remembers the play's origins and the way she represents Behan's role in writing it: the drunken Irishman constantly defaulting on his promises to supply a script; the Theatre Workshop team having to improvise the show which was so spectacularly successful.'[24] It is indicative of the complex and amorphous evolution of *The Hostage*, however, that accounts of its production are as dramatic and fictive as the play itself.

Behan worked on his translation of *The Hostage* while he was in Galway, then in Sweden in the summer of 1958, and later in Joan Littlewood's house in London as the opening night of the play approached. As it transpired, Behan attempted not so much a translation as a transformation of the play. He made more of the brothel setting of the play by introducing two whores, a social worker, a homosexual navvy and his black boyfriend, a Russian sailor, and a pianist. These characters dilute the nationalist focus of the plot, and introduce a range of issues such as class differences, homosexuality and cold war politics calculated to appeal to an English audience. They also contribute, as Richard Wall argues, to the more bawdy, music-hall tone of *The Hostage* compared to *An Giall*.[25] Many of these characters are caricatures, played for comic effect to offset the tragic action unfolding before them in the brothel. Their effect is immediately noticeable in comparison to *An Giall*. *An Giall* opens with dialogue between Patrick and Kate on the IRA boy who is to be hanged in Belfast jail, and on Patrick's part in the war of independence. The same opening conversation in *The Hostage* between Pat and Meg is interrupted by Rio Rita and Princess Grace, the two homosexual characters, who joke about having to earn their rent upstairs. *An Giall* is not without bawdy humour, or the frivolous joke, but these aspects are exaggerated further in *The Hostage*.

There are important differences between both plays, which are not just explained by the divergent styles of their directors, Frank Dermody and Joan Littlewood. *An Giall* begins with a pipe lament, played in sorrow for the boy held in Belfast, and ends with Teresa weeping over the body of Leslie, who has been suffocated accidentally in a cupboard. Behan refrained from using the device he deployed in the poignant scene in *The Quare Fellow*, in which humour deflates the sentimental tragedy of the hanging. In the final scene of *An Giall*, the audience is invited to participate in mourning the tragic death of Leslie in a cathartic revulsion at the futility of political causes. *The Hostage*, in contrast, opens with a wild jig, and closes with a fantasy scene in which Leslie rises from the dead and sings the curtain song. *An Giall* is dramatic, integrating song and

23 Ibid., p. 529.   24 N. Grene, *The Politics of Irish Drama: Plays in Context from Boucicault to Friel* (1999), p. 161.   25 Wall, 'Introduction', in Behan, *An Giall/The Hostage*, p. 13.

humour into the development of the plot, while *The Hostage* diverges from this integral model of theatre towards a model of theatrical diversity, spectacle and sensation. *The Hostage* is carnivalesque in contrast to the more sombre moods of *An Giall*, shifting register in the course of translation from tragedy to farce, but this is not, I would suggest, to the detriment of either play. This is especially the case if one concedes that Behan set out in the summer of 1958 not to take *An Giall* to an English audience, but to convert *An Giall* into a form sensitive to the theatrical vocabulary of an English audience.

An Giall registered the cultural and political contexts of de Valera's Ireland, with a smattering of allusions to Jayne Mansfield, Marilyn Monroe, Edmund Hillary, and the British interventions in Cyprus and Africa, which acknowledged the inseparability of Irish culture from Anglophone culture generally. As Kiberd argues, Behan's achievement in *An Giall* was to develop the 'unashamed experimentalism and expressionist sequences [which] proved that a Gaelic modernism had belatedly arrived.'[26] But Behan's task in *The Hostage* was not to showcase Gaelic experimentalism to a London audience, but to tap into the equivalent cultural and theatrical resources within the contexts of modern British theatre. *The Hostage* alludes more widely to debates on the monarchy, homosexuality, decolonisation, class, and political treachery, debates which were contemporary to English culture and indeed to English theatre. But the changes between the two plays were not merely a matter of content, for there was also, as already noted from the critical reception to the play, considerable controversy about the shifting form of the play. A Gaelic tragedy became an English music-hall farce, reason enough for the play's notoriety, but I want to argue that the formal differences between the two plays register the ways in which the plays necessarily respond differently to their divergent cultural and political contexts.

The melodramatic imagination

Behan's sense of national identity, and much of his knowledge of Irish history, derived from his early familiarity with the Queen's theatre, which was managed by his uncle, the actor-dramatist, P.J. Bourke. In the late 1920s and throughout the 1930s, when Behan frequented the theatre, renowned as 'the poor man's Abbey,' with his family, Bourke's repertoire of plays had not changed significantly from the diet the Queen's served up to audiences from the 1890s until the First World War. As both Cheryl Herr and Stephen Watt argue, the Queen's theatre, by producing mass-oriented, 'emotionally charged melo-

26 Kiberd, 'Introduction', in Behan, *Poems and a Play in Irish*, p. 10.

dramas, had primed Dublin's theatergoing audience at all levels to an interactive and subliminally politicized response.'[27] Herr then argues that the interaction between the Abbey theatre and its audiences can only be acknowledged and understood in relation to the ways in which the Queen's theatre had created and popularised the theatrical conventions of nationalist drama, while Watt insists that Joyce and O'Casey 'in crucial respects "see" and "know" the world in ways determined by popular dramatic and theatrical conventions' established by the melodramas produced by the Queen's theatre.[28] Dion Boucicault was a favourite of the Queen's well into the 1930s, with *The Colleen Bawn*, *Arrah-na-Pogue*, and *The Shaughraun* performed frequently, while the historical dramas of J.W. Whitbread, H.C. Mangan, and P.J. Bourke himself continued to appeal to post-independence audiences, even after it could be argued that O'Casey had parodied and deflated them of their political impact. Herr argues that Whitbread's plays, *Lord Edward* and *Wolfe Tone*, and Bourke's *When Wexford Rose* and *For the Land She Loved*, helped to shape and mobilise the cultural and political nationalism of the early twentieth century, but they, and other nationalist melodramas, continued to find resonance in the complex shifts in nationalist sentiment and ideology throughout the 1930s. Behan dismissed the idea that he had learned anything from seeing these plays at his uncle's theatre, as he dismissed possessing any form of prior literary or theatrical education,[29] but, as Ted Boyle argues, Behan drew upon his extensive knowledge of popular theatre when he wrote *The Hostage*, and, I would add, its Gaelic precursor, *An Giall*.[30]

An Giall mobilises and inverts the conventions of Irish political melodrama. It plays out a dramatic scenario in which IRA gunmen respond desperately to the threatened execution of one of their comrades in a Belfast jail by taking and keeping as hostage a young British soldier. There are, in effect, two plays running concurrently in *An Giall*: the play off-stage in which the boy in Belfast waits to be hanged; and the play on-stage in which the fate of Leslie, the British soldier, at the hands of his IRA captors depends upon what happens in Belfast. The conventional nationalist melodrama thus takes place off-stage, and is reported to the audience in conversations between characters and in radio transmissions. As in *The Quare Fellow*, Behan's *An Giall* focuses as much on the reaction to the hanging as it does on the story of the hanging itself. Monsúr, for

---

27 Cheryl Herr, *For The Land They Loved: Irish Political Melodramas, 1890–1925* (1991), pp 17–18. **28** S. Watt, *Joyce, O'Casey, and the Irish Popular Theater* (1991), p. 47. **29** B. Behan, 'Letter to Bob Bradshaw', (4 December 1943), in Mikhail (ed.), *The Letters of Brendan Behan*, p. 27. Behan writes that he 'never went to a play except to be entertained and sometimes even left the theatre then before the third act had got under way in pursuit of drink', and then professes ignorance of stage-craft and playwrighting techniques. In a similar vein, Behan often gave the impression that his writing was spontaneous and unrevised, as if the inspired outpourings of an instinctive artist, but almost all of his writings were written in several versions, and in the case of *Borstal Boy*, in particular, revised constantly and extensively. **30** T. E. Boyle, *Brendan Behan* (1969), p. 18.

example, represents the stubborn adherence to the nationalist cause and its iconography of sacrifice and martyrdom when he articulates the familiar melodramatic response to the news of the boy about to be hanged:

> KATE: Isn't it a terrible thing, Monsúr, they are after refusing mercy for that poor boy in Belfast. He will be hanged tomorrow morning at eight o'clock.
> TERESA: Wouldn't it break your heart to be thinking about it.
> MONSÚR: It wouldn't make me sad. It wouldn't make me sad at all, but proud and joy in my heart that the old cause is alive yet, and that there are splendid young men willing and ready to go out and stand their ground in the face of the English ... I would give anything I have to stand on the gallows tomorrow in place of that man. He is a lucky young man.
> PATRICK: Yet, it's a terrible pity that he didn't buy a Sweep ticket beforehand.[31]

Monsúr's sentiments echo the rhetoric of nationalist melodrama which celebrates the deaths of such figures as Robert Emmet, Patrick Pearse, and Wolfe Tone as heroic acts of self-sacrifice made in the service of a noble cause. His character resembles so many of the 'noble leaders of the cause' paraded before audiences at the Queen's Theatre, articulating the ideological foundations of modern political nationalism and its armed struggle against colonial oppression. In *An Giall*, however, he is played to such melodramatic excess that he becomes a caricature, playing the bagpipes at every available opportunity and failing to notice that his IRA barracks is in fact a brothel. Moreover, the characters around him consistently undermine his eulogies on the virtues of nationalist martyrdom. Kate and Teresa mourn the futility of the boy's death in Belfast, echoing the response of O'Casey's Juno to Johnny's sacrifice in *Juno and the Paycock*. Patrick, on the other hand, is the voice of cynicism and irony throughout the play, his sardonic comments constantly illustrating the weakness of Monsúr's sentiments.

Melodrama, as Peter Brooks has argued, is not so much a theme or set of themes 'as a mode of conception and expression, as a certain fictional system for making sense of experience, as a semantic field of force.'[32] Irish political

---

31 B. Behan, *An Giall/The Hostage* (1987), pp 45–46. All subsequent quotations from or references to *An Giall* and *The Hostage* are taken from this edition and are in parenthesis. *An Giall* is translated by Richard Wall, and Wall has chosen the 3rd edition of *The Hostage*, published first in 1962 after its successful runs in North America. There are some pertinent differences between various editions of *The Hostage*, and where appropriate I refer to such differences in the notes below, particularly comparisons between the 1st edition of the play published in 1958 and the revised text used in Wall's edition.   32 P. Brooks, *The Melodramatic Imagination: Balzac, Henry James, Melodrama, and the Mode of Excess* (1976), p. xiii.

melodramas of the late nineteenth and early twentieth centuries combined the various elements of this field of force – romantic, didactic, sentimental, spectacular, and moral – into a powerful tool for promoting the cause of Irish nationalism on the stage. It was a genre both adaptive and effective, borrowing from the melodramatic models of French and English theatre, and infusing the generic qualities of the form with the cultural politics of emergent nationalism. Herr argues indeed that the quintessential Victorian melodrama, such as Oxenford's *East Lynne* which was a favourite at the Queen's theatre, registered many of the issues 'of contested identity and forced disguise that also marked debates over national self-determination.'[33] Boucicault, and later Whitbread, Mangan, and Bourke among others, appropriated this model of popular theatre for Irish nationalism, focusing in particular on the mythology of the 1798 Rising in order to garner popular patriotic support for revolution and independence. As Daniel Gerould argues, melodrama as a substantive genre lent itself to the ideological vocabulary and iconography of revolutionary politics: 'melodrama's central theme of oppressed innocence has regularly been perceived as an incitement to rebellion against tyranny by audiences suffering similar victimisation.'[34]

An Giall manipulates the semantic codes of nationalist melodrama against itself, however. The 'oppressed innocence' familiar from melodramatic representations of nationalist heroism and martyrdom is in *An Giall* presented in the character of Leslie, the English soldier. Behan even deploys another stock characteristic of melodrama, the use of music as expressive technique to indicate character or mood, when he has Leslie enter the play to the sound of a hornpipe melody, 'The Blackbird,' which Wall tells us is a traditional metaphor for hero (48). If the audience fail to make this association between musical signifier and the hostage, they cannot help but notice that Leslie is, from his entrance at the end of Act One until his death in the final scene, unequivocally 'good.' He is the epitomé of good grace, the innocent victim of catastrophic circumstances and a political movement trapped within a circular system of atrocity and revenge. In the system of melodramatic signification, Leslie takes the place ironically of a Robert Emmet or Wolfe Tone, the object of sympathy for all in the play except for the cold, puritanical henchmen of the IRA, who are of course the 'persecuting villains' of the piece. The dramatic intensity of such sympathy is in evidence in the final scene of the play in which all of the characters gather round the dead body of Leslie, and Teresa weeps for him: 'There were none of your people to lament you, my darling. I'll be a mother to you, a sister to you, a lover to you, and I will not forget you' (74). *An Giall* juxtaposes the simplicity of such

---

33 Herr, *For The Land They Loved*, p. 11.   **34** D. Gerould, 'Melodrama and Revolution', in J. Bratton, J. Cook, and C. Gledhill (eds), *Melodrama: Stage, Picture, Screen* (1994), p. 185.

romantic sentiments between Teresa and Leslie with both the cynicism of Patrick and the antiquated puritanism of the IRA men.

Leslie is killed accidentally, of course, from suffocation in the press in which he is hidden for the duration of the police raid. That his death is accidental adds ironic force to the tragic circumstances in which he is held hostage in the first place. *An Giall* works outwards from sympathy with the 'oppressed innocence' of the hostage to circumscribing the discursive formations within which his death is imagined and then realised. Ultimately the ironic inversions which occur throughout the play produce an aesthetic which is anti-melodramatic, delineating the wider social and political causes for the tragic events depicted in the play. In this regard, *An Giall* is as much the product of Brecht as it is of Boucicault, although the form in which such causes are revealed is frequently didactic. Teresa says to Patrick in her grief for Leslie, for example, that 'it wasn't the six counties that were bothering you. You were trying to bring back two things which cannot be brought back – your youth and your lost leg' (74). This final accusation builds on the representation of the IRA throughout the play as a force locked into an anachronistic struggle which repeats the terms of colonial discourses. Leslie dies not because of the pursuit of political goals, but because his death is required to legitimate the continuation of a struggle which, like Monsúr, has ceased to remain sentient of contemporary circumstances.

An Giall does not merely criticise the individual actions and ideologies of post-independence fugitive nationalism, however, but suggests a more general critique of the derivative forms in which modern nationalism expresses and manifests itself. Monsúr borrows from an early Anglo-Norman phrase for conquering Ireland when he describes the IRA's strategy: 'One-by-one the castles were built' (31). Monsúr exemplifies throughout the indebtedness of modern nationalism to colonial discourses, since his ardent nationalism is explained as the product of an English education which romanticises 'Irishness.' But the consequences of the dialectic between English colonialism and Irish nationalism is a circular system of representation in which nationalism is condemned to express itself in terms either of mimicry or disavowal. The play articulates this system in its very form, paralleling the victimisation of Leslie on-stage with the concurrent victimisation of the boy in Belfast off-stage, but Leslie himself realises this connection towards the climax of the play:

> LESLIE: ... I'm an important prisoner. As important as the other boy who's up in Belfast. Perhaps he read the papers about me tonight. I don't know if he'd get a paper. We didn't know that we were connected in any way a little while ago. Tomorrow morning – I don't know about those things, but if there's anything in religion, we'll meet one another. (70)

Leslie's predicament is shown to be equivalent to the situation of the boy in Belfast. Elsewhere in the play there is reference made to the English 'hanging poor people and manipulating them always ... in every place – in Africa, in Cyprus and in Ireland' (54), but *An Giall* explicitly equates the fate of Leslie with the form of oppression practised under colonialism. Nationalism is critiqued for its unbridled reversion to forms of colonial oppression, a critique which Behan makes of state nationalism in its continuation of capital punishment in *The Quare Fellow*, but which he extends to the practices of fugitive nationalism in *An Giall* and *The Hostage*.

An Giall was written and produced in what Peter Brooks suggests in his conclusion to *The Melodramatic Imagination* is a post-melodramatic, or anti-melodramatic, age. Behan's play deploys the same 'radically ironic' stance, the same 'language of deflationary suspicion' as Brooks detects in Maupassant, Flaubert, Joyce and Beckett.[35] Melodrama promised what Brooks calls a 'morally legible universe' to which modernist and post-modernist writers could no longer subscribe, and yet the characteristic emphasis on theatricality and fictionality in melodrama provides an important basis for the self-reflexive and parodic forms which prevail in twentieth-century literature. *An Giall* occupies a curiously significant point of interface between these two modes of modern literature, for it mimics the generic conventions of melodrama in its presentation of dramatic conflicts between the innocent and the villainous at the same time as it persistently undermines the moral imperatives of its protagonists with irony and sardonic wit. Behan's play adopted the classic structure of Irish political melodrama, moving from the opening crises in the moral order of the nation to its sentimental resolution through martyrdom, and yet it subverts the nationalist iconography of heroism and martyrdom throughout. The ingredients of *An Giall* included the same thematic emphases on national heroism, historical inevitability, and political division as popularised in the dramas of J.W. Whitbread, but it shared Joyce's suspicion of such discourses in its comic and tragic deflation of nationalist rhetoric and language. Few sentiments of nationalist ardour are expressed without receiving ironic and excoriating reply.

Irish political melodrama emerged within what Seamus Deane calls the 'transitional condition' of nineteenth-century Ireland, in which, he argues, 'the cultural politics [of the period] was dominated by the need to find sufficient emblems of adversity in which this tragic transition could be exemplified.'[36] Behan's *An Giall* emerged within the cultural politics of another 'transitional condition,' in which the mindset of both state and fugitive nationalism had yet to be decolonised, in which the melodramatic struggle between colonialism and

---

35 Brooks, *The Melodramatic Imagination*, p. 198. **36** S. Deane, *Strange Country: Modernity and Nationhood in Irish Writing Since 1790* (1997), p. 51.

nationalism permeated the discourses of post-independence culture and politics. But like the melodramas of the late nineteenth century, *An Giall* sought to
make coherent the ruptures in contemporary nationalism by adapting the
conventions of melodrama in order to redirect its ends towards new ethical
imperatives. By figuring the death of Leslie as equivalent to, and as tragic as, the
death of the IRA boy in Belfast, Behan was not just resolving nationalist dilem-
mas within an international humanism, but deconstructing the melodramatic
excesses of nationalism itself.

Translation and transculturation

According to Ted Boyle, few of the original audiences of *An Giall* recognised
the subversive uses to which Behan was putting the conventions of Gaelic
drama. Behan mocked several sacred cows of Gaelic League culture, and even
swiped at the pretensions of his own patrons, Gael Linn, in caricaturing the
fashion promoted by that organisation for wearing the fáinne. *An Giall* was
profoundly ambivalent and critical about the dominant modes of Irish nationalism, yet it was solicited, commissioned, and produced under the auspices of an
organisation which shared the cultural assumptions of the nationalist state.
Despite its persistent critique and comic deflation of nationalist icons, Boyle
argues, 'the play had a routine run and apparently offended none of the
Dubliners who viewed it, probably because very few of them could understand
Irish well enough to be aware of the bitterness with which Behan was attacking
Irish shibboleths.'[37] A more likely explanation of the difference between the
benign reception of *An Giall* and the criticisms levelled at the anti-nationalism
of *The Hostage*, however, is the transgressive act of translation itself. *An Giall*
voiced its dissent from the myths of cultural nationalism in the Gaelic language,
performing to a small self-selecting audience of fluent Gaelic speakers and Gael
Linn officials who were invited to laugh at themselves. *The Hostage* flaunted the
caricatured fallacies and blunders of contemporary nationalism before an
international audience who were enticed to make fun of the Irish. Thus, while
An Giall appeared replete with revolutionary impetus, marking the arrival of a
political avant-garde in modern Gaelic theatre, *The Hostage* seemed in contrast
to return to the neo-colonial stage-Irish drama of the eighteenth century.

Littlewood's methods placed priority on keeping the audiences entertained,
and the revelry and farce of Behan's play provided ample opportunities to offset
the tragic plot line with amusement. Behan's own antics fuelled this effect, as he
frequently interrupted his own productions with songs and comic asides. But

37 Boyle, *Brendan Behan*, p. 86.

Behan recognised too that Littlewood's methods were not wholly designed to pander to the audience:

> She has the same views on the theatre that I have, which is that the music hall is the thing to aim at for to amuse people and any time they get bored, divert them with a song or a dance. I've always thought T.S. Eliot wasn't far wrong when he said that the main problem of the dramatist today was to keep his audience amused; and that while they were laughing their heads off, you could be up to any bloody thing behind their backs; and it was what you were doing behind their bloody backs that made your play great.[38]

Behan believed that Littlewood's ideas of drama held together seemingly contradictory impulses in modern theatre, the social unity enjoined by cathartic laughter, and the dislocation of the audience's ideological assumptions and beliefs. Both Behan and Littlewood drew upon the resources of popular culture, particularly from melodrama and the music hall. Moreover, Behan's regular visits to London pubs during the rehearsals for *The Hostage* were not wholly unproductive, since he borrowed from and adapted the humour and songs he found there. Littlewood encouraged such creative adaptation in her actors too, inviting them to contribute jokes, allusions and songs to the play as it evolved. Such methods have attracted disdain from Behan's critics, particularly Wall and O'Connor, who argue that the integrity of *An Giall* was destroyed in its conversion into what O'Connor describes as 'a platform for the queer camp current at that time.'[39] But neither Littlewood's production techniques nor Behan's urge to entertain English audiences with buffoonery are wholly responsible for the divergent reputations of *An Giall* and *The Hostage*.

    The Hostage is controversial for its representations of the follies and tragedies of nationalism to a metropolitan audience. Although various aspects of its production and translation add significantly to its capacity to offend nationalist sensibilities, it is the context in which the play was produced which lends itself most forcefully to the charge of stage-Irishry. 'The theatre history of *The Hostage*,' writes Nicholas Grene, 'brings up sharply the question of who created or controlled its images of Ireland.'[40] The question never arose about the critical portraits of nationalism in *An Giall*, largely because of an implicit assumption in cultural nationalism that to write in Gaelic is to express in intimate terms the nation to itself, while to write in English is to expose Ireland to foreign scrutiny. It is indisputable that *The Hostage* was written with an

---

38 Behan, *Brendan Behan's Island*, p. 17. **39** O'Connor, *Brendan Behan*, p. 215. **40** Grene, *The Politics of Irish Drama*, p. 139.

English audience in mind. The references to specific Irish contexts such as de Valera's government and the Gaelic league were pruned, while contemporary debates and issues in English culture were added. The history of political relations between the IRA and British forces was made clear through songs and dialogue, so that the play became more accessible to an English public often confused about Anglo-Irish relations. *The Hostage* also sharpens the sense in which Leslie and Monsewer represent different class identities within English culture, which Leslie articulates as 'racial' opposition between 'a cricket person' and 'a soccer person' (130). The play thus foregrounds English social and cultural divisions, as well as making connections for English audiences between the post-colonial discontents of Ireland, Cyprus, and Kenya.

The enlargement of the play's representation of English issues may not be simply a crude attempt to pander to the audience, however. Arguably, *The Hostage* begins to represent Irish nationalism within this system of cross-cultural representations as the paradoxical product of certain strands within English culture. Monsewer's particularly myopic adherence to violent national-ism, for example, is shown to be the mirror image of empire loyalism, while the puritanical nationalism of the IRA officer is constructed in opposition to colonial stereotypes, and yet he behaves in exactly the same way as a colonial administrator. *The Hostage*, in other words, may not be simply an exploitative representation of the quaint follies of Irish nationalism for a metropolitan audience. There may be the alternative possibility that *The Hostage* speaks back to the metropolis, and, moreover, that it uses the language and cultural forms of the metropolis to construct its reply.

Mary Louise Pratt uses the term 'transculturation' to describe this process whereby metropolitan modes of representation are absorbed and adapted in colonised and post-colonial cultures.[41] In the argument elaborated here, it refers to the degree to which Behan did not just translate *An Giall* for a metropolitan audience, but re-invented *An Giall* within the terms of metro-politan culture itself. Thus, not only does *The Hostage* realign the nationalism it depicts within the cultural dynamics of English society and re-orient its humour and politics to make sense to English audiences, but it does so within the form of music hall drama, a popular form of entertainment which had enjoyed immense success both in England and in Anglophone Irish culture. Music hall is present in traces in *An Giall*, but it becomes the prevailing mode of *The Hostage*, within which the diverse elements of song, dance, drama and farce cohere and make sense, and against which the play exerts ironic and parodic pressure.

---

41 M. L. Pratt, *Imperial Eyes: Travel Writing and Transculturation* (1992), p. 6.

The Hostage *and an east end music hall*

John Russell Taylor considers omitting Brendan Behan from *Anger and After*, his influential early study of the 'new wave' of playwrights in postwar Britain, since, he writes, Behan is 'in almost every respect foreign and irrelevant.'[42] The grounds for Behan's inclusion, however, are 'his roughness, his irreverence, his distaste for any establishment, even the establishment of rebellion' which he shares with 'the more notable of the new English writers.'[43] But Behan might equally be included for his interest in forging contemporary theatre in the spirit of the dying art of music hall, which interested such diverse figures in the British theatrical scene as John Osborne, Shelagh Delaney, Frank Norman, and, of course, Joan Littlewood. It could be argued indeed that *The Hostage* participated in the contemporary experiment to fuse the popularity of music hall entertainment with the subversive undertones of political theatre. Although the play would later transfer to the West End, and enjoy successful runs in theatres across Europe and the United States, it was apt that *The Hostage* opened in a former music hall theatre.

Littlewood recalls in her autobiography that the Theatre Royal at Stratford East, the home of her Theatre Workshop, and the theatre at which both *The Quare Fellow* and *The Hostage* became international successes, had been an important venue for music hall and melodramatic theatre in London's East End. In the 1880s and 1890s, Charles Dillon's theatre produced '*The Streets of London, The Colleen Bawn, Hamlet, East Lynne, Richard III, Don Caesar de Bazan, The Devil in Paris, The Shaughraun*, and *Belphagor*,' and later 'third-rate variety and striptease shows.'[44] The theatre attracted the suspicion of the local vicar in 1884, who worried that it would 'necessitate a low kind of drama; the place will become the resort of the worst characters of the neighbourhood.' Littlewood joked that in the 1950s the actors were the 'worst characters of the neighbour-hood.'[45] Under her direction, the Theatre Royal returned to the melodramatic and music hall proclivities of Dillon's time, but introduced recurrent political themes which alluded insistently to international socialism, post-colonial conflicts, and the internal class struggles of British society.

An Giall would have suited this diet of theatrical modes and themes even in a literal translation, but *The Hostage* pushed further into the realms of the music hall, perhaps most clearly in its loose structure and its rapid effusion of gags, bawdy songs, dances, farcical action, and quick-witted dialogue. These formal innovations proved controversial, with a number of critics and reviewers complaining of the constant, 'irrelevant' interruptions to the plot, while Behan's

42 J. Russell Taylor, *Anger and After: A Guide to the New British Drama* (1963), p. 104.   **43** Ibid., p. 105.   **44** Littlewood, *Joan's Book*, pp 444–46.   **45** Ibid., pp 444–45.

most enthusiastic champion, Kenneth Tynan, recognised that the play's form was its novelty: 'conventional terminology is totally inept to describe the uses to which Mr Behan and his director, Joan Littlewood, are trying to put the theatre. The old pigeon holes will no longer serve.'[46] Like Boucicault and O'Casey, Behan crossbred the naive romantic and political sentiments of melodrama with comedy, but Behan pushed further the parodic and subversive comic forms of the music hall.

The Hostage borrows from the music hall forms of Boucicault in adapting song and comic asides, and in attempting to effect a sentimental and comic reconciliation between the divided characters. We see in *The Hostage*, then, characters such as Pat, who like Myles-na-Coppaleen of Boucicault's *The Colleen Bawn*, continually makes comic asides, while we see also the absent figure of nationalist heroism in the young boy who is to be hanged in a Belfast jail, and the romantic nationalist image of feminine purity and innocence in the character of Teresa. As Stephen Watt argues, many similar ingredients are present in O'Casey's plays, including the stage-Irish comic character, the virtuous, downtrodden Irish woman, and the self-sacrificing hero, but O'Casey allows these conventional characters to settle in before overturning them.[47] Behan's play from the very beginning, although it includes these stock ingredients, never allows them to raise expectations of conventional plot or character resolution. The melodramatic opening scene is immediately interrupted with comedy and farce, and the play continues in much the same vein, interspersing the situation comedy of the IRA keeping safe house in a brothel with music-hall 'stand-up' comedy, noted for its one-line witticisms.

Like *An Giall*, *The Hostage* alludes to the routine reference points of popular cultural nationalism – the Shan van Vocht, 1916, 1798, Patrick Pearse, 'the Laughing Boy,' and heroic self-sacrifice – only to combine these with references to the hydrogen bomb, Jayne Mansfield, Harold Macmillan, and Krushchev. The songs about what the IRA did to the Black and Tans are followed by songs romanticising the life of a colonial administrator, nostalgic for 'dear old England' (131). So too, the conventional romantic plot of nationalist melodrama, in which the innocent Irish girl idealises the nationalist hero, is subverted in *The Hostage* when Teresa falls in love with the English soldier, Leslie. Together, they embody the sentimental reconciliation familiar from Boucicault, and explore the common cultural connections between an Irish countrygirl and a Cockney soldier. But even in this they subvert conventions. Teresa abandons the mask of countrygirl innocence when she leaps into bed with Leslie, for example, while Leslie mocks English political and imperialist

46 K. Tynan, 'New Amalgam', *The Observer*, 19 October 1958, p. 19.   47 S. Watt, *Joyce, O'Casey, and the Irish Popular Theater*, pp 143–87.

élites, in contrast to the leader of his IRA captors, Monsewer, who sings nostalgically about 'the playing fields of Eton' (131). *The Hostage* adopts and subverts almost every characteristic of political melodrama, using the popular comic and singing routines of the music hall to parody and undermine the customary devices of cultural nationalist forms.

Music hall is, of course, a notoriously indefinite term for a set of analogous entertainment patterns and tastes of the late nineteenth and early twentieth centuries, which enjoyed considerable success in the major urban centres of the British Isles. As Peter Bailey argues, 'the term mobilises a limited but still resonant set of associations that fall into place in a familiar collage of names and images: Marie Lloyd, Dan Leno; the Old Met, Collins'; "Boiled Beef and Carrots", "Down at the Old Bull and Bush"; the sing-song and the comic turn.'[48] As a genre of popular entertainment, it entailed a diverse but closely linked assembly of comedy, sketch dramas, song, music, dance, novelty acts, and other forms of spectacular performance such as tightrope and trapeze acts. The emphases of music hall veered towards either the spectacle, in the case of performance acts, or the induction of collective participation in song, particularly comic song. Nostalgic constructions of the music hall prevailed in Behan's time, celebrating it as an authentic expression of working-class folk culture, but this view tended to ignore the degree to which the success of music hall was the product of its incorporation into an expanding leisure industry in the mid-nineteenth century, and its commodification as a form of mass entertainment in the urban marketplace. Nevertheless, in the 1950s the music hall served as a model, particularly for Littlewood's Theatre Workshop, for the integration of diverse and eclectic cultural elements into an immersive experience of theatre. The ingredients for such theatre included silly or frivolous comic songs (which Bailey argues gave music hall its distinctive voice),[49] athletic displays of physical comedy or clown acts, episodic or fragmentary drama, and various kinds of parodic performances which targeted pretension and authority for mockery.

The Hostage contains and integrates all of these elements into its structure, giving some, notably the Lord Chamberlain's office, the impression that the play was merely a frame on which to hang 'low' forms of entertainment.[50] Many of its songs and jokes are both well worn and frivolous, including some which seemed to be borrowed haphazardly from Behan's other writings. But they do perform a function within the play, even if often it is for immediate subversive effect. This is made explicit at various times in the play, when Mulleady, Rio Rita, and Princess Grace sing 'We're here because we're queer,' for example:

48 P. Bailey, 'Introduction: Making Sense of Music Hall', in Peter Bailey (ed.), *Music Hall: The Business of Pleasure* (1986), p. viii. **49** Ibid., p. x. **50** C.D. Herriot, Reader's Report, Lord Chamberlain's Office, 1 October 1958.

When Socrates in Ancient Greece,
Sat in his Turkish bath,
He rubbed himself, and scrubbed himself,
And steamed both fore and aft.

He sang the songs the sirens sang,
With Oscar and Shakespeare,
We're here because we're queer,
Because we're queer because we're here. (159)

On one hand, it is easy to see why the Lord Chamberlain's reader, C.D. Herriot, believed the play was 'a mere excuse ... for stupidly indecent songs.'[51] Such songs appear regularly and indiscriminately throughout the play, breaking up the progress of the plot in order to keep the audience amused with frivolity and camp humour. Perversely, however, the reaction of the censor indicates the reason why the song is included in the play in the first place. After this song Princess Grace remarks to the audience: 'The trouble we had getting that past the nice Lord Chamberlain' (159).[52] The song is designed in part to test the response of the Lord Chamberlain's office, and, moreover, to show the audience that there is a moral code against which the play has been and continues to be policed and sanctioned. It serves to remind the audience of the moral and social contexts in which they are watching three 'queers' gyrating across the stage, and of the presence of an authority which seeks to keep theatrical performances within the bounds of some nebulous notions of moral respectability. The song is at its most truthful in its refrain, 'we're here because we're queer,' since the 'queer' characters singing it were indeed on stage solely to make visible the place of homosexuality on the contemporary moral agenda. This is, in part, the function of music hall, and other forms of popular entertainment, as George Orwell argued in 1941, to pit obscenity and bawdiness against systems of law and morality.[53]

'This next bit's even worse,' says Princess Grace after his reference to the Lord Chamberlain (159), performing the role of a compère or continuity announcer who functioned in the music hall to connect acts together into a seamless line of entertainment. Behan uses this device a number of times in the play, in the comic or acerbic asides of Meg and Pat, for example, which indicates

---

51 Ibid.   52 In the 1st edition of the play (1958), Princess Grace says 'The trouble we had getting that past the nice Earl of Scarborough', who was of course the then Lord Chamberlain, responsible for censoring theatre productions. As with many of the changes between editions of *The Hostage*, such allusions were made clearer, or more general, in order to make sense to different audiences. 53 G. Orwell, 'The Art of Donald McGill', *Decline of the English Murder and Other Essays* (1965), p. 152.

the ways in which *The Hostage* is constructed in the image of a variety show performance. The play can be analysed as a typical series of component acts within a variety show. Meg and Pat play the comic double act, whose 'almost marital' relationship revolves around stereotypical music hall notions of men as drunken dreamers and liars and women as acid-tongued, pragmatic whores. In between their banter, Monsewer plays the stage-Irish caricature, wheezing on the bagpipes and muttering about martyrs, but, with a touch of Shaw, Behan subverts Monsewer's stage-Irishry by confusing Scottish with Irish customs, and making him the Hibernophile product of Eton rather than the nationalist 'graduate' of Mountjoy. Other caricatures crowd and dance across the stage – the camp queers who waltz in and out of the action, and turn out in the end to be secret policemen; the prim and sanctimonious Miss Gilchrist, who oscillates between puritanical devotion to Catholicism and extreme protestations of empire loyalism. Leslie and Teresa, with the two IRA gunmen lurking sometimes menacingly, sometimes farcically in the background, provide the continuous sketches of melodrama and sentiment in the play, but even here Behan introduces music hall elements in the form of jokes and songs which have no obvious function in the plot.

The Hostage inclines frequently towards frivolity, a mode of comedy which delights in the pursuit of laughter for its own sake. The play abounds with examples, from the opening scene in which Pat tells us, for no apparent reason, that 'Killymanjaro' is 'a noted mountain off the south coast of Switzerland' (83), through to the conclusion in which Mulleady declares 'I'm a secret policeman and I don't care who knows it' (167). Behan's songs and jokes are often ludicrous or inane, played for momentary effect, such as the song Miss Gilchrist and Mulleady sing in Act One, consisting of the line 'Our souls. Our souls. Our souls,' which the stage directions indicate should be *'slurred to sound – "Our souls. Are souls. Arseholes"'* (100). The humour is neither subtle nor inventive, a point made by the censor when he asked Theatre Workshop to remove the Gaelic word 'focail' from the text because, he wrote, 'it is obvious that it will be played for a dirty laugh.'[54] *The Hostage* repeatedly deviates from its story line in order to achieve an instant effect – laughter or surprise – but, as Derrida argues, frivolity is in essence a deviant form, pursuing desire as an end in itself.[55] The frivolous instances of *The Hostage* work within an aesthetic of 'pure' theatre, which privileges spectacle and catharsis over what were believed to be the more edifying influences of melodrama. More importantly, frivolity performs a key function in relation to the political themes of the play, undermining the effectivity of political melodrama by deflating sentimentality consistently. No

54 Herriot, Reader's Report, 1st October 1958. **55** J. Derrida, *The Archeology of the Frivolous*, trans.. J. P. Leavey, Jr. (1987), pp 134–35.

one sentiment or mood is allowed space to develop or endure, since whenever the drama approaches resolution the play rapidly alters its tone with a dance, song, or comic routine.

The Hostage mobilises contradictory impulses towards melodramatic sentiment on the one hand, and frivolous momentary pleasure on the other. Melodrama, particularly in political form, aspires towards the condition of memory, raising up the events of the past within a sentimental order in order to awaken political consciousness in the present. It demands, therefore, to be remembered, to make a *lasting* impression on its audience. The frivolity of the music hall form, in contrast, aspires towards the instantaneous. Derrida defines frivolity as 'the arrangement of hollow or unnecessary signs,' in which identity is confronted constantly with the marks of its arbitrariness and disposability.[56] This is especially evident in the relationship between frivolity and identity in *The Hostage*. The melodramatic scenes in *The Hostage* work towards bolstering particular notions of identity and history. In Act Two, for example, Meg chants menacingly at the English soldier, Leslie, a song chastising English imperialism and lauding the history of nationalist struggle:

> Who fears to speak of Easter Week
> That week of famed renown,
> When the boys in green went out to fight
> The forces of the Crown.
>
> With Mausers bold, and hearts of gold,
> The Red Countess dressed in green,
> And high above the GPO
> The rebel flag was seen. (139–40)

Meg's song, in common with nationalist rebel songs more generally, represents an historical rupture responsible for the emergence of modern Republican identity. It draws upon the renowned song, 'Who fears to speak of '98?,' adapting it to tell the story of the Easter Rising of 1916. Meg uses it to explain to Leslie the historical reasons for his predicament as a hostage, replicating the melodramatic dialectic between English oppression and Irish nationalist identity. But the play immediately disturbs and subverts the effect of this song, firstly by commenting self-reflexively on the author, who Pat says would 'sell his country for a pint' (141), and secondly, by mocking as farce the whole issue of political identifications, as indicated in the stage directions for this scene:

> *What happens next is not very clear. There are a number of arguments all going on at once. Free-Staters against Republicanism, Irish against English, homo-*

56 Ibid., p. 119.

sexuals against heterosexuals, and in the confusion all the quarrels get mixed up and it looks as though everyone is fighting everyone else. In the centre of the mêlée, MISS GILCHRIST *is standing on the table singing "Land of Hope and Glory". The* IRA OFFICER *has one chair and is waving a Free State flag and singing "The Soldier's Song", while the* RUSSIAN SAILOR *has the other and sings the Soviet National Anthem. The* NEGRO *parades through the room carrying a large banner inscribed* "KEEP IRELAND BLACK". *The piano plays through out. Suddenly the* VOLUNTEER *attacks the* SOLDIER *and the* RUSSIAN *joins in the fight. The* VOLUNTEER, *somewhat dazed, sees the* RUSSIAN'S *red flag and thinks he has been promoted to guard. He blows his railway whistle and the fight breaks up into a wild dance in which they all join on the train behind the* VOLUNTEER *and rush round the room in a circle.* (141)[57]

The delineation of political identities is here mocked as pantomime, and reduced quickly and farcically into incoherent chaos. The activities described in these stage directions mock with irony the identity politics of contemporary Britain and Ireland, confusing the signs of their various affiliations and roles, until descending into a '*wild dance.*' Behan does not resolve this scene by plunging his characters meaninglessly into hectic dancing, however, for the dance breaks up so that '*the dancers are left in the position of forming a ring round* LESLIE *which resembles a prison cage*' (141). Their formation implies that the political posturing which they have just performed is responsible for Leslie's captivity. The formation of the characters on the stage continues to tell its own story. As Leslie discovers that he is to be shot by the IRA in reprisal for the hanging in Belfast, the dancers creep away from him, '*leaving him alone in the room*' to sing his mock sentimental song, 'I am a happy English lad' (142). The disappearance of all other characters from the stage, and his condemnation of them for doing so, implies the hypocrisy of their political flag-waving. In their eagerness to parade meaningless symbols of political loyalty, they are complicit in Leslie's fate. The music hall capers of Behan's characters, frivolous and futile as they might appear to be, do engage in critical dialogue with the melodramatic sentiment of the play.

This is evident in the final scene of the play, too, in which the dead body of Leslie yields a '*ghostly green light*' from which he rises from the dead to sing the curtain song:

---

57 These stage directions appear in revised versions of *The Hostage*. In the first edition of the play, a similar scene occurs which is given less specific direction. Meg's Republican song is followed by '*Rock and Roll. Everybody dances*', which breaks up the menacing political tones of her song with frivolous dancing.

> The bells of hell,
> Go ting-a-ling-a-ling,
> For you but not for me,
> Oh death, where is thy sting-a-ling-a-ling?
> Or grave thy victory? (168)

The whole cast joins in the repetition of this chorus, facing the audience, turning self-reflexively on the distinction between the theatrical and the real. The bells toll for the audience, not the actors. Here, *The Hostage* celebrates cheerfully its cultural hybridity, in which Irish nationalists and English soldiers, secret policemen and prostitutes can sing together a song indebted both to the bible and to British army folk culture of World War One; and in which the political effectivity of melodrama is fused with and deflated by the theatrical self-parody of music hall. Music hall interludes function throughout the play to frustrate and contradict the continuity and resolution of melodramatic plot.

Behan's play activates contradiction as the principal instrument for displacing the politics of identity at every turn. Sometimes, these contradictions take the form of inconsistencies. Meg is shocked when told that Monsewer's father was a bishop, but later admits casually that her father was the parish priest, for example; Teresa complains prudishly when Leslie attempts to touch her, then leaps jauntily into bed with him; she also understands Cockney dialect at one moment and not at another. Such inconsistencies destabilise the fixity of character in the play, and undermine the conventions of naturalist drama. At other times, the play stresses the ironic or paradoxical as forms of contradiction which reveal comic fallacies in the characters' own self-awareness: Monsewer as the rabid Irish nationalist nostalgic for Eton and the colonial service; Miss Gilchrist as the puritan Irish Catholic who adores English monarchy and sings patriotic English songs. Irony and contradiction are deployed frequently and effectively in *An Giall*, but in *The Hostage* they are developed further so as to exceed and frustrate the sentimental plot.

The Hostage is routinely represented as the bowdlerised, corrupted version of a moving Gaelic tragedy, the pitiable product of an author in declining health and a producer intent on cannibalising his play for a variety show. But the form of the play is both more complex and more coherent than this idea of *The Hostage* allows. *The Hostage* is, in some senses, a relentless parody of *An Giall* (which is itself parodic). It mobilises various modes of cultural subversion – frivolity, irony, parody, contradiction, irreverence, bawdiness – to displace the tragic and melodramatic aspects of *An Giall*. Behan constructs an intense dialogic interplay in *The Hostage* between its melodramatic plot and the stylistic instruments of disruption and subversion. The routine deployment of songs, jokes, malapropisms, dances, fights, anecdotes and farces dislodges and interrupts the progress of the drama. Displacement becomes a stylistic principle in *The Hostage*, refusing to allow the play to settle into sentimental or melo-dramatic resolution. *An Giall*, as we have seen, is subversive in its own right, but in a way which required a familiarity with the codes of nationalist melodrama in order to function effectively. In translating *An Giall* for the London stage, Behan recognised the necessity of translating the play's form as well as its content, its cultural modes of expression and performance as well as its allusions and idioms. *The Hostage* may be considered properly, therefore, not simply or wholly an Irish play, but a play inscribed within codes and contexts of English theatre and culture, as a play which resituates the subversive potential of *An Giall* within the language, forms and cultural politics of mid-century England.

The politics of cultural hybridity

The Hostage exploits the conventions of intensely theatrical forms, melodrama and the music hall, to give expression to its cultural and political critiques. In doing so, Behan's play participated in the appropriation of commodified forms of mass entertainment for experimental British culture in the mid century. This trend in the contemporary arts ranged from the paintings of Richard Hamilton and David Hockney, on the one hand, which constructed parodic collages comprised of images drawn from popular magazines and advertisements, to the writings of John Osborne and Colin MacInnes, on the other, which drew upon popular music and culture, including the dying art of music hall, to make sense of the changing dynamics of English society and culture. Behan's play engages productively with both English and Irish cultural contexts, recovering through the character of Leslie the cultural affinities between the working classes of both cultures, and recovering the shared hybrid cultural forms of Ireland and England through melodrama and music hall.

Bertolt Brecht once celebrated George Bernard Shaw as a 'terrorist,' whose principle weapons were his humour and his boisterous irreverence.[58] In similar terms, Gus Martin celebrated the work of Brendan Behan, for the 'minor explosions' his work caused wherever it was produced.[59] In *The Hostage*, Behan deployed irony and farce to destabilise the political identities produced in the competing discourses of nationalism and colonialism, and to reflect critically on politics, class, and morality. The parodic and self-reflexive devices assembled and played out in *The Hostage* reveal that modern political discourses borrow extensively from, and are disturbingly analogous to, theatrical spectacle and

58 B. Brecht, 'Three Cheers for Shaw', in *Brecht on Theatre*, ed. J. Willett (1974), p. 10.   59 A. Martin, 'Brendan Behan', *Threshold*, 18 (1963), p. 22.

caricature. Thus, empire loyalism and militant republicanism, stage-Irishry and Cockney buffoonery, are roles and masks as phoney and effective as each other, which blur the boundaries of the theatrical and the political.

For Behan, all Irishmen and women were hyphenated, an idea which could be as abusive as when he wrote that 'Paddy the wanker peasant and poet' Kavanagh would be more at home in Boston or New York than in Dublin,[60] or as benign as when he described how Dublin street-traders would treat Liverpool as an extension of Ireland.[61] Behan's representation of the hyphen between England and Ireland is not a reversion to the imperialist narrative of Anglo-Irish relations, but rather seeks a return to the hybridised culture produced in what W.J. McCormack has called the 'metropolitan colony.'[62] Behan's Dublin was as suffused with the ex-British army culture common to London and Liverpool, and as captivated by Victorian ideals and cultural forms, as it was comprised of nationalist culture and tradition. Behan recovers a fractured and contested notion of Englishness in *The Hostage* through the humour and irreverence of Leslie, just as he figures Irish nationalism as a reactive imitation of colonial discourses of control as correctives to the myopic political visions of both Irish nationalism and English imperialism.

Both *An Giall* and *The Hostage* effect small but significant shifts on the cultural politics of some of the principal literary genres through which nationalism and imperialism were conducted and popularised. Melodrama played as important a part in communicating the ideological foundations of modern Irish nationalism as music hall gave popular expression to English nationalism at the height of empire. Behan's plays constitute what Franco Moretti calls 'micro-evolutionary events'[63] in the history of these genres, re-assembling the conventions of melodrama and music hall within the cultural politics of postcolonial revisionism. Moreover, the differences between *An Giall* and *The Hostage* represent in themselves a shift away from the tragi-comic conventions of naturalist theatre towards the exaggerated theatricality and self-parody of the post-modern play. Behan's plays are thus situated at a crucial nexus in the relationship between popular literary genres and the avant-garde cultural politics of postcolonial and postmodern aesthetics. Both *An Giall* and *The Hostage* mobilise oppositional modes of appropriation, subversion, parody and irony to undermine and resist the politics of identity, and to displace the ethical imperatives of popular cultural forms towards recognising and legitimating the postcolonial politics of cultural hybridity.

60 B. Behan, 'Letter to Sindbad Vail', (October 1952), in Mikhail (ed.), *The Letters of Brendan Behan*, p. 53.   61 B. Behan, 'I Meet the Hyphenated Irishmen', *The Dubbalin Man* (1997), p. 51.   62 See W. J. McCormack, *From Burke to Beckett: Ascendancy, Tradition and Betrayal in Literary History* (1994).   63 F. Moretti, *Signs Taken for Wonders: Essays in the Sociology of Literary Forms*, trans. S. Fischer, D. Forgacs and D. Miller (1988), p. 269.

I have been arguing in this chapter that the hybrid forms of Behan's works constitute an avant-garde within the cultural politics of Irish postcolonialism. *The Hostage* was especially susceptible to the charge by Irish critics that Behan was exploiting stage-Irish comic stereotypes for the amusement of an English audience, but this is a crude reading of the play. It is to underestimate the extent to which *The Hostage* was performing a valuable function in English theatre, alongside Shelagh Delaney and John Osborne, in finding a place for the music hall form in 'serious' theatre, and in subverting the cultural politics of music hall against both Irish nationalism and English imperialism. This is, I want to conclude, one of the most revealing facets of Behan's work, that it found a function and a place in English literary culture and history as readily and comfortably as it did in the Irish literary tradition. *The Hostage* alluded to Ireland in the same breath as Cyprus and Kenya, thus implying the post-imperial agenda which followed in the wake of the Suez crisis, just as it showed through farcical music hall comedy routines the futility of both imperialist and nationalist wars. Behan's oeuvre can be narrated and contextualised in relation to the cultural trends of England in the postwar years as cogently as it can be situated in Irish contexts. This should alert us both to the inadequacies of literary histories which take the nation as the fundamental unit of explanation, and to the extraordinary fluidity of Behan's writings, which frequently took as their subjects the hyphen between English and Irish, between London and Dublin.

5 / *Borstal Boy:* colonialism, nationalism and carceral liminality

Carceral cartographies

> Each narrow cell in which we dwell
> Is a foul and dark latrine,
> And the fetid breath of living Death
> Chokes up each grated screen,
> And all, but Lust, is turned to dust
> In Humanity's machine.

Oscar Wilde, *The Ballad of Reading Gaol*[1]

Wilde's poem draws together much that is emblematic of the literary topo-graphy of imprisonment: its humanist extrapolation of the significance for issues of civilisation and society of specific instances of confinement, depriva-tion and punishment, its attention to the architectonics of carceral space and of the body, its intensification of sexual desire, and its sanctification of an imagined community of subaltern delinquents made the scapegoats of humanity's 'sins.' In its repeated imagery of prisoners looking 'with such a wistful eye/ Upon that little tent of blue/ Which prisoners call the sky,' the poem recapitulates the characteristic ingressive and egressive metaphors which structure the literal and figurative cartographies of the prison. Wilde figures the prison as self, as death, as language, as hell, as huddled community of outcasts, as the demarcated shame of modern society, but without permitting the epistemological reality of imprisonment to slide into abstracted metaphors for the human condition. But the metaphorical economy of incarceration in Wilde's poem works to secure the association of the disciplinary and punitive practices of prison with the domain of 'liberal society,' thus establishing the interdependence of incarceration and social 'freedom.'

The metaphorical capabilities of imprisonment function in a way which, for Wilde, invites liberal critique. But they have other functions too. For Genet, prison was the source of love, for he wrote in *Miracle of the Rose* 'it is the rigors of prison that drive us toward each other in bursts of love without which we could not live.'[2] Genet, like Foucault, conceived of the ambivalence and

---

1 O. Wilde [C.3.3.], *The Ballad of Reading Gaol* (1898), p. 27.   2 J. Genet, *Miracle of the Rose*, trans. B. Frechtman (1966), p. 1.

liminality of the prison as a disciplinary institution, of its role in the production of desire as well as deprivation, of love as much as violation. Brombert in *The Romantic Prison* delineates a particularly Gothic vision of imprisonment, embedded in complex interplay between fantasy and fear, and signifying release as well as constraint.[3] Carnochan argues indeed that the metaphorical potency of the prison tends rather to prevail over its concrete existence, and even that the 'reality follows rather than precedes metaphor,'[4] a notion which resonates through Foucault's explication of the discursive formation of disciplinary power.[5] Literary prisons, whether the subject of fictional, poetic or autobiographical writings, function largely in metaphorical economies in which confinement and punishment inevitably have corporeal manifestations, but have more pertinent symbolic ends.

The symbolic significance of imprisonment is particularly apparent in the literature of Irish nationalism, of course, which since the 1790s has employed narratives of penal discipline to produce its own mythology of martyrdom, sacrifice, protest and regeneration. This is especially the case in the nationalist testimonies of the nineteenth century: John Mitchel's *Jail Journal*, John Devoy's *Recollections of an Irish Rebel*, Jeremiah O'Donovan Rossa's *Prison Life*, Michael Davitt's *Leaves from a Prison Diary*, Wolfe Tone's *The Autobiography*, and Thomas Clarke's *Glimpses of an Irish Felon's Prison Life*.[6] Such narratives work to transform the punishment of nationalist rebellion into the heroic election of sacrifice, and to organise the political failure of rebellion into a mythic pantheon of Christlike martyrs. The narratives of Mitchel, Clarke and O'Donovan Rossa in particular, represented the dark, solitary confines of English prisons as the testing grounds of the spirit and determination of Irish nationalism, while Davitt, Tone and Devoy are concerned more with justifying and explaining the basis for nationalist rebellion in which imprisonment and punishment are merely extensions of the machinery of colonial government. Each of these narratives were written either as records or responses to the experience of rebellion and punishment, from Tone's *Autobiography* written in the 1790s, to the narratives of Clarke and Devoy, who were instrumental in organising the nationalist campaigns of the 1880s and of 1916. Common to all of them is the notion that suffering and death are the symbolic rituals through which the national cause will be served and won, that endurance and martyrdom are as essential to revolution as arms and men.

---

3 V. Brombert, *The Romantic Prison: The French Tradition* (1978).   **4** W.B. Carnochan, *Confinement and Flight: An Essay on English Literature of the Eighteenth Century* (1977), p. 4.   **5** M. Foucault, *Discipline and Punish: The Birth of the Prison*, trans. A.M. Sheridan Smith (1979).   **6** J. Mitchel, *Jail Journal* (1854); J. Devoy, *Recollections of an Irish Rebel* (1929); J. O'Donovan Rossa, *My Years in English Jails* [*Prison Life*] (1874); M. Davitt, *Leaves from a Prison Diary; or, Lectures to a 'Solitary' Audience* (1885); W. Tone, *The Autobiography*, ed. R. Barry O'Brien (1826); T. J. Clarke, *Glimpses of an Irish Felon's Prison Life* (1913).

Failure, and indeed the endurance of deprivation and confinement, was thus by the late nineteenth century a necessary component in the construction of a sacred myth of heroic struggle, which required its register of executions, deportations, penal colonists and prisoners in order to sanction the violence of the present. Mitchel records his contentment in *Jail Journal* at being deported and exiled from his native land, since it strengthens the nationalist case against British injustice. To be a failure in one's struggle against imperialism, to be captured, deported, or executed, earned neither notoriety nor oblivion, but instead secured a place in the nationalist canon of heroic martyrs and champions. Terence MacSwiney, jailed in Reading prison, reflected in his diary on the scenes of celebration among the Irish nationalist prisoners on the execution of Roger Casement in 1916:

> The English have immortalised another day in Irish history. Today they executed Casement for his attempt to restore Ireland's independence ... He died in a manner worthy of our comrades who have already failed in the same cause and worthy of the heroic line of martyrs to English misrule ... When we read of the execution in the evening papers it was a consolation to learn how splendidly he faced death with a reverence with which the Irish people always like their leaders to die.[7]

For MacSwiney, Casement's death is important for its participation in a long line of heroic failures, just as his own death by hunger strike in 1920 would enlist him to the ranks of historic martyrdom. Imprisonment, deportation, and execution, in the language and iconography of modern cultural nationalism, paradoxically signified the legitimation of the struggle against British imperialism, and the prison thus became a metaphorical projection both of colonial rule and of its limits.

While imprisonment signified endurance and transcendence, the nationalist imagination reserved the rhetoric and imagery of resurrection for the apotheosis of imperial punishment, execution. Thomas MacDonagh, for example, executed for his part in the nationalist uprising of 1916, concluded his speech from the dock with an emboldened summons to 'Take me away, and let my blood bedew the sacred soil of Ireland. I die in the certainty that once more the seed will fructify.'[8] The metaphors for 'blood sacrifice' were abundant in the literary construction of the 1916 Rising, in particular, drawing upon the ballads and narratives of the nineteenth century to ritualise the foredoomed Rising as yet another glorious failure. From the 1890s onwards, militant nationalism was

7 Quoted in F. J. Costello, *Enduring the Most: The Life and Death of Terence MacSwiney* (1995), pp 75–76.

potent in its adept fusion of nationalist rhetoric with Catholic imagery of crucifixion and resurrection, drawing together the resurgent devotional practices of Catholic Ireland and the growing tide of support for Home Rule.[9] The trial reports and 'speeches from the dock' of those who were to be executed, and the prison memoirs of those who endured penal servitude, formed a popular genre of reading during this period. They served to dramatise the struggle between the oppressor and the oppressed further, so that badly planned and executed uprisings seemed mere preludes to the more significant and climactic representational conflicts which took place in the courtrooms.

In the early twentieth century, therefore, the iconography of nationalism was deeply indebted to the prison scenario, and particularly to imprisonment as the inevitable prelude to the rekindling of the flame of rebellion. Nationalist narratives of imprisonment tend to suggest the unequivocal identification of the individual with the nation, so that, as Sean Ryder has argued, 'the historical, contingent subject ... appears to achieve authenticity and completion – its heroic realisation – through identification with the transcendent, impersonal entity known as "the nation".'[10] The disparate experiences and emotions of the individual are thus made coherent only through a sustained allegorical projection of the individual onto the evolving drama of the national destiny. This is the familiar resort of many Irish writers in the nineteenth and twentieth centuries, including Mangan, Mitchel, Pearse, Corkery and O'Connor. It is the 'tradition,' or discourse, in which Brendan Behan and his autobiographical novel, *Borstal Boy*, are thoroughly, irretrievably immersed.[11]

Borstal Boy

Borstal Boy was first published in 1958 as an autobiographical account of Behan's imprisonment in England between 1939 and 1941. When he first conceived of writing a book of his experiences in 1943, when he was in Mountjoy jail in Dublin for shooting at a detective, Behan professed the book to have the wider scope of narrating the history of the IRA campaign of 1939, and to be entitled, *The Green Invader*.[12] He had already published a draft of the opening section of

---

8 T. MacDonagh, quoted in *Speeches from the Dock*, ed. by T.D., A.M. and D.B. Sullivan (1968), p. 340.   **9** See also F. O'Connor's intriguing suggestion of the influence of English Romanticism on the nationalist iconography of sacrifice and death, in *An Only Child* (1961), pp 253–54. Richard English traces the significance of O'Connor's suggestion for Irish nationalism in the early twentieth century, and specifically on romanticist manifestations in the life of E. O'Malley in *Ernie O'Malley: IRA Intellectual* (1998), p. 117.   **10** S. Ryder, 'Male Autobiography and Irish Cultural Nationalism: John Mitchel and James Clarence Mangan', *The Irish Review*, 13 (Winter 1992/93), p. 70.   **11** B. Behan, *Borstal Boy* (1961 – orig. 1958). All page references to *Borstal Boy* are subsequently cited in parenthesis.   **12** See Behan's letter to B. Bradshaw, December 4th 1943, in Mikhail (ed.), *The*

Borstal Boy, entitled 'I Become a Borstal Boy,' in Sean O'Faolain's *The Bell* in 1942, and would later publish extracts in *Points*. John Ryan recalls that Behan sent him a draft entitled *Another Twisting of the Rope* in 1951, and Ryan suggested that he should call it *Bridewell Revisited*, a literary pun obviously on Evelyn Waugh's famous novel of 1945. 'When it did see the light of publishing day,' Ryan records, 'it was under the bland and un-inventive title of *Borstal Boy*, a title which, no doubt, the pass B.A. reader who read it for his publisher, bearing in mind the possibilities of a *News of the World* readership, had thought terribly swinging.'[13] Ryan perhaps overemphasises the degree to which the book was swept into the sensitivities and demands of the English book trade, but his response reflects the view that *Borstal Boy* evolved considerably from its genesis as a history of a Republican bombing campaign. By 1958, when it was published, Behan had already become a success in London with *The Quare Fellow*, and *Borstal Boy* seemed to tap into prevailing English concerns with juvenile delinquency and criminal justice reform as much as it told the story of a teenage IRA bomber.

Nevertheless, *Borstal Boy* appears to conform to the generic conventions of nationalist prison narratives, from the opening scene in which Behan is captured in England, which he compares to the arrest and trial of the Fenian, Thomas Clarke, to the conclusion in which Behan returns to Dublin, which bears striking similarities to John Mitchel's final passage to New York in his *Jail Journal*. At the age of sixteen, Behan was arrested in Liverpool and sentenced to three years borstal detention for carrying explosive charges into England, allegedly to cause explosion either at Cammell Lairds shipyard or a city centre department store, and *Borstal Boy* is the narrative of his experiences in the English carceral system between 1939 and 1941.[14] When a detective voices

Letters of Brendan Behan (1992), pp 27–28. Behan writes that he has been accepted by his IRA comrades as the official historian of the campaign of 1939, and that he is engaged in writing a long work on the subject, entitled *The Green Invader*.   13 J. Ryan, *Remembering How We Stood: Bohemian Dublin at the Mid-Century* (1975), p. 67. In recalling seeing a draft of *Borstal Boy* entitled *Another Twisting of the Rope*, Ryan may be confusing the evolution of *Borstal Boy* with that of *The Quare Fellow*, for which of course the reference to Hyde's *Casadh an tSugáin* is more appropriate. See Chapter 3.   14 Behan joined the Irish Republican Army (IRA) in 1937, at the age of fourteen, having been a member of its youth organisation, the Fianna Eireann. The IRA at this time was a faction of the Irish Volunteer movement which had fought for and negotiated the independence of the twenty-six 'southern' counties of the island of Ireland from British rule. Its members continued to fight for the six 'northern' counties still under British rule, and in 1939 launched a bombing campaign in England, the aim of which was to terrorise the British government into ceding Northern Ireland to the Irish Free State. It is, however, unclear as to whether Behan was ordered to carry explosives into England on the occasion described in *Borstal Boy*. He may have acted on his own initiative. See U. O'Connor, *Brendan Behan* (1993) and M. O'Sullivan, *Brendan Behan: A Life* (1997). Throughout *Borstal Boy* Behan's republicanism is of a peculiarly aestheticised and romantic kind, which is constructed more often through songs, ballads and literary references than through

disgust at Behan's actions – 'You facquing bestud, how would you like to see a woman cut in two by a plate-glass window?' – Behan conceives of his desperate ploy as the only recourse of men engaged in anti-colonial war, and the inevitable reply to colonial atrocities (10). Behan's own part in the IRA bombing campaign against England in 1939 is the silent subtext for his exploration throughout *Borstal Boy* of nationalist ideology and anti-colonial struggle. It is rarely mentioned beyond the first scene, but it informs and fuels the identity crisis with which Behan wrestles throughout the narrative.

The novel begins with a scene in which Behan is cast as the tough rebel, defiant of his captors and scornful of England. 'If I'd have had a gun you wouldn't have come through the door so shagging easy,' he tells the detectives who arrive to arrest him (9). There follow scenes in which he conforms to the expected role of a Republican prisoner:

> I was brought to the C.I.D. headquarters in Lime Street. In accordance with instructions, I refused to answer questions. I agreed to make a statement, with a view to propaganda for the cause. It would look well at home, too. I often read speeches from the dock, and thought the better of the brave and defiant men that made them so far from friends or dear ones.
>
> 'My name is Brendan Behan. I came over here to fight for the Irish Workers' and Small Farmers' Republic for a full and free life, for my countrymen, North and South, and for the removal of the baneful influence of British Imperialism from Irish affairs. God save Ireland.' (12–13)

Behan's statement is elaborated further in his speech from the dock of his trial, which is barely tolerated in court, and, similar to the accounts of Robert Emmet's speech from the dock, is interrupted by the judge (143–44).[15] In addressing the court, and constructing himself within the mould of the nationalist martyrs and heroes of previous struggles, Behan advertises his conformity to the conventions of nationalist iconography. 'I was a good volunteer,' he writes, 'captured carrying the struggle to England's doorstep' (13).

political arguments or debate. The IRA were, at the time, supposed to be fighting for the liberation of the northern six counties of Ireland, but Behan refers to Northern Ireland hardly at all. The consequence is that Behan's republicanism appears to be anachronistic, similar to that of his caricature, Monsewer, in *The Hostage*, who wanders around an IRA safe house in the 1950s believing that the war of independence is still being fought.   **15** R. Emmet's speech from the dock is quoted in Sullivan et al, *Speeches from the Dock*, pp 31–44. Behan was well versed in Republican speeches and, as a young child, could recite every word from Emmet's famous speech from 1803. One of his favourite plays was H.C. Mangan's *Robert Emmet: A History Play in Three Acts* which was performed at the Queen's theatre in Dublin with Behan's uncle, P. J. Bourke in the lead role. Mangan's play emphasises the Republican ideology of martyrdom and sacrifice, with Emmet

As Colbert Kearney argues, what we find in Behan's narrative is that 'the narrator is perpetually posing and examining the pose.'[16] After he has made his statement, he compares himself to the Manchester Martyrs.[17] When he is being searched in prison he alludes to Tom Clarke's description of prison searches in *Glimpses of an Irish Felon's Prison Life*. Throughout the narrative, Behan intersperses his descriptions and reflections on prison life with the verses from Irish nationalist ballads and songs, seeming to construct his own prison experiences through the echoed voices and cries of nationalist heroes – 'In boyhood's bloom and manhood's pride,/ Foredoomed by alien laws,/ Some on the scaffold proudly died,/ For Ireland's holy cause' (93).

Imprisonment in England seems to validate Behan's self-image as Republican hero, an image which he works frequently to underpin in the narrative through allusion to nationalist culture and heroics. He rarely considers the crime for which he has been imprisoned, and instead imagines imprisonment as a censure of national difference. The prison is for him an extension of colonial rule – he is jailed, it appears, for being an Irish nationalist. His treatment seems to him particularly punitive when he is forbidden to express what he considers to be his national culture – he is excommunicated by the priest from Catholic services, for example, and beaten severely when he shouts nationalist criticism at the priest for colluding with imperialism. For Behan, the prison frequently seems to be the site of fraught colonial struggle, governed by a 'tired old consul, weary from his labours amongst the lesser breeds' (90), and policed by colonial warriors in flight from the impending demise of the empire. Carceral space is thus for Behan the extended instrument of colonial rule, its regimes and strategies calculated to undermine and censure his sense of national identity.

Behan's imaginative reaction to the cold realisation of his plight in the English prison system is to resort to the characteristic typologies of nationalist separatism. Reeling in defence from the brutality of warders and the stark disciplinary codes of imprisonment, he elects to distinguish between the English and the Irish on racial grounds. On several occasions in his early experiences of prison, Behan considers the shared ancestry and racial characteristics of the English and the Germans as 'a master race that would burn a black man alive or put a pregnant woman out the side of the road in the interests of stern duty' (49). In contrast he considers the Catholic allegiances and affiliations

declaring that 'The hope that has lived for centuries can be crushed only by the extermination of our people' (7). See H.C. Mangan, *Robert Emmet: A History Play in Three Acts* (1904). **16** C. Kearney, 'Borstal Boy: A Portrait of the Artist as a Young Prisoner', in E.H. Mikhail (ed.), *The Art of Brendan Behan* (1979), p. 108. **17** The Manchester Martyrs were W. O'Meara Allen, Michael Larkin and W. O'Brien, who were hanged for their part in the murder of a police sergeant who was shot in a bid by the Fenians (a nationalist insurrectionary movement) to rescue two Fenian prisoners in 1867. The hangings provoked a wave of popular support for the Fenian cause in Ireland.

which bring the Irish closer to the culture and humour of the Mediterranean. He pictures the common cultures of 'Dante, Villon, Eoghan Ruadh O'Sullivan, in warmer, more humorous parts of the world than this nineteenth-century English lavatory, in Florence, in France, in Kerry, where the arbutus grows and the fuchsia glows on the dusty hedges in the soft light of the summer evening' (61). Behan mobilises a number of familiar stereotypes of the distinction between the English and Irish here: Protestant against Catholic, duty against humour, the rational against the poetic, the clinical against the cultural. In doing so, he recapitulates the terms of the nationalist categorisation of 'two civilisations,' pitched in opposition against one another, familiar in the work of Behan's precursors, Daniel Corkery, Sean O'Faolain, and Frank O'Connor, who themselves borrowed the separatist mould from D.P. Moran. But it is familiar to Behan by other means too, in the melodramas performed at the Queen's theatre in Dublin, under the management of Behan's uncle, P.J. Bourke, for example. 'God placed our islands and our souls apart,' says the heroic figure, Robert Emmet, in a play written by H.C. Mangan with Bourke playing the lead role, 'we do not *think* as they do.'[18] To distinguish the English racially and culturally from the Irish is Behan's defensive reaction against his early treatment in the prison. It is his attempt to assert his own authority over a system in which he has no control, and to reclaim his masculine self-esteem by identifying with the nationalist tradition of aggressive separatism. But such moments occur not as instances of regeneration or motivation, but as crises in Behan's sense of identity, both as a young, aggressive male made submissive within the prison system, and as an Irish nationalist forced to submit to his English captors.

Carceral masculinities

Colonial topographies are, of course, strongly gendered, and, as Ashis Nandy noted, the consequence of the association of the imperial ruler with masculinity, and the effective 'feminisation' of the colonised, is the aggressive assertion of masculinity in anti-colonial discourse.[19] Masculinity becomes the absolute gender of the colonial struggle, with the inevitable negation of femininity, and the recapitulation of imperialist terms of conflict. 'Even in its oppositional stance,' writes David Lloyd, 'nationalism repeats the master narrative of imperialism,'[20] which means, among other things, that the obsessive concern with martial prowess and the sexualisation of violence in imperialist discourse is

---

18 Mangan, *Robert Emmet*, p. 7. **19** A. Nandy, *The Intimate Enemy: Loss and Recovery of Self Under Colonialism* (1998). See particularly Nandy's first essay, 'The Psychology of Colonialism', pp 1–63. **20** D. Lloyd, *Anomalous States: Irish Writing and the Post-Colonial Moment* (1993), p. 54.

replicated and reproduced in nationalist discourse. In the prison scenario, the gendered terms of this conflict are exaggerated still further. The threatened violence of nationalism can only be treated by the systematic application of violence against the body – not just the beatings which Behan receives, but also the deprivation and containment of the body which Foucault observed as the focal point of disciplinary power. The masculine authority of the warders and the prison regime is designed to emasculate the prisoners, by compelling them into submission and silence. This strategy is particularly evident in Clarke's narrative. But similarly, the means for resistance and subterfuge are inevitably defined too by masculine tropes: when Behan is threatened by anti-Irish intimidation in the prison his instinctive response is to demonstrate his masculine authority through a brutal display of violence.

Fanon argued that the violence of anti-colonial struggle was 'a cleansing force,' which freed 'the native from his inferiority complex,' but at the same time that nationalist violence was the product of the imperialist, 'the bringer of violence into the home and into the mind of the native.'[21] John Mitchel makes much the same argument in *Jail Journal*, arguing that it is 'the prerogative of man to bear arms' in colonial conditions, since the use of violence 'under bayonet tuition, is a secret we cannot but learn.'[22] The violence of the coloniser breeds the violence of the colonised, according to Mitchel. The effect in the colonial struggle is to produce a competitive masculinity, which in terms of violence produces the cyclical rivalry of meeting force with force, atrocity for atrocity. The atrocities at Cork and Balbriggan are thus the justification Behan offers for his attempt to bomb Liverpool.[23] But the competitive masculinity of Behan's nationalism sometimes assumes comic proportions too, when, for example, he believes he may have lost his girlfriend in Dublin to a fellow Republican who has been sentenced to fourteen years penal servitude, which, compared to his three years borstal detention, somehow makes him less attractive (281). The nationalist call to arms, it seems, is also a call to manliness and virility, and Behan experiences his imprisonment as the necessary authentication of his masculine credentials, but also as the sustained attempt by the imperial power to undermine and negate his masculinity.

The power to subject Behan to discipline, to make him passive and submissive is manifest in the topography of imprisonment. The spatial rigours of imprisonment discipline the body into new habits of walking, sleeping,

---

21 F. Fanon, *The Wretched of the Earth*, trans. Constance Farrington (London: Penguin, 1967), p. 74, p. 29. 22 Mitchel, *Jail Journal*, p. 114, p. 144. 23 Behan is referring to the reprisal attacks by British police auxiliaries in 1920 on Cork and Balbriggan, after Irish Volunteers had successfully ambushed British forces. These reprisals were largely characterised by undisciplined looting, burning and destruction of property. In Cork, much of the city centre was burned to the ground while police auxiliaries obstructed fire fighters from attending the scene.

excretion, communication, reading and thinking. Every aspect of Behan's life as a prisoner in Walton jail, for example, is subject to control – not merely because his freedom to move and communicate is at the mercy of lock and key, but because, in the course of the narrative, prisoners are regulated as to when they may defecate, when light permits them to read, when their behaviour controls their rations of food. 'Systems of punishment,' Foucault writes, 'are to be situated in a certain "political economy" of the body: even if they do not make use of violent or bloody punishment, even when they use "lenient" methods involving confinement or correction, it is always the body that is at issue – the body and its forces, their utility and their docility, their distribution and their submission.'[24]

When Behan enters Walton jail for the first time, he is first placed in a line of other prisoners and abused and beaten by two warders who pounce on his omission of the word 'sir,' and then stripped of his clothes and made to bathe. These are the routine instruments of carceral discipline, but they demand passivity and submission. In his confrontation with the two warders, Behan considers the nationalist mythology which might sustain him and inspire his defiance – 'Young Cuchulainn, after the battle of the ford of Ferdia, on guard the gap of Ulster, with his enemies ringed around him, held his back to a tree and, supported by it, called on the gods of death and grandeur to hold him up till his last blood flowed' (41). Behan here draws upon the eighth-century Irish mythological figure, Cuchulainn, and his legendary defiance of his 'ringed enemies,' a figure of nationalist heroism which was revived and appropriated in the Rising of 1916, and central to nationalist iconography ever since.[25] Yeats figured Cuchulainn in his final play, *The Death of Cuchulain* (1939), as the Nietzschean 'superman,' while the leader of the 1916 Rising, Patrick Pearse, made a sacred cult of the mythic hero as the model of masculine strength and nobility in his school. For Pearse and his contemporaries, the mythic power and self-sacrifice of Cuchulainn served as the counterpoint to the emasculation of colonised men. 'We of this generation are not in any real sense men,' wrote Pearse, 'for we suffer things that men do not suffer, and we seek to redress grievances by means which men do not employ.'[26] To summon Cuchulainn was, therefore, to attempt to renew masculine authority and power, to reclaim the right to defiance and independence. But however heroic, the myth of Cuchulainn fails to mean anything to Behan when confronted with the impending

---

24 M. Foucault, *Discipline and Punish*, p. 25. **25** P. Pearse, the leader of the 1916 Rising, in particular, was renowned for the cult of Cuchulainn which he fostered in his school, St Enda's, in Dublin, but W.B. Yeats, Lady Gregory and others contributed to the revival of the mythological figure, too, partly in publishing the ancient stories and myths of Ireland in collected volumes, but also in theatre productions. **26** P. Pearse, 'The Coming Revolution', in *The Field Day Anthology of Irish Writing: Volume Two*, ed. S. Deane (1991), p. 557.

violence which British warders will inflict on a Republican prisoner. He submits to the demands of the warders, and surrenders his defiance to the dawning realisation of the inflated reputation of martyrdom. 'They could easily kill you,' he reflects at another point in the narrative, 'Who would give a fish's tit about you over here?' (21–22). This signals a turn in Behan's conception of his role as a nationalist – the symbols and ideology of sacrifice and endurance prove difficult to mobilise when faced with the threat of death. Behan fails to be a martyr, or even a hero, to the cause.

In the early scenes in *Borstal Boy* Behan proves all too willing at times to play the rebel hero – when he shouts 'Up the Republic!' in the Assizes in Liverpool, for example – but the limitations of the heroic mask become all too apparent to him. When a fellow Republican prisoner, Callan, in a cell below Behan's, incites him to shout 'Up the Republic' later in Walton jail, Behan discreetly fakes a defiant shout by whispering down the ventilator and telling Callan that the walls are too thick to hear him shouting. Callan is beaten by the warders for his gesture, while Behan is found reading Mrs Gaskell's *Cranford* on his bed when the warders check his cell (140–41). Behan is caught between the demands of his Republican fellows to answer the historic call to sacrifice, and the pressures imposed upon him to submit to the disciplinary violence of the prison. He cowers from the opportunity to defy his captors, and instead offers himself up as the ideal subject for reform. Behan's cowardice may be a matter of prudence, strategy, or even instinctive preservation, but it also signifies the failure of nationalist imagery of masculinity. In refusing the call to defy the authority of his jailers, he elects the passivity and malleability which prison requires of him.

Submission and resistance

Behan is not merely the willing dupe of the prison guards, however. There is, I want to argue, a certain seduction taking place, whereby Behan submits the alluring image of a model prisoner up to his jailers without relinquishing his capacity for less obtrusive means of resistance. If he recognises that the effective locus of prison discipline and punishment is the body of the prisoner, he also remembers that the body can be the locus of resistance. When he is confined to his cell and deprived of food for assaulting another prisoner, he is reminded of the hunger strikes of Republican prisoners of a previous generation, in particular of Terence MacSwiney – 'seventy-eight days and no scoff at all' (95):[27]

27 MacSwiney was the most renowned of the Irish prisoners on hunger strike during the war of independence against Britain (1919–21). He died in Brixton jail, London, on 25th October 1920, after a hunger strike which lasted 74 days. He had been elected Lord Mayor of Cork as a nationalist candidate earlier in 1920. The hunger strike as used by nationalist prisoners in the war of

MacSwiney had the eyes of the world on him, and knew that it must be driving these bastards mad from the publicity it was getting. They were up and offering him every conceivable delicacy, chicken, ham, turkey, roast pork, steak, oh for the love of Jesus, give over, me mouth is watering. If Johnston came up and said, 'Here you are, sing two lines of "God Save the King" and I'll give you this piece of round steak,' would I take it? Would I what? Jesus, Mary and Joseph, he'd be a lucky man that I didn't take the hand and all off him. And sing a High Mass, never mind a couple of lines of "God Save the King" for it, aye or for the half of it. (96)

The hunger strike is an effective mode of resistance, Behan knows, because it threatens to remove the only weapon available to prison authorities. A dead prisoner is a martyr, not a warning of the power of punishment, and a hunger strike has the effect of winning the sympathy of the public for the corporeal deprivation which the prisoner is willing to endure for an ideal or principle. Like Patrick Pearse and Thomas MacDonagh, MacSwiney shrouded his Republicanism in the language and imagery of the sacrifice of Christ, thus concocting a powerful discourse which represented nationalist struggle as, above all, a spiritual struggle, in which the demands of the body had to be forsaken for the spiritual needs of the nation. Behan confesses, however, to being incapable of such sacrifice, and the fact that he compares his own punishment of one day on 'bread and water' diet with MacSwiney's hunger strike, and later with the Irish Famine, reveals the pathetic disparity between Behan and the nationalist icons to whom he compares himself.[28] This is just one of many moments in *Borstal Boy* in which Behan deflates the potent symbolism and mythology of Republicanism – with its litany of famines, hunger strikes, executions and injustices – with a comic, often irreverent, contrast. But there is reverence in Behan's narrative too, for he recognises in MacSwiney's protest the power of appropriating the weapons of incarceration, and turning them into acts of resistance. MacSwiney symbolises the equivocal relationship between prison and prisoner, between coloniser and colonised, for his protest shows that the power to deprive the body is, as Foucault suggests, 'exercised rather than possessed' (174). It is not the sole preserve of the warders, but can be utilised by

independence is thought to have derived from Suffragette tactics in England. It has since become a powerful weapon for protest for nationalists in Ireland, not in winning concessions from governments so much as winning popular sympathy and support. **28** The disparity functions to enable Behan to contextualise his lonely struggle against imperialism, and the comparatively lenient ways in which he is treated in British prisons, in relation to the martyr figures of nationalist history. The comparison tends to reduce Behan's occasional encounter with official disapproval, beatings and short periods of deprivation of privileges to insignificance. The effect is almost comic in suggesting both that British imperialism now treats a potential terrorist as if he has stolen a watch, and that Behan's republicanism falls pathetically short of the nationalist ideal.

those who are dominated too. This is most clearly visible in *Borstal Boy* in the sexual relations between the prisoners.

There are faint intimations of homoerotic desire from an early point in the narrative. When Behan first meets Charlie Millwall, the young sailor remanded for stealing, he admires the line of his neck, and they indulge in a kind of light petting as Behan towels Charlie dry and Charlie puts his hands into Behan's pockets and shirt. There follows a number of subdued courtship rituals in which Behan sings Charlie a love song (24), Charlie bids Behan good night through the aperture on his cell door (26), and they continue their relationship in the washroom every morning (28). More important is the symbolic conversion of carceral spaces of containment into the sites of sexual desire. Behan and Charlie, along with another inmate, Ginger, are not humiliated by the ritual at Walton jail of being forced to strip naked in front of each other and bathe. Instead, in a scene which is repeated several times in *Borstal Boy*, the three young men stand admiring each other. The boys are occasionally interrupted by an older man who makes crude homosexual jokes and asks if they want to be helped to bathe, but Behan contrasts the idealised homoeroticism of the boys with the older man's crudity. Desire, it seems, is a more potent force than sexual release, and works to transform the spaces of containment and repression into sites of fantasy, perhaps even, as Genet described, of love.

Behan and his intimates transform the reception room, a panopticon space of surveillance and exposure, into a space of secret sexual desire, imposing their own subaltern 'counterdesign' on the authoritarian architecture of the penitentiary.[29] Behan recognises the functional design of Walton jail, with its various spaces of containment, isolation, and exposure, and recognises in it what Thomas Clarke called 'a refined system of cruelty.'[30] Indeed, he contrasts the Victorian architecture of incarceration in Walton with the model of liberal reform typified in the open design of Hollesley Bay borstal. In each case, however, Behan and his fellow prisoners find ways of transforming the spaces of imprisonment to their own advantage, utilising the disciplinary apparatus to accommodate desire and liberation. Thus, while Clarke's account of being imprisoned in an English jail contains little other than despairing scenes of deprivation, madness and humiliation, Behan's narrative is sometimes idyllic, manifested either in Behan's imaginative transformations of his dismal surroundings into reminders of his home, or in the arcadian scenes of playing and swimming with his fellow inmates in the fields and waters around the borstal. In part, this is because *Borstal Boy* is as much *bildungsroman* as it is prison narrative, indebted as much to *A Portrait of the Artist as a Young Man* as to *Jail*

29 See B. Tschumi, *Architecture and Disjunction* (1996), in which he argues that architecture consistently collides with events which it hosts: 'A building is a point of reference for the activities set to negate it' (132). 30 Clarke, *Glimpses of an Irish Felon's Prison Life*, p. 17.

Journal, but it is also because Behan finds in the English carceral system a contentment and love unknown to him before. 'I loved Borstal Boys and they loved me,' he wrote (but never published),[31] a sentiment which is reflected in the utopian scenes of homosocial, and sometimes homoerotic, intimacy and contentment.

Behan is not so much departing from conventional nationalist representations of relations between men in prison as appropriating and converting a consistent feature of nationalist prison narratives – the celebration of masculine homosociality. In *Jail Journal*, for example, John Mitchel begins to recognise in the course of his sea-voyage to Australia a strong camaraderie with his shipmates, which does not manifest itself in overtly erotic terms, but finds expression in Mitchel's increasing emphasis on a Carlylean notion of masculine 'greatness.' Mitchel asserts that it is the duty of great men to lead, to carry themselves above the 'subterhuman' lower classes of convicts and fiends, to bear arms nobly and bravely, and to raise other men up to follow glorious causes. 'We must openly glorify arms,' he writes, 'until young Irishmen burn to handle them.'[32] Manhood is also about the capacity to absorb punishment, and to endure sacrifice, however. Thus, Mitchel dismisses suicide as a solution to his misery in captivity because it is unmanly: 'sometimes to suffer manfully is the best thing man can do.'[33] For Thomas Clarke, too, prison is experienced as 'a test of manhood as severe and searching as mortal man could be subject to,' which he endures through his intimacy with other 'manly, self-reliant men.'[34]

Nationalist prison narratives tend to emphasise, perhaps defensively, the 'manliness' of their bonds and experiences, the resort to homosocial notions of shared bravery and vigour. The epigraph to *Borstal Boy*, taken from Virginia Woolf's *Orlando*, promises the homosocial imagery which pervades the narrative, as well as suggesting the celebration of irreverence and youthful rebellion:

> One crew of young watermen or postboys ... roared and shouted the lewdest tavern songs, as if in bravado, and were dashed against a tree and sunk with blasphemies on their lips. An old nobleman – for such his furred gown and golden chain of office proclaimed him – went down not far from where Orlando stood, calling vengeance upon the Irish rebels, who, he cried with his last breath, had plotted this devilry. (6)[35]

Behan is quoting from the first chapter of *Orlando*, in which, in his male persona in Elizabethan England, Orlando watches as a sudden thaw of the river Thames

31 Quoted in O'Sullivan, *Brendan Behan*, p. 69. 32 Mitchel, *Jail Journal*, p. 52. 33 Ibid., p. 61.
34 Clarke, *Glimpses of an Irish Felon's Prison Life*, p. 13. 35 See V. Woolf, *Orlando: A Biography* (1993), p. 45.

sweeps young boatmen and a nobleman to their deaths. The nobleman blames Irish rebels for the flood with his dying words, thus suggesting at once for Behan the historical longevity of the collision between English and Irish cultures, as well as the hyperbolized abilities of Irish rebels.[36] So too, the epigraph encapsulates an image of Behan and his fellow inmates as the lewd, daring boatmen, fated to die with tavern songs and blasphemies on their lips. In *Borstal Boy*, Behan exaggerates the erotic identification which such notions of youthful homosociality contain, distinguishing (in a passage omitted from the published novel) between the homoeroticism of 'the youth of healthy muscle and slim-wrought form' and that of 'the powdered pansy.'[37] Effeminacy had no place in Behan's erotic identification with his fellow prisoners, in keeping with Mitchel, Clarke and O'Donovan Rossa, but his relationship with Charlie Millwall threatens to subvert other conventions of nationalist prison narratives besides their celebration of masculine homosociality. Charlie is a common criminal, a thief, while Behan is, in nationalist terms, a political prisoner. Behan's identification with him rather than his IRA comrades offends the distinction made particularly by Mitchel and Clarke between the noble, splendid men serving the cause of Irish freedom and what Clarke calls the 'dregs' of English society.[38]

Behan's relationship to Charlie Millwall occupies a muted but central role in the narrative, developing out of sensuous gazes in part one of *Borstal Boy*, into mutual dependence in part two, and finally into Charlie's jealousy and resentment of Behan's new friends in part three. Behan's behaviour alters with every passing stage in their relationship, and, when he receives word of Charlie's death as a sailor on board the *Southampton*, he becomes silent, mournful and restless. That Behan and Charlie are homosexual lovers in the narrative is not made explicit, but the imagery and language of homoeroticism need not constitute a dissident sexual identity in order to make transgressive the relationships between the boys. Behan reacts coldly to jokes about sodomy, for example, and rejects identification with a homosexual subculture, yet his depiction of boys bathing naked together in the sea at Hollesley Bay Borstal suggests an idyll of homoerotic love which, in its subtlety and openness, threatens to draw the homosocial into the realm of desire and the erotic, and thus, to disrupt radically the sexual order of incarceration.[39]

When prison becomes the site of homoerotic initiation, and the symbolic spaces of punishment are appropriated in acts of desire, the languages and

36 That an Irish rebel is blamed for the death of young English boatmen in this epigraph has obvious resonances with the story that Behan was intent on blowing up a naval dockyard when he was arrested.   37 Quoted in O'Sullivan, *Brendan Behan*, p. 69.   38 Clarke, *Glimpses of an Irish Felon's Prison Life*, p. 41.   39 On the potential transgression of drawing the homosocial into the homoerotic, see E. Kosofsky Sedgwick, *Between Men: English Literature and Male Homosocial Desire*

ideologies of imprisonment begin to falter, especially because there is no discernible transgressive practice to be policed or punished. Behan's homoeroticism works not by subterfuge or conflict with the prison system, but by borrowing from the homosocial bonds encouraged within the prison itself. In Hollesley Bay, for example, the Governor encourages manly camaraderie between the boys, organising them into 'houses' modelled on the public school system, and cultivating a love of sports and fitness, but this has the effect on Behan of aestheticising and eroticising male bonds and bodies. Thus, Behan draws homosocial bonds into the realm of the homoerotic, borrowing not just from nationalist imagery of masculine intimacy, but also from the icons and images of manhood associated with the English empire, from 'boy's own' adventure stories, and from the camaraderie of sporting, scouting and soldiering experiences. Behan delineates the masculine homoeroticism which is suggested in *Borstal Boy* more clearly in his story, 'After the Wake,' published in *Points* in Paris in 1950. He describes the process whereby he persuades a heterosexual man of the attractions of homosexual love:

> The first step – to make him think it manly, ordinary to manly men, the British Navy, "Porthole Duff", "Navy Cake", stories of the Hitler Youth in captivity, told me by Irish soldiers on leave from guarding them; to remove the taint of "cissiness", effeminacy, how the German Army had encouraged it in Cadet Schools, to harden the boy-officers, making their love a muscular clasp of friendship, independent of women, the British Public Schools, young Boxers I'd known (most of it about the Boxers was true), that Lord Alfred Douglas was son to the Marquess of Queensbury and a good man to use his dukes himself, Oscar Wilde throwing 'Q' down the stairs and after him his Ballyboy attendant. On the other front, appealing to that hope of culture – Socrates, Shakespeare, Marlow – lies, truth and half-truth.[40]

Behan utilises in *Borstal Boy*, as in 'After the Wake,' the same appeal to the imagery and iconography of masculine authority and affection. His homoerotic imagery is effective because it is unobtrusive without being secret – it is formed and practised under the watchful, oblivious eyes of the warders, arrogating for itself only those spaces and relationships which carceral discipline permits and fosters, appropriating only those images and experiences which are encouraged and forged by the prison authorities.

(1985) and *Epistemology of the Closet* (1991).   **40** Ibid., p. 48.

Liminality and transgression

The homoerotic relationships in *Borstal Boy* are not significant for their sexual transgressiveness, then, but because they cut across the other relationships between the boys. In Behan's case, the fact that he has been suspected of planning to blow up a naval dockyard and proceeds to have homoerotic relations with a naval rating emphasises the transgressive potential of same-sex relations in relation to the homosocial discourses of imperialism and nationalism. While this is hardly a startling revelation about a writer who celebrated Wilde for having it 'both ways,'[41] it does perform a more specific and more dynamic function in *Borstal Boy*, of radically altering the terms in which Behan conceives of, and relates to, his imprisonment. If prison is experienced at first as the colonial censure of his national identity, the validation of his Republican persona, it becomes instead the condition in which he is compelled to re-imagine his cultural identity in relation to others, specifically those 'others' he once construed in absolutist terms as opposites. He comes to the realisation that he'd 'rather be with Charlie and Ginger and Browny in Borstal than with my own comrades and countrymen any place else. It seemed a bit disloyal to me, that I should prefer to be with boys from English cities than with my own countrymen and comrades from Ireland's hills and glens' (129). However ashamed of this disloyalty he may be, it is merely a passing reservation which does not impede his growing sense of fraternity and intimacy with young Englishmen. Behan becomes entangled in an elaborate negotiation of national and sexual identities, in which, as Sedgwick argues of Oscar Wilde and Roger Casement, 'the question of the Other of a national, as of a sexual, identity was an irreducibly – and *sometimes* an enablingly – complex one.'[42]

Much of *Borstal Boy* is concerned with exploring and interrogating Behan's shifting notions of cultural identity, from his initial mimicry of the role of militant Republican to his later ventures into defining his cultural, political, sexual and social moorings. He discovers a common culture in songs and stories between Irish Republicanism and the British Army, identifies his shared working-class sensibility with boys from Newcastle, Cardiff and London, and finds in his discussions with English inmates and his readings of English literature a counter-narrative to Anglophobe nationalism. In an implicit criticism of the nationalist tradition in which he has been immersed, Behan lauds the English for their modernity: 'the English can love people without their being seven foot tall or a hundred years dead' (310). Behan depicts the English as a people without memory, whose tolerance is the product of a self-

41 See B. Behan, 'Oscar Wilde', *Poems and a Play in Irish* (1981). **42** E. Kosofsky Sedgwick, 'Nationalisms and Sexualities', *Tendencies* (1994), p. 152.

willing amnesia, whereby Behan's loud, defiant Irish rebel songs are enjoyed as if they bore no relation to England. So, an English Colonel's loyalist speech about 'this perilous but glorious time in our island story,' is greeted with the same rapturous applause as are Behan's songs about English oppression in Ireland (288–93). Whilst Behan recognises in this amnesia a distasteful propensity towards indifference of other cultures, he is also contrasting the tolerance with which his attempted acts of sabotage are forgotten, with the 'historically informed and obscene' consciousness of Irish nationalism. In construing this amnesia in English culture as an indication of tolerance, Behan shares with other postcolonial writers in England in the 1950s – notably from the West Indies – a cautious belief in the inclusivist properties of modern English society, a belief which would be severely questioned by later generations of postcolonial writers.[43]

If the communal spaces of prison enable Behan to explore his cultural and sexual identifications with others, the constraints of his own cell prove to be no less enabling. Colbert Kearney has argued that the prison in *Borstal Boy* serves as metaphor for the unfolding and evolving personality of the young Behan: 'the penal institutions bear much the same relationship to *Borstal Boy* as the island does to *Robinson Crusoe*. Beneath the illusion of actuality is a structure which expresses the development of a personality.'[44] The metaphorical relation between Behan and the confined space of his cell, however, pertains neither to insularity nor to coherent identity, but, I would argue, to the liminality of both spaces.

As Monika Fludernik argues, the delimiting barriers of the cell – the walls, the door, the window, the body – are 'breachable and permeable boundaries that incorporate a transitional area of interfacing.'[45] Confined to his cell, Behan is also such a transitional space – the median point of imperialist and nationalist discourses, the interface between hermetic inside and expansive outside, the site of translation of writings, noises, and gestures from beyond his cell into the language and imagery of his own confinement. This process, of the transformation of the limits of his confinement into figures of his own liminality, is clearly at work when Behan reads. Behan remarks throughout his narrative on the progress and content of his reading, from his stolen glances at the *News of the World* in the washroom in Walton, to his intense consumption of novels by

---

43 See in particular A. Sinfield's arguments concerning Sam Selvon's *The Lonely Londoners* in *Literature, Politics and Culture in Postwar Britain* (1989), p. 126, in which Sinfield argues that Selvon's novel belongs to an era of liberal optimism about English tolerance which was interrupted in 1958 by race riots. See also my chapter on postcolonial writers in England from 1945 to 1965 in *Literature and Culture in England, 1945–1965* (2002).   44 Kearney, 'Borstal Boy', p. 108.   45 M. Fludernik, 'Carceral topography: spatiality, liminality and corporality in the literary prison', *Textual Practice*, 13, 1 (Spring 1999), p. 64.

Hardy, Mrs Gaskell, Joyce, plays by Shaw, O'Casey, Synge, and an assortment of biographies, histories and memoirs. In part, his reading sustains an important link with Ireland while he languishes in an English jail – hence his enjoyment of Joyce, Synge, and O'Casey as well as Robert Lynd and Robert Collis – but reading also enables him to explore his cultural 'other,' to discover the meanings and representations of 'Englishness' outside of Ireland.

Reading is Behan's endeavour to metamorphose his surroundings into the desired (and desiring) landscape of the imagination, by which he can simulate the effect of transcendence. He rations his reading over time, 'saving' it up as self-indulgent play. Behan gives himself over to the narratives, reporting his engagement with the characters and plots of the books he reads, but there is also an important process of cultural conversion taking place in his readings. Behan inserts himself into his reading of Thomas Hardy's *Under the Greenwood Tree*, for example. He appropriates a song from Hardy's novel, putting a Christmas Carol from the novel to the tune of the 'Famine Song,' as Behan points out, 'my situation being more like Famine than like Christmas' (96). Here Behan clearly signals the necessity of reading one's self into a text, and of making the reading conform to his own situation. In other readings he resists conforming to the cultural assumptions and identities of that text. Hardy's novel at times becomes allegorical of idyllic English rural life, the tree itself used as a microcosm of this idyll which spawns tribes and families, and provides 'healthy exercise ground.'[46] This is also where Fancy, newly wed to Dick Dewy, marks the passing of ancient manners into new ways, and the marriage of Dick and Fancy seems to herald in new times, celebrated on this exercise ground. But Behan converts the novel through his own reading, and performance of the text, to new purposes. The ending of Hardy's novel, where Thomas Leaf, whom Behan calls an amadán (Gaelic for fool), tells his 'half-arsed class of a story,' finds the tranter speaking of Leaf's wish to join the party:

> 'Poor feller!' said the tranter, turning to Geoffrey.
> 'Suppose we must let en come? His looks are rather against en, and he is terrible silly; but 'a never been in jail, and 'a won't do no harm.'[47]

In Behan's performance of the novel a different voice speaks out of Hardy's characters:

> 'Let the poor bastard in,' says the Tranter, 'he's a bit silly-looking but I never heard he was in jail.' Sure, if he was itself, there was as good as ever he was in it. (99)

---

46 Thomas Hardy, *Under the Greenwood Tree* (1994), p. 216. **47** Ibid., p. 212.

Behan inserts his own voice into Hardy's story, converting Hardy's story of idyllic rural England into a working-class Dubliner's story. Behan appropriates the power of English symbolic representations, and exerts an ironic manoeuvre in his writing which undermines English cultural power. This move is described by Ashcroft, Griffiths and Tiffin in *The Empire Writes Back* as abrogation and appropriation, that of simultaneously denying privilege to the metropolitan centre while seizing and adapting the language of the centre for the colonised.[48] In this case, the language which Behan translates Hardy's novel into is comic farce. This comic device is also a critical manoeuvre whereby Behan draws attention to the obscene disparity between an idyllic representation of rural England and his situation in prison, between English cultural power, exemplified in the idyllic novel, and Irish rebel culture, exemplified in the Famine song. This puts Behan back into a situation in which he is affirming Irish national identity as being different from English national identity, and yet at the same time he is showing how English culture is permeable to an Irish rebel. It doesn't exclude or marginalise him. In fact, it allows him to find his own identity, and to add his own voice. The characters in Hardy's novel remind him of his family, 'even their speech when they said "carrel" and "traypsing and rambling about" was like Dublin speech' (81).

That Behan reads into Hardy's novel his cultural identity as a working-class Dubliner, and his situation as a prisoner in an English jail, reveals not only the cultural permeability enacted in the process of reading, but also that there is no 'pure' transcendence for Behan. Reading is rather an extension of that condition of liminality by which Behan shows that prison is not absolute containment either. Just as he can 'resist' the cultural imperatives of Hardy's novel, he can also resist the imposed limitations and constraints of imprisonment. Kearney remarks on the metamorphic qualities of Behan's narrative: 'prison food is often described with a relish normally reserved for more imaginative cuisine, reading a book is made to seem a feast, a mishap to a member of the staff provokes an orgy of pleasure.'[49] This is a consistent feature of Behan's interaction with his surroundings. Both Walton jail and Hollesley Bay borstal remind him in different ways of life in Dublin (27; 212–13). The gardens around the borstal prompt him to cite a passage from Brian Merriman's Gaelic poem, *The Midnight Court*, which describes his scene perfectly (319–20). In part, this feature of Behan's narrative is a conservative conversion of difference into the same – it enables Behan to bolster his sense of 'Irishness' by appropriating the materials of his 'foreign' surroundings, and thus works to foreground the nationalist dialectic of sameness and difference. But, as in Behan's reading of Hardy, it also

48 B. Ashcroft, Gareth Griffiths and Helen Tiffin, *The Empire Writes Back: Theory and Practice in Post-colonial Literatures* (1989), p. 38.   **49** Kearney, 'Borstal Boy', p. 115.

suggests the permeability of English and Irish cultures to each other, that they can be read in and through each other. In every instance of Behan's engagement with English culture and landscape, in fact, he exhibits that 'exquisitely exacerbated sensitivity' which Sedgwick observes in Wilde as to 'how by turns porous, brittle, elastic, chafing, embracing, exclusive, murderous, in every way contestable and contested were the membranes of "domestic" national defini-tion signified by the ductile and elusive terms of England, Britain, Ireland.'[50]

Nationalism and the subaltern

Behan complicates the 'simple' narratives of nationalist incarceration as his story unfolds, therefore, after finding himself incapable of identifying with, or mobilising the resources of, what David Lloyd calls 'the monologic desire of cultural nationalism,'[51] and after failing to isolate the distinctive characteristics of a national culture required in the ideology of separatist nationalism. In iden-tifying with West Country dialects, Cockney humour or Lancashire bluffness, each of which delineate and reiterate discrete regional stereotypes, Behan resi-tuates his own sense of cultural distinction within a diffusive field of hybridised identities and cultures. At stake in this contrivance is not just his recognition that he shares more in common culturally with a Londoner than with an Irish farmer, but also that he can no longer accommodate the stories he wishes to construct of himself comfortably within the province of Irish nationalism.

In thinking of Wilde, for example, he realises that his upbringing has equipped him inadequately to conceptualise Wilde's rebelliousness. Behan's mother tells him that Wilde was brought down by sex, just like the nationalist party leader, Parnell, but Behan discerns that Wilde's 'fall' was profoundly incompatible with the language and ideology in which Parnell's ruin was explained (253–55). Similarly, Behan's own embarrassment about his love for English boys is, in part, recognition of the awkward incongruity of his new relationships with the cultural baggage of both colonialism and nationalism. It seems not to fit into the available typology, nor do many of Behan's associations accord with all his friends and overseers, particularly because he learns in the course of his incarceration to cut across class, sexual, religious, political and national boundaries:

> The other fellows might give me a rub about Ireland or about the bombing campaign, and that was seldom enough, and I was never short of an answer, historically informed and obscene, for them. But I was nearer to them than they would ever let Ken be. I had the same rearing

---

50 Sedgwick, 'Nationalisms and Sexualities', p. 151.   **51** D. Lloyd, *Anomalous States: Irish Writing and the Post-Colonial Moment* (1993), p. 89.

as most of them, Dublin, Liverpool, Manchester, Glasgow, London. All our mothers had all done the pawn – pledging on Monday, releasing on Saturday. We all knew the chip shop and the picture house and the fourpenny rush of a Saturday afternoon, and the summer swimming in the canal and being chased along the railway by the cops. But Ken they would never accept. In a way, as the middle and upper class in England spent so much money and energy in maintaining the difference between themselves and the working class, Ken was only getting what his people paid for but, still and all, I couldn't help being sorry for him, for he was more of a foreigner than I, and it's a lonely thing to be a stranger in a strange land. (241–42)

When Behan explores his interactions with fellow inmates, as he does in this passage, he finds a mess of contradictory, complex subject positions which shift constantly, from defending Irish nationalism, to identifying a common culture shared with the English urban working class, and to seeing his own alterity reflected in an English middle class boy alienated in the borstal. There is no sense of transcendence in any of these subject positions, nor does Behan adopt one over the other in anything but the most contingent fashion, but each rebuts and intersects with the others. Irish nationalism can weaken English imperialist assumptions by being 'historically informed and obscene,' by which Behan means that he interrupts colonial myths with terse, 'obscene' reminders of colonial atrocities. So too, the separatist assumptions of Irish nationalism are undermined by the common social history which Behan identifies between Dublin, Liverpool, Glasgow, Manchester and London. Colonialism has forged a common heritage for London and Dublin: an urban industrial and artisan working class which communicates in English, and which shares specific forms of cultural expression and entertainment. The heritage is still valid enough so that Behan is closer to the English working class characters than they are to Ken, the alienated middle class inmate, but it is not strong enough to cancel the differentiation which Behan's English friends make by unanimously referring to him as 'Paddy.' Behan's residual sense of alienation also enables him, para-doxically, to identify with Ken in a way which seems to be impossible for the other inmates.

Borstal Boy inclines towards an inclusivist narrative of expansive and magna-nimous cross-cultural identifications rather than defining a specific identity *per se*. Behan's identity is thus transgressive even if only in the literal sense that it crosses over various class, sexual, religious, political and national boundaries, but, significantly, by the end of the novel, he is not encapsulated or defined by any one trope or idiom of identity. Behan begins his narrative by defining himself exclusively, single-mindedly, as a Republican soldier following in the tradition of his heroes and ancestors, but he proceeds to revise and expand the terms of his nationalism beyond the myopic dogma of his upbringing. He does this partly by demonstrating the readability of English and Irish cultures to each other, partly by articulating dissent from the élite nationalism defined by state and church authorities, and partly also by reading nationalism in provocative and innovative ways. The latter strategy is at stake when he reads Irish voices into Hardy's novel, for example, but it is also in evidence when he reads Robert Collis' autobiographical narrative of his experiences as an Irish rugby international, *The Silver Fleece*. Rugby, as Behan explains, is a game associated in the minds of Irish nationalism with the cultural legacy of imperialism: 'it was a game for the Protestant and the shop-keeping Catholic, and I never thought it had anything to do with me' (360). But Behan identifies with rugby, through the martial metaphors of Collis' descriptions of rugby charges and victories, and appropriates it as an icon of nationalist contest. 'The way that he wrote about the Irish forward line would set your blood pumping like "Speeches from the Dock",' Behan remarks of Collis' book, or, again, 'the way he described an Irish forward rush would put you in mind of "Fontenoy" by Thomas Davis' (360). Behan's identification with Collis' descriptions of the excitements of rugby is partly an imaginative projection of himself in the Irish forward charge against an English line. Thus, in similar terms to C.L.R. James' appropriation of cricket as an expression of West Indian cultural identity, Behan pulls rugby across the colonial divide, so that a game representing Englishness in Ireland seems to speak the language of anti-colonial struggle. In one sense this is a colonising gesture on behalf of Irish nationalism, appropriating the other within the discourse of anti-colonialism, but it is also a provocative and expansive manoeuvre on Behan's part, like his many identifications and comparisons of Irish experiences with other cultures, of opening nationalism up to the possibility of productive engagement with its 'others.'

Throughout *Borstal Boy*, and increasingly as the narrative progresses, Behan explores and delineates the subaltern positions which become available to him through the enabling metaphors of class, sexuality, politics and religion. Subalternity, as Guha suggests in his conception of it as the unspoken, unintegrated residue of nationalism and colonialism, is not equivalent to the subcultural, which is constructed necessarily as a minority culture.[52] It crosses over and speaks from within hegemonic discourses, mobilising contradictions and weaknesses within such discourses. The subaltern, as Veena Das argues, is not a 'morphological category,' not an individual subjectivity, but a perspective which necessitates a new topography of the relations between imperialism and nationalism.[53] Behan refuses to formulate a specific, transgressive subjectivity

52 R. Guha, 'On Some Aspects of the Historiography of Colonial India', *Subaltern Studies I: Writings on South Asian History and Society* (1994), pp 1–8. 53 V. Das, 'Subaltern as Perspective',

which might encompass and authenticate the various forms of his engagement with subaltern positions. This is particularly evident when he arrives back in Dublin after his release in the conclusion to his narrative, a conclusion which resists resolving his borstal experiences and discoveries into a coherent identity. 'It must be wonderful to be free,' says the immigration officer in Dublin who studies Behan's expulsion order. '"It must", said I, walked down the gangway, past a detective, and got on the train for Dublin' (378–79). In this final scene of *Borstal Boy*, Behan conceives of his liberty in ironic terms, and, in playing inter- textually with John Mitchel's exile to New York at the end of *Jail Journal*, Behan situates Dublin as the location of his exile even as he recounts its familiarity.

Borstal Boy concludes ironically, therefore, by suggesting that the carceral condition is not defined by prison walls, and that post-colonial Dublin is as much bound up in the legacy of imperialism as the 'six counties' for which Behan was apparently prepared to bomb Liverpool. The project of 'national liberation,' it turns out, is more difficult than it seemed, as much an intellectual struggle within nationalism, as a military struggle against imperialism. If Behan's narrative begins by recapitulating the terms in which nationalism imagined colonial incarceration as the necessary and paradoxical condition for producing the symbolic resources of nationalist resurrection, Behan finds that his time in an English prison has exerted an equally paradoxical effect in him, of emancipating him from the psychological binds both of colonial stereotypes and nationalist iconography. His 'emancipation' is, of course, contingent and contradictory, never transcendent, but it begins to delineate what Fanon called the 'new humanism' which would emerge in the wake of anti-colonial national- ism. 'After the conflict,' Fanon wrote, 'there is not only the disappearance of colonialism but also the disappearance of the colonized man.'[54]

In moving beyond the weary subject positions which colonial relations bestowed as their legacy, Behan's narrative glimpses the contours of what Andrew Murphy calls an 'ante-colonial' project, which moves beyond the 'simple colonial narrative.'[55] *Borstal Boy* mimics the *anti*-colonial discourse of Irish nationalism in Behan's refusal to atone for his attempted atrocity, in justifying his 'mission' through epigrammatic history lessons, and in advertising his struggle in isolation against the brutal, degrading machinery of incarceration. But it deviates considerably from the popular Irish prison narratives in which it is immersed, by identifying, culturally and erotically, with Englishmen, and by refusing the call to open defiance. Behan refuses to be consoled or enlightened by the prospect of sacrifice, suffering, or martyrdom,

Subaltern Studies VI: Writings on South Asian History and Society, ed. R. Guha (1989), pp 310–24.
54 Fanon, *The Wretched of the Earth*, p. 198.   **55** A. Murphy, 'Ireland and Ante/anti-colonial Theory', *Irish Studies Review*, 7, 2 (August 1999), p. 160.

and thus chooses to abandon his faith in the redemptive properties of nationalist struggle.

It is the ironic consequence of the penal demand for the malleable subject that produces in Behan his erotic identification with English 'otherness,' his rejection of the timeworn casts of nationalist martyrology, and his subaltern realignment of the colonial and carceral paradigm. Just as the prison of his captivity becomes for Behan the metamorphic site of his reform, so 'England's doorstep' becomes the metaphor for his discovery of the potentially liberating thresholds of post-colonial relations. As an Irish nationalist captive in an English jail, Behan negotiates what Mary Louise Pratt calls the 'contact zone,' in which the fraught struggle between disparate cultures is telescoped into a contested social and symbolic space.[56] Behan's narrative begins, in common with the narratives of Mitchel, Clarke, Devoy, O'Donovan Rossa, and others, with the clash of two antithetical cultures, English imperialism and Irish postcolonial nationalism, but it collapses these opposed cultures in the course of exploring his subaltern resistances to both, and in identifying the hybrid cultures to which both he and his fellow prisoners belong. Behan discovers in the mobilising contradictions of post-colonial hybridity the potential to move beyond the 'perceptual prison' of colonialism.[57]

---

56 M. L. Pratt, *Imperial Eyes: Travel Writing and Transculturation* (1992), p. 4.   57 'Perceptual prison' is a term used to describe the vicious circle of colonial stereotypes and neo-colonial behaviour by R. N. Lebow, *White Britain, Black Ireland: The Influence of Stereotypes on Colonial Policy* (1976).

6 / Late writings: confessions and autobiographical epitaphs

A man of letters

'If I am anything at all, I am a man of letters. I'm a writer.'[1] Ironically, Behan dictated this description of himself into a tape-recorder, which was then transcribed and edited by Rae Jeffs. In the last three years of his life, Behan suffered bouts of serious illness, from the combination of his continuing dependence on alcohol and his diabetic condition, which made it difficult for him to write at any length. Jeffs, who had been his editor at Hutchinson, became more of a collaborator and co-author for his final publications. The last three of his books – *Brendan Behan's Island*, *Brendan Behan's New York*, and *Confessions of an Irish Rebel* – were dictated and transcribed, and, as the titles imply, relied heavily on the cult of Behan's formidable and ebullient personality. Behan provided the anecdotes, the wit, and the memories, but Jeffs was left with what she described as 'the monumental task' of giving Behan's late publications their artistic shapes.[2] Paradoxically, then, Behan's late writings are not properly *his* writings at all, but the products of desperate acts of collaboration and co-dependence between a failing writer and publishers eager to capitalise on a celebrity cult. 'They require their pound of flesh,' Behan remarked to his friend, John Ryan, of the publishers who pursued him for publications, 'and I suppose I owe it to them.'[3]

Behan's increasing sense of despondency and incapacity marks each of his late works, and indeed, after 1958, it could be argued that he failed to complete a single work. *Richard's Cork Leg*, his final play, was completed by Alan Simpson. *The Catacombs*, which was to be his second novel, reached twelve thousand words before Behan ran dry of ideas and stamina, and remains incomplete. Jeffs completed *Brendan Behan's Island*, *Brendan Behan's New York*, and *Confessions of an Irish Rebel* by adding material published previously, or by including sketched drawings of some of the places Behan reminisced about in his narratives. Two of the books he published in the year of his death were merely compilations of his earlier writings. *The Scarperer*, the serialised novel which he had written for the *Irish Times* in 1953, was published in book form in 1964, as was an edition of Behan's writings for the *Irish Press*, selected and edited by Jeffs, which was

---

1 B. Behan, *Confessions of an Irish Rebel* (1985), p. 219.   **2** Ibid., p. 11.   **3** Quoted in M. O'Sullivan, *Brendan Behan: A Life* (1997), p. 295.

entitled, *Hold Your Hour and Have Another*. 'A faded print is better than none at all,' Jeffs wrote of Behan's later works, justifying her role as 'literary midwife.'[4] But these parasitic, repetitious publications do not just pale in comparison to works such as *The Quare Fellow*, *The Hostage*, and *Borstal Boy*. By turning to formulaic, artless imitations of the styles and structures of Behan's successful works, the late writings seem to parody and mock the comic and inventive qualities of the earlier texts. Read in the contexts of popular theatrical and music hall styles, *The Hostage* is an imaginative, playful fusion of styles and themes. Read in relation to *Richard's Cork Leg*, *The Hostage* seems an amorphous, futile collection of inane jokes and farcical plots.

Behan's literary and artistic reputation, in other words, seems impoverished by the commercial exploitation of his last, desperate attempts at creative endeavour. 'To look back now over Behan's work is to see how terribly repetitive he was,' wrote Christopher Ricks shortly after Behan's death, 'The jokes, the songs, the historical incidents – all return word for word again and again and again. Not because they are obsessions, but because Behan was short of material.'[5] Partly, the responsibility for the repetition of Behan's material lies with his publishers and editors, since his late works were discovered to be too short to publish without some padding. *Brendan Behan's Island* included his radio play, *The Big House*, two of his poems and two of his short stories. Jeffs also worked several of Behan's column pieces for the *Irish Press*, written between 1954 and 1956, into the text of *Confessions of an Irish Rebel*, which also retold (in less artistic fashion) some of *Borstal Boy*. Behan did repeat the same jokes and anecdotes, and his fund of stories did appear to reach its limits at an early stage in his career, but this effect is even more exaggerated because of the publishing practices to which he submitted himself in his later years.

Behan's writings drew extensively upon his experiences as a member of the IRA in the thirties and forties, and on his bohemian lifestyle in Dublin and occasionally in England and France in the late forties and early fifties. There is little evidence to suggest that Behan was attempting to move beyond these experiences in his later writings. Much of his later writings are attempts to feed off the legends he had created of himself in the past, rather than finding new subjects and styles for the future. His flawed method of working for *Richard's Cork Leg*, according to Colbert Kearney, was based on his attribution of the success of his earlier plays to an established recipe: 'Choose a setting which is visually striking, bring on a few colourful characters, introduce sex, religion and politics, and baste well with song-and-dance, stand-up jokes, slapstick business and some reference to himself.'[6] Behan's bankruptcy as a writer came to haunt

---

4 Behan, *Confessions*, p. 12.   5 C. Ricks, 'Bee-keeper', *The New York Review of Books*, 11, no. 12 (30 July 1964), p. 9.   6 C. Kearney, *The Writings of Brendan Behan* (1977), pp 140–41.

his later years, as his biographers, Ulick O'Connor and Michael O'Sullivan, have attested.[7] His failure to generate new material became apparent even to those eager for his success. Joan Littlewood's Theatre Workshop rejected *Richard's Cork Leg* when Behan submitted a rough incomplete draft of the play in 1960, while another of his early benefactors, Gael Linn, rejected a shorter, Irish language version of the same play. There are characters in Behan's last play – the Leper Cronin and the two 'bawds' – who might have become rich veins of comedy and parody had they been revised and reworked. Equally, *The Catacombs* begins with provocative promise, with the story of a girl who has returned from having an abortion in England. But Behan became incapable of the labour and energy required to write, and consequently sunk further into disillusionment and into morbid reflections on the poverty of his artistic legacy.

In Behan's later writings, there is, one could argue, the overwhelming sense of an impending end. Where his early writings are characterised by an open experimentation with style and form, the later works resort to predictable and weary formulae. Where Behan's early texts shaped his experiences into artistic form and resonated with urgent contemporary social and political issues, his late texts became increasingly preoccupied with telling perfunctory narratives of his own past exploits. The early writings engage in productive dialogue with a rich variety of literary and cultural traditions, while the late writings resort to superficial anecdotes about spurious encounters with contemporary writers and celebrities. There is, in short, a sense of exhaustion and aridity about Behan's late writings which suggest terminal decline. In his late writings, Behan seems condemned to circle desperately around the ghostly traces of his earlier writings, increasingly drawn towards the compelling appeal of closure and totalisation which autobiographical narratives promise to yield. The argument of this chapter is that Behan's publications in the last years of his life, particularly *Brendan Behan's Island, Richard's Cork Leg*, and *Confessions of an Irish Rebel*, repeatedly return to representations of memory, subjectivity, and morbidity, to produce a kind of 'epitaphic' discourse. Death was an important theme of his early writings, particularly as the product of political violence, but it became an intense preoccupation in his late writings.

Essays upon epitaphs

'Epitaphs,' Wordsworth writes, 'personate the dead, and represent him as speaking from his own tomb-stone.'[8] As such they are exemplary figures of prosopopoeia, of giving a voice 'to the language of the senseless stone.'[9] The

7 See U. O'Connor, *Brendan Behan* (1993), and O'Sullivan, *Brendan Behan: A Life*. 8 W. Wordsworth, 'Essays upon Epitaphs', *Wordsworth's Literary Criticism*, ed. W.J.B. Owen (1974), p. 132. 9 Ibid., p. 125.

function of the epitaph, according to Wordsworth's essay, is not merely to pay tribute to a life that has passed, but also to preserve the memory of the dead. Preservation, in this sense, is a fictional prolongation of life, the attempt to retain vocal and spatial presence. A memorial monument may mark the feelings of the living towards the achievements and life-histories of the dead, but an epitaph attempts to 'personate' the dead, to breathe life into the inanimate. 'All prosopopoeias are visits to the underworld,' writes Hillis Miller,[10] epitaphic representations perhaps more so than most. But if this is the case, they do so only to return familiarity to the dead, and to death itself. The epitaph is a source of consolation, of restoration, which performs the illusion of 'prolonged companionship.'[11] As such, as Wordsworth argues, it is an imaginative site, 'a shrine to which the fancies of a scattered family may repair in pilgrimage; the thoughts of the individuals, without any communication with each other, must oftentimes meet here.'[12] Wordsworth represents epitaphs in much the same terms as poetry, or narrative, as symbolic or imaginative spaces in which the minds of their readers may meet in 'shadowy' unison, now and again.

In Wordsworth's conception of the epitaph, then, form plays a more important role than content. What is inscribed on the tomb of the dead is less significant than the fact that it is inscribed at all. Thus, towards the end of his essay, he sharply upbraids Addison for his remark that memorials which bear nothing but the name and dates of the dead are 'a kind of satire upon the departed persons.'[13] Even these brief, minimal epitaphs, in Wordsworth's mind, contain immense symbolic significance, by providing that imaginative space through which the relationship between the dead and the living is prolonged, and through which the relations of the deceased maintain a kind of attachment and community. Even the frailest of memorials might conjoin individuals into recognition of their affinities and bonds, and might therefore feed, in Wordsworth's terms, 'the tap-root of the tree of Patriotism.'[14] What matters is not the artistic merits, nor the emotional depths, of the epitaph, but instead its figuration of acts of remembrance and imaginative communion.

Wordsworth's essay is confined to the place and function of the epitaph and memorial architecture, but the notions elaborated in that essay might be extended to what I will discuss as an 'epitaphic discourse' in Behan's late writings. As Edna Longley argues, 'Commemoration is a means whereby communities renew their own *religio*.'[15] There is an implicit acknowledgement of this connection between commemoration and cultural identity throughout Behan's writings. In a piece written for the *Irish Press* in 1954, Behan railed against what he called 'the alien monuments' of British rule in Ireland, and

10 J. H. Miller, *Topographies* (1995), p. 72.   **11** Wordsworth, 'Essays upon Epitaphs', p. 162.   **12** Ibid., p. 162.   **13** Ibid., p. 162.   **14** Ibid., p. 162.   **15** Edna Longley, *The Living Stream: Literature and Revisionism in Ireland* (1994), p. 67.

argued that 'the obelisk in the park [the Wellington monument] was put there by the enemies of the people of Ireland, and should be shifted, now that they are no longer powerful enough to enforce its preservation.'[16] It was an argument he extended to Nelson's Pillar in O'Connell Street, in a piece which reflected on the grandeur of nineteenth-century British memorial architecture, as well as the contentious issues of nomenclature and memorials in general. Memorial architecture is one way in which cultural identity is inscribed and, following Behan's argument, imposed, although, as his article goes on to show, it may also serve merely to remark upon the alienation of the people from the sentiments expressed in monumental representation.

At stake in Behan's criticism of memorial architecture in Dublin is the correlation between a particular community and its representations. Nelson and Wellington are not, in Behan's mind, worthy subjects for the Dublin people to preserve and commemorate, and part of his argument rests on mocking the individuals themselves. 'If [Wellington] is remembered for any law, it is the Poor Law, if for any building, it is the workhouse,' Behan writes, and similarly, of Nelson, he paraphrases Shaw's jibe that Nelson had 'won victories he'd have been deservedly shot for losing, and anyway has nothing to do with us.'[17] The 'us' here is of crucial significance, for there is a process of cultural identification taking place which is inclusive only of those who share the particular strand of Anglophobic nationalism being implicitly peddled. This piece, among others, seems to jar against the liberal nationalism of many of Behan's other writings of the time, in which pro-British sentiments are neither uncommon nor undesirable.

In Behan's more substantial writings, the relationship between commemoration and cultural identity owes more to a liberal and critical suspicion of cultural nationalism. The hanging of 'the quare fellow' in the play of that title sounds a death knell for humanist values, and the victory for the exclusivist function of nationalist identifications. 'One off, one away' is the slogan which prisoners cry out when 'the quare fellow' is executed, mocking the prison warders, but implicitly remarking upon the ritual exclusion of the condemned man from human society.[18] The prisoners fight for the hanged man's letters, the obligatory figures of prosopopoeia in this play, in order to sell them on to the newspapers, a final act of inhuman desperation which signifies the debasement of commemoration in a society which devalues human life. The epitaph carved on the tombstone of the hanged man is significant here too, for Behan seems to echo Addison's remark about minimal epitaphs when his characters chisel the dead man's number on to the stone incorrectly. He is remembered not by his name, nor even by his number, E779, but as a '7' is easier to carve than a '9,' the

16 B. Behan, 'These alien monuments – thoughts before the Albert Memorial', *The Dubbalin Man* (1997), p. 41.   17 Ibid., p. 41.   18 B. Behan, *The Quare Fellow*, in *The Complete Plays* (1978), p. 121.

epitaph of 'the quare fellow' reads simply 'E777.' The epitaph here is no satire upon the deceased, however, but a satirical indictment of the living.

In *The Hostage*, when the British soldier, Leslie, is killed accidentally at the end of the play, he is commemorated by his lover, an Irish convent girl, Teresa. She mourns that he died 'in a strange land,' and vows her own epitaph for him: 'I'll never forget you, Leslie, till the end of time.'[19] Teresa's decision to commemorate Leslie is constructed in opposition to the political iconographies of sacrifice and retribution which have caused his death, and thus serve to critique the nationalist and imperialist ideologies which are figured in conflict throughout the play. Leslie himself then rises from the dead and sings: 'Oh death, where is thy sting-a-ling-a-ling? Or grave thy victory?'[20] Leslie's resurrection signifies that same symbolic renewal central to Christian and Republican ideologies, the notion that death produces remembrance, and remembrance continually reinscribes and defines the identity and community of the living. Or, as Bloom thinks in *Ulysses*, standing in Glasnevin cemetery, 'In the midst of death we are in life.'[21]

Bloom reflects on how 'both ends meet,' life and death, while thinking of stories of prostitutes bringing their clients to graveyards. Behan's final play, *Richard's Cork Leg*, was based on the story that when Joyce had a play rejected as too gloomy, he retorted that he should have given his character, Richard, a cork leg. Behan took the title for his play, and the implication that, as Colbert Kearney says, he 'was willing to "jolly things up" to suit the public,' where Joyce declined.[22] But *Richard's Cork Leg* also dramatises the scenes that Bloom only imagines in the 'Hades' chapter of *Ulysses*. Like *The Hostage*, in Behan's final play whores and patriots meet again, but this time in the graveyard rather than the brothel. 'I always think graveyards and patriots goes together,' one prostitute tells the Leper Cronin, a thought never very far from Bloom's mind in 'Hades.'[23] *Richard's Cork Leg* contains the barest of plots, and seems to strive vainly towards the successful mixture of farce, music and irreverence achieved in Behan's earlier plays. At its core, however, is a series of dramatic meditations on death, memorials, and prosopopoeia.

In *Richard's Cork Leg*, there is something resembling Beckett's attention to what Steven Connor calls 'a poetics of poverty and an art of impotence, incompetence or failure.'[24] Behan's prostitutes bring their own 'dunlopillos' and wait on the tombstones in the hope that they might attract customers from the passing funeral processions. They meet up instead with two blind men, who turn out to be Republicans awaiting the arrival of Blueshirts. Other characters

19 B. Behan, *The Hostage*, in *The Complete Plays*, p. 236.   **20** Ibid., p. 236.   **21** J. Joyce, *Ulysses: Annotated Students Edition* (1992), p. 136.   **22** Kearney, *The Writings of Brendan Behan*, p. 141.   **23** B. Behan and A. Simpson, *Richard's Cork Leg*, in *The Complete Plays*, p. 247.   **24** S. Connor, *Theory and Cultural Value* (1992), p. 80.

arrive, never to much effect, other than to offer ways of passing the time with songs, wit, and stories. Simpson may be partly responsible for the similarities to Beckett, here, as his reputation as a theatre producer in Dublin rested upon the fact that he brought both Behan and Beckett to Dublin audiences. The tone is markedly and widely different from Beckett's, however, and falls far short of the poetic economy of Beckett's work. This is best exemplified in the scene in the graveyard in which American technologies of commemoration coagulate in a bizarre and farcical fashion with Irish commemorative practices. The manager of the graveyard, now owned by a Californian company called 'Forest Lawn,' demonstrates to the assembled crowd of prostitutes and patriots his vision of the future of memorial architecture and rituals:

> PRINCE: ... I believe in a happy Eternal Life ... I therefore prayerfully resolve that I shall endeavour to build Forest Lawn ... as unlike other cemeteries ... as Eternal Life is unlike death ... a park filled with sweeping lawns, beautiful statuary, noble architecture [....] With interiors full of light and colour, and redolent of the world's best history and romances. [....] For those who request it we have tape-recordings especially made of the Loved One's voice, electronically co-ordinated with instruments in the body of the Loved One to give the appearance of life. [....] It has proved a great comfort to many Waiting Ones to once again hear the voices of those who have gone before.[25]

There follows a demonstration of the technique which Prince describes, in which a corpse sits up from his coffin and proceeds to speak, 'You'd think there was someone dead around here ... heh, heh, heh, that's good that is.'[26] The device of the talking corpse was used widely in modern Irish literature, from Synge's *In the Shadow of the Glen* to Joyce's *Finnegans Wake*. It was the central theme and apparatus of Máirtín Ó Cadhain's *Cré na Cille*, in which the dead converse from their graves about news of the living. Behan's representations of the talking corpse differ somewhat, in its figuration of the re-animated corpse as an automaton, uncannily bearing the voice of the deceased. Behan's graveyard humour in *Richard's Cork Leg* turns upon figures of resurrection and preservation, and plays with a technological fantasy of prosopopoeia, in which the dead are artificially re-animated and given a voice.

Here, Behan extends his fascination with American technologies of burial and mourning, exemplified in the conclusion to his story 'After the Wake,' in which he remarks upon the emphasis on cosmetic techniques in American mortuaries. This scene in *Richard's Cork Leg* imagines the cross-fertilisation of

---

25 Behan and Simpson, *Richard's Cork Leg*, p. 261. The ellipses in parenthesis are mine.   26 Ibid., p. 261.

American funerary technologies with Irish burial customs and beliefs, and thus registers the way in which death is experienced in culturally distinctive ways. 'There are cultures of death,' Derrida writes, 'In crossing a border, one changes death ... Every culture has its own funerary rites, its representations of the dying, its ways of mourning or burying.'[27] Thus, as the prostitutes in *Richard's Cork Leg* suggest, we can know Ireland from its graveyards, from reading its cultural apprehensions of death.[28] The representation of the corpse returned to life, singing and joking, signals both the failure and the necessity of imagining death as familiar, as a kind of living on. Death is figured, therefore, as a kind of ghostly preservation. There are echoes certainly of *Krapp's Last Tape*, in which old Krapp is confronted with the uncanny voices of his past recorded on tape, but there are autobiographical resonances too. The notion of a speaking corpse, of the mechanical reproduction of the voice from beyond the grave, is embodied in the form of Behan's late autobiographical writings.

'Even the most perfect reproduction of a work of art is lacking in one element,' writes Walter Benjamin, 'its presence in time and space, its unique existence at the place where it happens to be.'[29] Behan's prose narrative works, from his early stories to the posthumous *Confessions*, rely heavily on the notion of a speaking presence, on the narrative persona of a storyteller or raconteur. The voice embodies the source of narrative authority, in this sense, effecting the illusion of presence, a speaker self-identical with the spoken word. Benjamin argues that the mechanical reproduction of art, whether by print, sound recording, photography, or otherwise, disembodies art of its 'aura,' or its presence, and becomes instead the ghostly trace of an original. In the case of *Confessions of an Irish Rebel*, the narrative becomes spectral through and through. Its posthumous construction is evident throughout, with commemorative tributes to Behan written after his death included in the narrative. It contains disembodied and partially reconstructed versions of earlier writings and narratives, so that to read *Confessions* is to be confronted constantly with the impression of revenance. Even the recording technologies by which *Confessions* came into existence, we might argue, place the narrative within what Julian Wolfreys calls 'a virtual network of spectro-technical relations.'[30] Behan's narrative is constructed in his absence from the recorded tapes of his monologues, and therefore at a double remove from the ontological notion of authorship. If, as I argued in chapter one, we can take Behan's collaborative

27 J. Derrida, *Aporias*, trans. T. Dutoit (1993), p. 24.   28 I discuss the relationship between death, writing and national identity from Derridean perspectives in 'Writing Determination: Reading Death in(to) Irish National Identity', in J. Brannigan, R. Robbins and J. Wolfreys (eds), *Applying: To Derrida* (1996), pp 55–70.   29 W. Benjamin, 'The Work of Art in the Age of Mechanical Reproduction', *Illuminations*, ed. H. Arendt, trans. H. Zohn (1992), p. 214.   30 J. Wolfreys, *Victorian Hauntings: Spectrality, Gothic, the Uncanny and Literature* (2001), p. 1.

methods of working as indicative of a socialised concept of authorship, the spectral tendencies of his late writings suggest instead the idea of decentred authorship, one in which the author is continually displaced and absent. 'When the very *first* perception of an image is linked to a structure of reproduction,' Derrida says in interview, 'then we are dealing with the realm of phantoms.'[31]

Spectres of Behan

The argument advanced here is that Behan's late writings, in form and content, became enmeshed in structures and discourses of spectrality, prosopopoeia, and epitaphic inscription. As Paul de Man argues, 'prosopopoeia is the trope of autobiography ... by which one's name is made as intelligible and memorable as a face.'[32] Behan's last three prose works, *Brendan Behan's Island*, *Brendan Behan's New York*, and *Confessions of an Irish Rebel*, are especially concerned with constituting the cult of the name, by which 'Behan' becomes synonymous with the objects with which he associates himself. Behan is projected as the locus of life in Ireland or New York, the centre around which the montage of experience is organised. 'Ireland' is read in *Brendan Behan's Island*, for example, as the assembled sum of Behan's autobiographical reminiscences, a feature not uncommon in other autobiographies of the time.[33] As Ted Boyle argues, however, this is a narrative which fails to discover or reveal anything about the identity of 'Ireland, its people, or Brendan Behan,' collapsing instead into a 'rambling and almost totally insignificant Behan monologue.'[34] It was intended to imitate the form and conception of Synge's *The Aran Islands*, but became instead a series of anecdotes and reminiscences strung loosely together and too short to form a book by itself.

Brendan Behan's Island mixes anecdotes about Behan's experiences with idiosyncratic explanations of Ireland's geography, history, and cultural traditions, but the focus throughout is on the performance of the speaking persona. As Louis MacNeice observed, Behan is better at narrative than exposition, process rather than revelation.[35] Behan performs as comedian, raconteur, songster, tour-guide, firebrand, and genial host, but the objects of his attention – Brendan Behan and Ireland – remain elusive. He concludes:

31 J. Derrida, 'The Ghost Dance: An Interview with Jacques Derrida', trans. J.-L. Svoboda, *Public* 2 (1989), p. 61.   **32** P. de Man, 'Autobiography as De-facement', *Modern Language Notes*, 94, no. 5 (Dec. 1979), p. 926.   **33** See, for examples, F. O'Connor, *An Only Child* (1961), S. O'Faolain, *Vive Moi* (1964), or P. Kavanagh, *Self-Portrait* (1964). Autobiographical narratives by nationalist insurgents such as E. O'Malley and D. Breen tended to make the same equation between self and nation. Perhaps E. de Valera exemplified this equation best, however, when he declared that he had only to look inside himself to see what the Irish people were thinking.   **34** T. Boyle, *Brendan Behan* (1969), pp 128–29.   **35** L. MacNeice, 'The Two Faces of Ireland', *The Observer*, Sept. 30th 1962, p. 29.

So there you are. Ireland is like that – a land of contrasts like every other country – rigid in some matters, free and easy in others. You can take it or leave it, and that's the end of my story and all I am going to tell you and thanks for coming along.[36]

Behan's conclusions, like his preceding narrative, fail to give either distinction or definition to his subjects. Behan, like Ireland, is merely the assemblage of his anecdotes, which themselves are frequently directed towards performance rather than revelation. The function of his narrative is, however, signalled in the final phrase, 'thanks for coming along,' which registers the act of reading as a form of attendance. *Brendan Behan's Island* functions to divert or delay the reader, to hold the reader's attention before the performance of the narrator. The object of this kind of autobiographical writing, as James Olney has argued, is to fix attention on the performance of 'being':

> The author of an autobiography gives a sort of relief to his image by reference to the environment with its independent existence, he looks at himself being and delights in being looked at – he calls himself as witness for himself.[37]

Autobiography is not just, then, as its etymology suggests, the writing of the self, but is also testimony to the self living. Behan begins with songs and stories of his birthplace and home – 'I come from the same area as Sean O'Casey' – and his concluding anecdote delights in the story of being discovered swimming naked by a group of Abbey actors, to whom he seems to flaunt his corporeality. In between, Behan's stories witness his joys and sorrows, and testify to the fact and significance of his presence. *Brendan Behan's Island* holds in tension the contradictory impulses of autobiographical writing, then, for in witnessing Behan's living self, it already announces the end of Behan – 'that's the end of my story' – but simultaneously must resist closure or totalisation. Thus, Behan also writes that his narrative is 'all I am going to tell you,' which suggests that auto-biographical writing is controlled disclosure, by which the writer reveals particular masks and performances, but always retains something more to tell. Behan's narrative requires the fiction of closure, of representing himself *as if* his life were complete, in order to witness the experience of his living. Auto-biography, as de Man argues, needs 'the fiction of the voice-from-beyond-the-grave,' while simultaneously demonstrating the impossibility of closure and totalisation.[38]

36 Behan, *Brendan Behan's Island*, p. 191.   **37** J. Olney, 'Autobiography and the Cultural Moment: A Thematic, Historical and Bibliographical Introduction', *Autobiography: Essays Theoretical and Critical*, ed. J. Olney (1980), p. 29.   **38** de Man, 'Autobiography as De-facement', p. 927.

While written in a similar style, and containing similar anecdotes of self-promotion, *Brendan Behan's New York* is necessarily more limited in scope than *Brendan Behan's Island*. The New York book is part travel guide, part celebration of city living, but mostly a collection of Behan's reminiscences of writers and dignitaries with whom he has been associated in the city. *Brendan Behan's Island* enables Behan to conflate self-identity with the nation, but New York can only be read partially and idiosyncratically through Behan's narrative. The style is mostly reportage, while the anecdotes tend towards the theme of Behan's own renown and fame among the notable intellectuals, politicians and celebrities of New York society. There is an incestuous flavour to the narrative too, as Behan records the praise afforded him by his various acquaintances at the same time as he heaps adulation on their writings, talents or activities. This is Behan as entertaining locus of a celebrity community, the Behan whom Norman Mailer once remarked had made the Beat writers acceptable in uptown New York. Behan addresses himself in particular to the Irish-American community, commenting not just on the landmarks and hangouts of this community, but establishing his own family credentials with the Irish-Americans. The book closes with some correspondence between his maternal grandfather's family who had emigrated to the United States, and a brief resume of his own parents' connections with people there. Thus, *Brendan Behan's New York* trawls through family history, besides his own anecdotes and experiences, to forge an odd, self-indulgent view of life in New York. It is a book which could only succeed on the back of Behan's personality, trading on the currency of his signature. It is a book, moreover, in which Behan becomes equated with memory, in which his achievements and fame are history, a history of which he is now merely the narrator, no longer the participant.

The reminiscent mode comes to dominate Behan's writings in his later years, forming a discourse in which there is no longer a future to be anticipated, merely a past to be retold and offered up again and again. *Confessions of an Irish Rebel* revisits the events of Behan's life from the time of his release from borstal in 1941, to his marriage to Beatrice ffrench-Salkeld in 1955. It pretends to be the second volume in Behan's autobiography, although it owes little to the literary styles and fictional conventions of *Borstal Boy*. And although it ends in 1955, prior to Behan's rise to fame and success in London and New York, it is markedly elegiac towards the end. The book finishes with a kind of epitaph of its own, in which Behan declares to his loved one, in sentimental quotation, 'I've been faithful to thee, after my fashion.'[39] This final line resonates with a sense of closure, of words spoken from a death bed, as if Behan is dictating how he wishes to be remembered.

---

39 Behan, *Confessions of an Irish Rebel*, p. 259.

This sense of fashioning his legacy pervades his description of his first success as a playwright too. In the course of narrating his ascent to fame with the first production of *The Quare Fellow*, Behan recollects the pride with which he watched his uncle, P.J. Bourke, playing scenes of 'good old melodrama' at the Queen's theatre in Dublin:

> 'The O'Grady is as proud a title as any of your earls or dukes, and bedamned to you. I may be an English officer, but I'm also an Irish gentleman!' And with that the hero of the play flung the scarlet coat, gold epaulettes and all, on the floor, and in a frenzy of fury, foaming at the mouth, to the cheers and shouts of 'Up the Republic!' and croaks of 'Up, Skin-the-Goat!' from the more venerable of the multitude, he leapt the high steps of a slip-jig on the cloth of scarlet and gold.
>
> 'God bless you, P.J.,' screeches an ould one from the gods. 'That's me dream out. You'll turn yet.'
>
> Rory and Séan, my step-brothers, and I looked round the parterre in a weakness of adoration, wishing there was someone there to tell the people to point from us to the stage and at the centre, glorious against the lights, a strapping lad from Kildare in his lawn shirt and velvet breeches, and to say: 'See those three kids there, and see your man there, the O'Grady, the Colonel that's after telling off the other rat of an English officer on the courtmartial? Well, he's their uncle' ...
>
> *The Quare Fellow* got good notices, and was pretty well packed for the twenty-eight performances, and I stood there thinking of my uncle, Paddy J. Bourke, and the times I had watched him performing in his own melodramas and in the plays of Dion Boucicault.[40]

This is a passage worth quoting at length for the connection it makes between the child Behan mesmerised by the glory and excitement of his uncle's performances on the stage and the aging, dying author, eager to fix the value and significance of his own artistic legacy. Here, Behan's uncle symbolises a fusion of theatrical performance with patriotic fervour, whipping up audiences into cathartic expressions of nationalist pride and solidarity. The child Behan longs for the glory and power of such a performance, the authority to entice audiences into emotional release. *The Quare Fellow* owes something of its humour and its dramatic style to melodrama, but it functions in a very different mode from the heroic, nationalist theatricality depicted in Behan's narrative above. It is critical in contrast to melodramatic glorification; it is grimly, grotesquely comic where melodrama is cathartic and jovial; it revolves around

---

40 Ibid., p. 258.

the absent anti-hero, 'the quare fellow,' where Bourke's performances required the commanding presence of the hero. Yet, Behan weighs and situates his own legacy among the popular theatrical heroes of his childhood.

Nostalgia, and a strong vein of family pride, play their parts in bringing Behan to this identification with popular patriotic drama. Such an identification is not unfounded, as is evident in the styles and theatrical conventions of *The Hostage*, but its significance in *Confessions of an Irish Rebel* is that it registers again the desire of the author not merely to leave behind an artistic legacy but to evaluate and situate that legacy himself. The passage quoted above appears towards the end of *Confessions*, and while it does not foreclose the possibility of an ensuing narrative about his experiences after 1955, it already begins to announce the end of Behan. A further volume of autobiography would, it seems, have continued in the same vein, talking about Behan's life as history, evaluating and contextualising his writings as if he were dead, as if he had become the biographer and critic of his own life and works. In part, as de Man suggests, this is a consequence of the generic composition of autobiographical writing – the fiction of death which enables the attempt to totalise – but in part too it is exemplary of the way in which Behan's writings become epitaphic in structure and style, scripting the final self-image by which he desires to be remembered.

The ends of Behan

At the end of the second chapter of *Confessions of an Irish Rebel*, after Behan has narrated his return to Ireland, and his reacquaintance with a girl dying young from consumption, he writes that 'if these are the confessions of an Irish rebel, they are indeed confessions.'[41] Confessional writing, as Jeremy Tambling has shown, is central to the production of subjectivity, and to the process of self-fashioning within a network of power relations.[42] The confessional entails a controlled divulgence of the self in order to legitimate modern categories of privacy and publicity. If this is the case, it is clear that Behan's *Confessions* is highly ambiguous as a confessional text. Its *modus operandi* is not self-divulgence but self-promotion; it is not submissive to the judgement of others but pre-emptive; it neither seeks nor requires the tolerance or forgiveness of others in order to sanction the self-fashioning which takes place there. That it seeks to be considered confessional is perhaps more pertinent, since the promise of submission and revelation are seductive narrative ploys with which to divert and hold the reader. Not all autobiographies are confessional, but the narrative

---

41 Ibid., p. 29.   42 See Jeremy Tambling, *Confession: Sexuality, Sin, the Subject* (1990).

conventions of the confessional can be usefully deployed in autobiographical writing in order to win much desired attention. Moreover, in Catholic ritual, the confessional is an important part of an individual's preparations for death, and itself forms a kind of auto-epitaphic rite through which the subject passes from the living to the dead. To confess is thus to offer up the final autobiographical version of one's life, to enact one final performance of self-fashioning, and this is the function of the confessional mode in Behan's late writings.

Maureen Waters wrote of Behan that 'the most compelling character he ever created was Brendan Behan.'[43] His late publications are increasingly obsessed with prolonging the narrative continuity of this character, but paradoxically succeed in creating an epitaphic discourse around Brendan Behan, speaking about him as if he were already dead. Writing, as Roland Barthes notes in the opening of his own confessional text, *Roland Barthes*, tends to monumentalise its autobiographical subject: 'Once I produce, once I write, it is the text itself which (fortunately) dispossesses me of my narrative continuity.'[44] Hence, the necessity of producing more books, to go on writing or talking, even when the subject of one's narrative has been exhausted. Behan's creative endeavours, the inventive fictions of his imagination, had come to an end long before he ceased to produce books. Speaking, he suggested to Rae Jeffs, was his way of continuing to write, to keep the narrative going, but it was also a desperate attempt to master narrative and subjective presence in the mode of absence.[45] In the years before his death, then, Behan was beginning to practice a kind of ghostwriting, returning to the narrative and fictions of his past through the spectral media of tape-recording and a willing amanuensis.

43 M. Waters, *The Comic Irishman* (1984), p. 166.   **44** R. Barthes, *Roland Barthes* (1995), p. 4.   **45** U. O'Connor, *Brendan Behan*, p. 249.

Conclusion

I want to return briefly in this conclusion to two suggestive moments in Behan's life, which exemplify the complex interaction between nationalism and writing which pervaded his life, and which continue to dominate critical and biographical constructions of Behan. The first moment took place on the evening of 30 November 1939, when Behan was sixteen years old. He went to his family home, 70 Kildare Road, in Dublin, and packed a suitcase. The suitcase contained chlorate of potash and paraffin wax, which was mixed with gelignite to form an explosive compound. It contained also ampoules of sulphuric acid, which, when inserted into wax-filled condoms, would corrode and ignite the explosives. While he packed his case, his tense, disapproving family gathered around his father at the fireside, who was reading aloud from a favourite book of Behan's childhood, Dickens' *The Pickwick Papers*. Behan left the house with familiar tales of Mr Pickwick, Mr Snodgrass, and Mr Winkle ringing in his ears. He arrived in Liverpool the following morning, where he went to a lodging house and began to prepare his bombs. He was arrested that afternoon by Liverpool CID before he could carry out his plans. Here was Behan the dedicated terrorist, preparing to bomb, according to different accounts, either British Navy ships at Cammell Lairds dockyards, or a department store in the centre of Liverpool. The second moment occurred almost twenty years later, on 3 April 1959. Behan sat in the back of a car being driven around Paris by a chauffeur, on the occasion of his play, *The Hostage*, representing Great Britain in the Theatre de Nations festival. Behan noticed that the Union Jack flag was flying on one side of the car. He leant forward to the driver and joked with him that if he stuck another Union Jack flag on the other side, he might drum up a bit more trade for his play.

I cite these two anecdotes from the life of Brendan Behan because of the narratives which seem to resonate between them, narratives of nationalism and betrayal, of commitment and compromise, of militancy and recalcitrance, and indeed of violence and writing. The critical reputation of Behan's writings has conventionally been determined by the oppositions and hierarchies suggested by these anecdotes: that Behan was a Republican who deserted his political commitments for the attractions of literary fame in England; that he turned from cultural nationalism to cultural anomie; that he allowed his writings to become the vehicles of stage-Irish amusements for the metropolitan audiences

165

of London's West End. I have been arguing throughout this book for an alternative conception of Behan's writings, in which these oppositions and hierarchies are inverted, in which writing enabled Behan to articulate dissident and critical perspectives on cultural nationalism in mid-century Ireland. Behan's writings, I have argued, participate in the emergence of revisionist and post-colonial critiques of modern nationalism, even, and especially, at the point at which those writings are indebted to nationalist discourses and iconographies.

There is, then, an alternative narrative between the two moments of Behan's life sketched above which I want to pursue briefly in the course of this conclusion, and which has both particular pertinence for Behan's writings, and general significance for the relationship between literature and nationalism. It is an argument which Simon During makes in an essay published initially in Homi Bhabha's collection, *Nation and Narration*, in 1990, where he contends that literature acts 'as other to, or resistance against' discourses of nationalism.[1] During constructs his argument as a sympathetic revision of Said's notion that literature 'belongs to, gains coherence from, and in a sense emanates out of, the concepts of nation, nationality and even of race.'[2] While During accepts that literature can and frequently does function in ways which legitimise national identities and indeed the nation-state, he proceeds to argue that literature exceeds the discursive and representational demands of nationalism, and that literature belongs more closely to a civil imaginary than the cultural constructions of nationalism. At its simplest level, During's argument is no more ambitious than to suggest that 'literature has operated in different social spaces than nationalism, employing different signifying practices.'[3] The implications of his argument, however, are more significant, that literature might embody, to adapt Fredric Jameson's phrase, the cultural and 'political unconscious' of nationalism.

As I argued in the introduction, the critical debates of this period were staging a struggle between alternative conceptions of Irish cultural identity. In this sense, there was an explicit acknowledgement of the constitutive role of literature in exercising what During calls the 'civil imaginary.' In practice, this took the form of a struggle between competing versions of cultural memory, in which 'memory' became the site of cultural and political contention. While the state nationalism of 'the age of de Valera' emphasised the memorial project of recovering an Irishness which was Gaelic, rural and Catholic, the literary and historical revisionism of the 1940s and 50s probed nationalism for the fissures and tensions already evident in its ideologies and its political and cultural practices. Such criticism is necessarily belated, returning to the theories and writings of the past in order to effect its own interventions and revisions.

1 S. During, 'Literature – Nationalism's other? The case for revision', in H. Bhabha (ed.), *Nation and Narration* (1990), pp 138–53. 2 E. Said, *The World, the Text, and the Critic* (1984), p. 169. 3 During, 'Literature – Nationalism's other?', p. 138.

The revisionist debates of the mid-century were embroiled in the cultural politics of Irish memory, in which incitements to memory and commemoration were imbricated within contested notions of Irishness. Behan's writings are inseparable from these debates, and themselves counterpose the amnesia of state nationalism by bearing witness to that which nationalism excludes and forgets – the executed of *The Quare Fellow*, as argued in chapter three, or the discontents of Behan's working-class Dublin. For Behan, memory played a crucial role in grounding identity, and this is the subject of his belated engagement with the nationalist mythologies of the revival.

In contrast to the cultural nationalism of his youth, Behan's writings frequently counter the logic of cultural anomaly and exclusivity by interrogating the analogous cultural experiences of Irish and English peoples. In *The Hostage*, this is symbolised in the cultural rapport which develops between the English hostage, Leslie, and his Irish captors, or indeed, at a formal level in his reworking of the common cultural forms of 'music hall' shared between Behan's Dublin upbringing and that of his audiences in London's East End. Behan comments upon the common class identifications which he shares with working-class English boys in *Borstal Boy*. His identification with English working-class culture is, I would suggest, not unaware of the degree to which such a culture had gained considerable authority and prestige in the literary marketplace in England in the 1950s. *Borstal Boy* shares with Alan Sillitoe, Frank Norman, and Colin MacInnes themes of juvenile delinquency, political disillusionment, and self-conscious masculinity which marked the emergence of what Alan Sillitoe described at the time as the new proletarian novel. Behan was not just plugging into the demands and fashions of the literary markets in England, however, for he had already delineated the contours of an Anglophone urban Ireland in his earlier writings for the *Irish Press*.

It is possible, of course, to represent Behan's depiction of Anglicised Ireland as the residual rumblings of neo-colonialism, as the return of stage-Irishry which his appearances in English and American media seemed so often to resemble. Behan seemed often all too willing to provide journalists and interviewers with stories of his drunkenness, boisterousness, or staged antics. The forms and contexts of his writings, however, frequently undercut notions of stage-Irishry, particularly when situated in relation to an emergent critical culture in Ireland, and in relation to the powerful texts and genres with which Behan's writings construct critical dialogues. The mythology surrounding Behan's life and public image has tended to discourage the task of situating Behan within critical contexts, within the cultural politics of his time. Gus Martin commented on a certain critical embarrassment in treating Behan's work seriously, in an essay Martin wrote while Behan was still alive:

Brendan Behan does not invite critical comment on his work. The whole character of the man discourages it. The public image that he has created is so tremendously alive and exuberant that one is inclined to regard the writing as a mere casual offshoot of his rollicking personality. As if, in fact, the work was there as an excuse to display the man. Again one feels a little silly in treating his work with more attention and respect than he allows it himself.[4]

Martin admirably proceeds to analyse Behan's writings critically, despite his reservations about the writer's personality. It is neither possible nor desirable to circumvent the author's biography entirely, but it is necessary to distinguish the writings from Behan's public image, which I have attempted to do here. For much of his literary career, Behan's writings tackled complex issues of culture and representation within inventive, experimental forms. Writing seemed to demand of Behan a form of critical interrogation and revision which it was not possible nor perhaps productive to do in speech. This is, in part, the reason why his later, spoken works not only suffer in quality in comparison to his writings, but also retreat considerably from the cultural complexity and critical oppositionality evident in *The Quare Fellow*, *The Hostage*, *Borstal Boy*, or even in his weekly columns for the *Irish Press*.

Writing, as Jean-François Lyotard argues, is a technology for remembering, for producing the past as 'an available, presentable and reactualizable memory.'[5] In this sense, writing serves as a site of political and cultural contest, in which acts of remembrance and representation perform the critical task not merely of remarking on the unrepresented, but also in forming a kind of oppositional counter-memory. Behan's writings worked in mid-century Irish literary culture to call back to memory the variegated cultural traditions and practices which composed Irishness, and to signal the disjunctive, contingent nature of cultural and national identities. Behan returned to formative texts and genres of the Irish literary revival in order to critique the forms of cultural nationalism which had become entrenched in the post-colonial state. Ali Behdad describes this work in general as an important dimension of postcolonial studies, which he argues are 'on the side of memory, their oppositionality a function of *anamnesia*, as they expose the genealogy of oppression and the oppressed.'[6] This is not to argue that postcolonial writings remember more or better than the cultural nationalism with which they are engaged in revising, but rather that postcolonial revisionism gathers its energies and critiques from the gaps and contradictions of nationalism.

4 A. Martin, 'Brendan Behan', *Threshold*, no. 18 (1963), p. 22.   5 J.-F. Lyotard, *The Inhuman: Reflections on Time*, trans. G. Bennington and R. Bowlby (1991), p. 48.   6 A. Behdad, *Belated Travelers: Orientalism in the Age of Colonial Dissolution* (1994), p. 6.

Revisionism is defined, in this sense, as the critical memory of the aporia and disjunction of nationalism.

To perform this task, the postcolonial revisionism which I have argued is evident in Behan's writings, is of necessity indebted to and imbricated in the structures and logic of nationalism. It is, in John Hutchinson's useful phrase, 'methodologically nationalist.'[7] Revisionist writing must return to the scene of nationalist writing in order to acquire its critical stimuli, in order to clear away 'the briars and the brambles' of history, as O'Faolain suggested in *The Bell*.[8] In the same way, as David Lloyd argues, modern nationalism is deeply rooted in colonial structures and ideologies. 'Nationalist monologism,' he writes, 'is a dialogic inversion of imperial ideology, caught willy-nilly in the position of a parody, antagonistic but dependent.'[9] It is this parodic relation between nationalism and imperialism which opens up the discursive space of postcolonial revisionism.

Literature, it seems to me, to return to During's argument, can participate in the construction of nationalism, or work to counter nationalism, or indeed can function in ways discrete from and oblivious to the demands of nationalism. I have been arguing that in mid-century Ireland, writing constituted a representational space in which the grounding of national identity and culture was subject to what Lyotard calls 'anamnesiac resistance.'[10] Behan's writings, like those of many of his contemporaries, were engaged in contentious dialogue between specific forms and practices of memory, in which the belatedness of his time gave rise to crises of memory and consequently crises of representation. The genres of representation central to Behan's work – autobiography, drama, anecdote – were associated principally with the cultural endeavours of early twentieth-century nationalism. Behan chose to refract critical and subaltern perspectives on state and fugitive nationalism through these forms of representation, and to engage in revisionary dialogue with nationalism as an emancipatory discourse.

I have been arguing in this book for particular ways in which we might re-examine the writings of Brendan Behan, and to situate Behan in the cultural and political contexts of Irish and English literature in the 1940s and 1950s. Behan turned from the political violence of his youth to examine and critique such violence in his writings, and this made him a controversial figure for Irish nationalism. He wavered between writing for an Irish audience, sometimes in the Irish language, and writing for the metropolitan audiences in England and North America, and thus registered the constitutive dilemma of Irish writing

---

7 J. Hutchinson, 'Irish Nationalism', in Boyce and O'Day (eds), *The Making of Modern Irish History: Revisionism and the Revisionist Controversy* (1996), p. 101. **8** S. O'Faolain, 'Editorial: This is Your Magazine', *The Bell*, 1, no. 1 (October 1940), p. 7. **9** D. Lloyd, *Anomalous States: Irish Writing and the Post-Colonial Moment* (1993), p. 112. **10** Lyotard, *The Inhuman*, p. 57.

after independence. His writings systematically engaged with and deconstructed modern discourses of nationalism and colonialism, but contained no vision of the future through which Ireland might be re-imagined as 'a different place.'[11] Brendan Behan remains, then, in the trajectory of modern Irish writing, a figure of considerable ambivalence, but his writings participated in the construction of a post-colonial, post-nationalist aesthetic, which continues to exercise itself in the literary imagination of contemporary Ireland.

11 B. Behan, *Brendan Behan's Island* (1965), p. 191.

Chronology

1923   Brendan Behan born, 9 February, to Kathleen (Kearney) and Stephen Behan. The Behan family live in a flat in 14 Russell Street, Dublin.

1928–34 Attends St Vincent's School, North William Street, Dublin.

1931   Joins Fianna Eireann (IRA youth movement).

1934–37 Attends St Canice's Christian Brothers' School, North Circular Road, Dublin.

1936   Behan publishes his first piece of writing, 'A Tantalising Tale' in *Fianna: The Voice of Young Ireland* (June).

1937   Attends Bolton Street Technical School to learn the trade of house painting. The Behan family are rehoused by the Dublin Corporation in 70 Kildare Road, Crumlin, in a new housing estate.

1939   Brendan Behan joins the IRA. He is arrested in Liverpool, 1 December, on charges of possession of explosives, and held in custody in Walton Jail.

1940   Behan sentenced to three years' borstal detention, 8 February, and moved initially to Feltham Boys' Prison, then to Hollesley Bay Borstal, where he is imprisoned until his release and expulsion to Ireland on 1 November 1941.

1942   Behan arrested for shooting at Dublin detectives, 10 April, and sentenced to fourteen years' penal servitude. He is imprisoned in Mountjoy Jail, then Arbour Hill Military Prison, and the Curragh Military Camp, until his release under general amnesty in September 1946. 'I Become a Borstal Boy' published in *The Bell* (June).

1947   Behan visits the Blasket Islands, Kerry (January). He is arrested and imprisoned in Strangeways Jail for three months for attempting to free an IRA prisoner from prison in Manchester (March-July).

1948   Behan serves one month in Mountjoy Jail, Dublin, for assaulting a policeman. He goes to live in Paris in August.

1950   'After the Wake' published in *Points* (December).

1952   Behan serves one month in Lewes Prison, Sussex, for breaking expulsion order (October).

1953   *The Scarperer* is published serially in the *Irish Times*, beginning on 19 October.

1954   Behan writes a weekly column for the *Irish Press*, April 1954– April 1956. *The Quare Fellow* opens at The Pike Theatre, Dublin, 19 November 1954.

1955   Behan marries Beatrice ffrench-Salkeld, 16 February.

1956   *The Quare Fellow* opens at the Theatre Royal, Stratford East, London, 24 May.

1958   *An Giall* opens at the Damer Hall, Dublin, 16 June. *The Hostage* opens at the Theatre Royal, Stratford East, London, 14 October. *Borstal Boy* is published by Hutchinson (London) on 20 October.

1952   Behan suffers epileptiform seizures (July).

1961   'The Big House' published in *Evergreen Review* (October).

1962   *Brendan Behan's Island* published (October).

1963   *Hold Your Hour and Have Another* published (September). Behan's daughter, Blanaid, is born, 24 November.

1964   Brendan Behan dies at the Meath Hospital, 20 March. *The Scarperer* published (June). *Brendan Behan's New York* published (September).

1965   *Confessions of an Irish Rebel* published (September).

1972   *Richard's Cork Leg* opens at the Peacock Theatre, Dublin, 14 March.

Bibliography

BRENDAN BEHAN'S WRITINGS

The following editions are those cited and used in this study:

An Giall/The Hostage, ed. Richard Wall (Washington D.C.: Catholic University of
America Press, 1987).
The Complete Plays (London: Methuen, 1978).
Borstal Boy (London: Corgi, 1961).
Confessions of an Irish Rebel (London: Arena, 1985).
Hold Your Hour and Have Another (London: Corgi, 1965).
The Dubbalin Man (Dublin: A. & A. Farmar, 1997).
After the Wake, ed. Peter Fallon (Dublin: O'Brien, 1981).
Poems and a Play in Irish (Oldcastle, Ireland: Gallery Press, 1981).
The Scarperer (New York: Doubleday, 1964).
Brendan Behan's Island (London: Corgi, 1965).
Brendan Behan's New York (London: Hutchinson, 1964).

The text also contains quotations from the following audio-visual sources:
Brendan Behan on Joyce, Folkways Records FL9826 (Behan's lecture to the James
Joyce Society in New York, 1960)
'On the Northside,' *Radio Éireann*, 11 September 1951.

GENERAL BIBLIOGRAPHY

Adorno, Theodor W., *Minima Moralia: Reflections from Damaged Life*, trans. E.F.N.
Jephcott (London: Verso, 1978).
Ashcroft, Bill, Griffiths, Gareth and Tiffin, Helen, *The Empire Writes Back: Theory and
Practice in Post-colonial Literatures* (London: Routledge, 1989).
Bailey, Peter (ed.), *Music Hall: The Business of Pleasure* (Milton Keynes, UK: Open
University Press, 1986).
Bakhtin, M.M., *The Dialogic Imagination: Four Essays*, ed. Michael Holquist, trans. Caryl
Emerson and Michael Holquist (Austin, Texas, USA: University of Texas Press,
1981).
Baldick, Chris, *The Social Mission of English Criticism, 1848–1932* (Oxford: Clarendon
Press, 1983).
Barthes, Roland, *Roland Barthes* (London: Papermac, 1995).

Baudrillard, Jean, *Seduction*, trans. Brian Singer (London: Macmillan, 1990).

Behan, Beatrice, *My Life with Brendan* (London: Leslie Frewin, 1973).

Behan, Brian, *With Breast Expanded* (London: MacGibbon and Kee, 1964).

— and Behan, Kathleen, *Mother of All the Behans* (Dublin: Poolbeg, 1994).

— and Dillon-Malone, Aubrey, *The Brothers Behan* (Dublin: Ashfield Press, 1998).

Behan, Dominic, *Teems of Times and Happy Returns* (London: Four Square, 1963).

—, *My Brother Brendan* (London: Four Square, 1966).

Behdad, Ali, *Belated Travelers: Orientalism in the Age of Colonial Dissolution* (Cork: Cork University Press, 1994).

Benjamin, Walter, *Illuminations*, trans. Harry Zohn (London: Fontana, 1992).

Bhabha, Homi (ed.), *Nation and Narration* (London: Routledge, 1990).

—, 'Representation and the Colonial Text,' *The Theory of Reading*, ed. Frank Gloversmith (Brighton: Harvester Press, 1984), pp 93–122.

—, *The Location of Culture* (London: Routledge, 1994).

Bloom, Harold, *The Anxiety of Influence: A Theory of Poetry* (New York: Oxford University Press, 1973).

Borges, Jorge Luis, *Labyrinths: Selected Stories and Other Writings* (London: Penguin, 1970).

Boyle, Ted E., *Brendan Behan* (New York: Twayne, 1969).

Brannigan, John, 'An Historical Accident: National Identity in the Writings of Brendan Behan,' *Irish Studies Review*, 13 (Winter 1995/96), pp 26–29.

—, '"Historically Informed and Obscene": Brendan Behan and the Politics of Comedy,' *Imprimatur*, 2, no. 1 (October 1996), pp 37–42.

—, 'Writing Determination: Reading Death in(to) Irish National Identity,' *Applying: To Derrida*, ed. John Brannigan, Ruth Robbins and Julian Wolfreys (Basingstoke, UK: Macmillan, 1996), pp 55–70.

Bratton, Jacky, Cook, Jim, and Gledhill, Christine (eds), *Melodrama: Stage, Picture, Screen* (London: British Film Institute, 1994).

Brecht, Bertolt, *Brecht on Theatre*, ed. John Willett (London: Eyre Methuen, 1974).

Brombert, Victor, *The Romantic Prison: The French Tradition* (Baltimore: Johns Hopkins University Press, 1978).

Brooks, Peter, *The Melodramatic Imagination: Balzac, Henry James, Melodrama, and the Mode of Excess* (New Haven: Yale University Press, 1976).

Brown, Terence, *Ireland: A Social and Cultural History, 1922–1985* (London: Fontana, 1985).

Bürger, Peter, *Theory of the Avant-Garde*, trans. Michael Shaw (Minneapolis: University of Minnesota Press, 1984).

Burke, Sean, *The Death and Return of the Author: Criticism and Subjectivity in Barthes, Foucault and Derrida* (Edinburgh: Edinburgh University Press, 1992).

Butler, Hubert, 'The Barriers,' *The Bell*, 2, no. 4 (July 1941), pp 40–46.

Carnochan, W.B., *Confinement and Flight: An Essay on English Literature of the Eighteenth Century* (Berkeley: University of California Press, 1977).

Chambers, Ross, *Story and Situation: Narrative Seduction and the Power of Fiction* (Manchester: Manchester University Press, 1984).

——, *Room for Maneuver: Reading (the) Oppositional (in) Narrative* (Chicago: University of Chicago Press, 1991).

Clarke, Thomas J., *Glimpses of an Irish Felon's Prison Life* (1913; reprinted Dublin: Maunsel and Roberts, 1922).

Connor, Steven, *Theory and Cultural Value* (Oxford: Blackwell, 1992).

Coogan, Tim Pat, *Ireland Since the Rising* (Westport, Connecticut: Greenwood Press, 1966).

Corcoran, Neil, *After Yeats and Joyce: Reading Modern Irish Literature* (Oxford: Oxford University Press, 1997).

Corkery, Daniel, *Synge and Anglo-Irish Literature* (Cork: Mercier, 1966).

——, 'The Hidden Force in Irish Revival,' *Sunday Press*, 4 May 1952.

Costello, Francis J., *Enduring the Most: The Life and Death of Terence MacSwiney* (Dingle, Ireland: Brandon Books, 1995).

Cottom, Daniel, *Ravishing Tradition: Cultural Forces and Literary History* (Ithaca, NY: Cornell University Press, 1996).

Cronin, Anthony, *Dead as Doornails: A Chronicle of Life* (Dublin: The Dolmen Press, 1976).

Das, Veena, 'Subaltern as Perspective,' *Subaltern Studies VI: Writings on South Asian History and Society*, ed. Ranajit Guha (Delhi: Oxford University Press, 1989), pp 310–24.

Davie, Donald, 'Reflections of an English Writer in Ireland,' *Studies*, 44 (Winter 1955), pp 439–45.

Davitt, Michael, *Leaves from a Prison Diary; or, Lectures to a 'Solitary' Audience* (London: Chapman and Hall, 1885).

Deane, Seamus, *Strange Country: Modernity and Nationhood in Irish Writing since 1790* (Oxford: Oxford University Press, 1997).

de Búrca, Séamus, *The Queen's Royal Theatre Dublin, 1829–1969* (Dublin: Séamus de Búrca, 1983).

——, *Brendan Behan: A Memoir* (Dublin: P.J. Bourke, 1993).

de Man, Paul, 'Autobiography as De-facement,' *Modern Language Notes*, 94, no. 5 (Dec. 1979), pp 919–30.

Derrida, Jacques, *The Archeology of the Frivolous*, trans. John P. Leavey, Jr. (Lincoln and London: University of Nebraska Press, 1987).

——, 'The Ghost Dance: An Interview with Jacques Derrida,' trans. Jean-Luc Svoboda, *Public* 2 (1989).

——, *Aporias*, trans. Thomas Dutoit (Stanford: Stanford University Press, 1993).

de Valera, Eamon, *Speeches and Statements, 1917–73*, ed. Maurice Moynihan (Dublin: Gill and Macmillan, 1980).

Devoy, John, *Recollections of an Irish Rebel* (1929; reprinted Shannon, Ireland: Irish University Press, 1969).

During, Simon, 'Literature – Nationalism's other? The case for revision,' *Nation and Narration*, ed. Homi Bhabha (London: Routledge, 1990), pp 138–53.

Eagleton, Terry, *The Function of Criticism: From* The Spectator *to Post-Structuralism* (London: Verso, 1984).

Eliot, T.S., *Selected Prose*, ed. John Hayward (London: Penguin, 1953).

English, Richard, *Ernie O'Malley: IRA Intellectual* (Oxford: Clarendon Press, 1998).

Falco, Raphael, *Conceived Presences: Literary Genealogy in Renaissance England* (Amherst: University of Massachusetts Press, 1994).

Fallon, Brian, *An Age of Innocence: Irish Culture, 1930–1960* (Dublin: Gill and Macmillan, 1999).

Fanon, Frantz, *The Wretched of the Earth*, trans. Constance Farrington (London: Penguin, 1967).

Fisk, Robert, *In Time of War: Ireland, Ulster and the Price of Neutrality, 1939–45* (Philadelphia: University of Pennsylvania Press, 1983).

Fleming, Deborah, *"A Man Who Does Not Exist": The Irish Peasant in the Work of W.B. Yeats and J.M. Synge* (Ann Arbor: University of Michigan Press, 1995).

Fludernik, Monika, 'Carceral topography: spatiality, liminality and corporality in the literary prison,' *Textual Practice*, 13, no. 1 (Spring 1999), pp 43–77.

Foucault, Michel, *Discipline and Punish: The Birth of the Prison*, trans. A.M. Sheridan Smith (London: Penguin, 1979).

Gerdes, Peter René, *The Major Works of Brendan Behan* (Frankfurt: Peter Lang, 1973).

Genet, Jean, *Miracle of the Rose*, trans. Bernard Frechtman (New York: Grove Press, 1966).

Gilroy, Paul, *'There Ain't No Black in the Union Jack': The Cultural Politics of Race and Nation* (London: Routledge, 1987).

Graham, Colin, '.'.. maybe that's just Blarney: Irish Culture and the Persistence of Authenticity,' *Ireland and Cultural Theory: The Mechanics of Authenticity*, ed. Colin Graham and Richard Kirkland (Basingstoke, UK: Macmillan, 1999), pp 7–28.

Gramsci, Antonio, *Selections from Prison Notebooks*, ed. and trans. Quintin Hoare and Geoffrey Nowell Smith (London: Lawrence and Wishart, 1971).

Greenblatt, Stephen, *Shakespearean Negotiations: The Circulation of Social Energy in Renaissance England* (Oxford: Clarendon Press, 1988).

——, *Marvelous Possessions: The Wonder of the New World* (Oxford: Clarendon Press, 1991).

Grene, Nicholas, *The Politics of Irish Drama: Plays in Context from Boucicault to Friel* (Cambridge: Cambridge University Press, 1999).

Guha, Ranajit, 'On Some Aspects of the Historiography of Colonial India,' *Subaltern Studies I: Writings on South Asian History and Society* (Delhi: Oxford University Press, 1994), pp 1–8.

Hardy, Thomas, *Under the Greenwood Tree* (London: Penguin, 1994).

Harmon, Maurice, *Sean O'Faolain: A Life* (London: Constable, 1994).

Hawkins, Maureen, 'Women, "Queers", Love, and Politics: *The Crying Game* as a Corrective Adaptation of/ Reply to *The Hostage*,' *Representing Ireland: Gender, Class, Nationality*, ed. Susan Shaw Sailer (Gainesville: University Press of Florida, 1997), pp 194–212.

Hermeren, Goran, *Influence in Art and Literature* (Princeton: Princeton University Press, 1975).

Herr, Cheryl, *For The Land They Loved: Irish Political Melodramas, 1890–1925* (New York: Syracuse University Press, 1991).

Hughes, Eamonn, 'Forgetting the Future: An Outline History of Irish Literary Studies,' *Irish Review*, 25 (Winter 1999/ Spring 2000), pp 1–15.

Hutchinson, John, 'Irish Nationalism,' *The Making of Modern Irish History: Revisionism and the Revisionist Controversy*, ed. D. George Boyce and Alan O'Day (London: Routledge, 1996), pp 100–19.

Hyde, Douglas, *A Literary History of Ireland from Earliest Times to the Present Day* (London: Fisher Unwin, 1899).

——, 'The Necessity of De-Anglicising Ireland,' *The Field Day Anthology of Irish Writing*, 2, ed. Seamus Deane (Derry, Northern Ireland: Field Day Publications, 1991), pp 527–33.

——, *Selected Plays* (Gerrards Cross, Bucks, UK: Colin Smythe, 1991).

Jameson, Fredric, *The Political Unconscious: Narrative as a Socially Symbolic Act* (London: Methuen, 1981).

Jeffs, Rae, *Brendan Behan: Man and Showman* (London: Corgi, 1968).

Joyce, James, *Ulysses: Annotated Students' Edition* (London: Penguin, 1992).

——, *The Critical Writings of James Joyce*, ed. Ellsworth Mason and Richard Ellmann (New York: Cornell University Press, 1989).

Kaestner, Jan, *Brendan Behan: Das Dramatische Werk* (Frankfurt: Peter Lang, 1978).

Kavanagh, Patrick, 'Diary,' *Envoy*, 1, no. 1 (December 1949), p.90.

——, 'Who Killed James Joyce?,' *Envoy*, 5, no. 17 (April 1951), p.12.

——, 'Editorial: Victory of Mediocrity,' *Kavanagh's Weekly*, no. 1 (12 April 1952), p.1.

——, 'Editorial,' *Kavanagh's Weekly*, 3 (26 April 1952), p.1.

Kearney, Colbert, *The Writings of Brendan Behan* (New York: St Martin's Press, 1977).

Kearney, Richard, *Transitions: Narratives in Modern Irish Culture* (Dublin: Wolfhound Press, 1988).

Kenny, Herbert A., *Literary Dublin: A History* (Dublin: Gill and Macmillan, 1974).

Kiberd, Declan, *Synge and the Irish Language* (Dublin: Gill and Macmillan, 1979).

——, 'The Fall of the Stage Irishman,' *Genre*, 12 (Winter 1979), pp 451–72.

——, 'Writers in Quarantine? The Case for Irish Studies,' *Crane Bag*, 3 (1979), pp 9–21.

—— and Gabriel Fitzmaurice (eds), *An Crann Faoi Blath: The Flowering Tree* (Dublin: Wolfhound, 1991).

——, *Inventing Ireland: The Literature of the Modern Nation* (London: Jonathan Cape, 1995).

Kiely, Benedict, *Modern Irish Fiction: A Critique* (Dublin: Golden Eagle Books, 1950).

Lamming, George, *The Pleasures of Exile* (London: Allison and Busby, 1984; orig. 1960).

Lazarus, Neil, *Nationalism and Cultural Practice in the Postcolonial World* (Cambridge: Cambridge University Press, 1999).

Lebow, Richard Ned, *White Britain, Black Ireland: The Influence of Stereotypes on Colonial Policy* (Philadelphia: Institute for the Study of Human Issues, 1976).

Le Brocquy, Anne Madden, *Seeing His Way: Louis le Brocquy – A Painter* (Dublin: Gill and Macmillan, 1994).

Littlewood, Joan, *Joan's Book: Joan Littlewood's Peculiar History as She Tells It* (London: Minerva, 1995).

Lloyd, David, *Nationalism and Minor Literature: James Clarence Mangan and the Emergence of Irish Cultural Nationalism* (Berkeley: University of California Press, 1987).

——, *Anomalous States: Irish Writing and the Post-Colonial Moment* (Dublin: Lilliput Press, 1993).

——, *Ireland after History* (Cork: Cork University Press, 1999).

Longley, Edna, *The Living Stream: Literature and Revisionism in Ireland* (Newcastle, UK: Bloodaxe Books, 1994).

Lyons, F.S.L., *Culture and Anarchy in Ireland, 1890–1939* (Oxford: Clarendon Press, 1979).

Lyotard, Jean-François, *The Inhuman: Reflections on Time*, trans. Geoffrey Bennington and Rachel Bowlby (Cambridge, UK: Polity Press, 1991).

MacDonagh, Thomas, *Literature in Ireland: Studies Irish and Anglo-Irish* (Nenagh, Ireland: Relay Books, 1996).

MacNamara, Desmond, 'Early and Late,' *New Statesman*, 72 (18 November 1966), p.750.

MacNeice, Louis, 'The Two Faces of Ireland,' *The Observer*, 30 Sept. 1962, p. 29.

——, *Collected Poems* (London: Faber and Faber, 1966).

Malley, Earnan O. [Ernie O'Malley], 'Louis le Brocquy,' *Horizon*, 14, no. 79 (July 1946), pp 32–7.

Mangan, H.C., *Robert Emmet: A History Play in Three Acts* (Dublin: Gill and Son, 1904).

Martin, Augustine, 'Brendan Behan,' *Threshold*, 18 (1963), pp 22–8.

——, 'Novelist and City: The Technical Challenge,' in Maurice Harmon (ed.), *The Irish Writer and the City* (Gerrards Cross, Bucks., UK: Colin Smythe, 1984), pp 37–51.

——, *Bearing Witness: Essays on Anglo-Irish Literature*, ed. Anthony Roche (Dublin: University College Dublin Press, 1996).

Matthew, James, *Voices: A Life of Frank O'Connor* (New York: Atheneum, 1983).

Maxwell, Desmond, 'Brendan Behan's Theatre,' *Irish Writers and the Theatre*, ed. Masuru Sekine (Gerrards Cross, Bucks., UK: Colin Smythe, 1986), pp 87–102.

McCann, Sean (ed.), *The World of Brendan Behan* (London: Four Square, 1965).

—— (ed.), *The Wit of Brendan Behan* (London: Leslie Frewin, 1968).

McCormack, W.J., *From Burke to Beckett: Ascendancy Tradition and Betrayal in Literary History* (Cork: Cork University Press, 1994).

——, 'Convergent Criticism: The *Biographia Literaria* of Vivian Mercier and the State of Irish Literary History,' *Bullán: An Irish Studies Journal*, 2, no. 1 (Summer 1995), pp 79–100.

McKeon, James, *Frank O'Connor: A Life* (Edinburgh: Mainstream, 1998).

McMahon, Frank, *Brendan Behan's Borstal Boy: Adapted for the Stage* (Dublin: Four Masters, 1971).

Mercier, Vivian, 'Dublin's Joyce,' *Irish Writing*, 35 (Summer 1956), pp 75–79.

Mikhail, E.H. (ed.), *The Art of Brendan Behan* (New York: Barnes and Noble, 1979).

——, *Brendan Behan: An Annotated Bibliography of Criticism* (New York: Barnes and Noble, 1980).

—— (ed.), *Brendan Behan: Interviews and Recollections* (London: Macmillan, 1982).

—— (ed.), *The Letters of Brendan Behan* (Basingstoke, UK: Macmillan, 1992).

Miller, J. Hillis, *Topographies* (Stanford: Stanford University Press, 1995).

Miner, Earl, *Literary Transmission and Authority: Dryden and Other Writers* (Cambridge: Cambridge University Press, 1993).

Mitchel, John, *Jail Journal* (Washington D.C.: Woodstock Books, 1996).

Montague, John, *Collected Poems* (Oldcastle, Co. Meath, Ireland: Gallery Press, 1995).

Moretti, Franco, *Signs Taken for Wonders: Essays in the Sociology of Literary Forms*, trans. Susan Fischer, David Forgacs and David Miller (London: Verso, 1988).

Morrison, Blake, *The Movement: English Poetry and Fiction of the 1950s* (Oxford: Oxford University Press, 1980).

Mulhern, Francis, *The Present Lasts a Long Time: Essays in Cultural Politics* (Cork: Cork University Press, 1998).

Murphy, Andrew, 'Ireland and Ante/anti-colonial Theory,' *Irish Studies Review*, 7, no. 2 (August 1999), pp 153–61.

Murray, Christopher, *Twentieth-Century Irish Drama: Mirror up to Nation* (Manchester: Manchester University Press, 1997).

Nandy, Ashis, *The Intimate Enemy: Loss and Recovery of Self under Colonialism* (Delhi: Oxford University Press, 1998).

Nash, John, 'Counterparts before the Law: Mimicry and Exclusion,' *Re: Joyce – Text, Culture, Politics*, ed. John Brannigan, Geoff Ward and Julian Wolfreys (Basingstoke, UK: Macmillan, 1997), pp 3–16.

Ó Briain, Seán, 'Brendan Behan,' *Irish Press*, 21 May 1964, p.8.

O'Brien, Flann, *At Swim-Two-Birds* (London: Penguin, 1967).

O'Connor, Frank, *An Only Child* (London: Macmillan, 1961).

——, 'He was so much larger than life,' *Sunday Independent*, 22 March 1964, p.7.

——, 'Guests of the Nation,' *Guests of the Nation* (Dublin: Poolbeg, 1985), pp 5–18.

O'Connor, Ulick, *Life Styles* (Dublin: The Dolmen Press, 1973).

——, *Brendan Behan* (London: Abacus, 1993 [1970]).

O'Donovan Rossa, Jeremiah, *My Years in English Jails* [*Prison Life*] (1874; reprinted Tralee, Ireland: Anvil Books, 1967).

O'Faolain, Sean, 'Editorial: This is Your Magazine,' *The Bell*, 1, no. 1 (October 1940), p.5–10.

——, 'Editorial: Standards and Taste,' *The Bell*, 2, no. 3 (June 1941), pp 5–11.

——, 'Editorial: New Wine in Old Bottles,' *The Bell*, 4, no. 6 (September 1942), p.381–88.

——, 'Editorial: Signing Off,' *The Bell*, 12, no. 1 (April 1946), pp 5–8.

——, 'The Bombshop,' *Midsummer Night Madness: Collected Short Stories, 1* (London: Penguin, 1982).

O'Hehir, Brendan, 'Re-Grafting a Severed Tongue: The Pains and Politics of Reviving Irish,' *World Literature Today*, vol. 54, no.2 (Spring 1980), pp 213–17.

O'Neill, Michael, *The Abbey at the Queen's: The History of the Irish National Theatre in Exile* (Nepean, Ontario, Canada: Borealis Press, 1999).

Olney, James (ed.), *Autobiography: Essays Theoretical and Critical* (Princeton, NJ, USA: Princeton University Press, 1980).

Orwell, George, *Decline of the English Murder and Other Essays* (London: Penguin, 1965).

O'Sullivan, Michael, *Brendan Behan: A Life* (Dublin: Blackwater Press, 1997).

O'Toole, Fintan, 'Going West: the Country versus the City in Irish Writing,' *Crane Bag*, 9, no. 2 (1985), pp 111–16.

——, 'The Southern Question,' *Letters from the New Island*, ed. Dermot Bolger (Dublin: Raven Arts Press, 1991), pp 15–43.

Ó Tuathaigh, Gearóid and Lee, J.J. (eds), *The Age of de Valera* (Dublin: Ward River Press, 1982).

Pearse, Patrick, 'The Coming Revolution,' *The Field Day Anthology of Irish Writing: Volume Two*, ed. Seamus Deane (Derry, Northern Ireland: Field Day Publications, 1991), pp 556–8.

Porter, Raymond J., *Brendan Behan* (New York: Columbia University Press, 1973).

Pratt, Mary Louise, *Imperial Eyes: Travel Writing and Transculturation* (London: Routledge, 1992).

Ricks, Christopher, 'Bee-keeper,' *The New York Review of Books*, 11, no. 12 (30 July 1964), pp 8–9.

Roche, Anthony, *Contemporary Irish Drama: From Beckett to McGuinness* (Dublin: Gill and Macmillan, 1994).

Ryan, John, *Remembering How We Stood: Bohemian Dublin at the Mid-Century* (Dublin: Gill and Macmillan, 1975).

Ryder, Sean, 'Male Autobiography and Irish Cultural Nationalism: John Mitchel and James Clarence Mangan,' *Irish Review*, 13 (Winter 1992/93), pp 70–77.

Said, Edward, *The World, the Text, and the Critic* (London: Faber and Faber, 1984).

Sedgwick, Eve Kosofsky, *Between Men: English Literature and Male Homosocial Desire* (New York: Columbia University Press, 1985).

——, *Epistemology of the Closet* (Hemel Hempstead, Herts., UK: Harvester Wheatsheaf, 1991).

——, *Tendencies* (London: Routledge, 1994).

Shulman, Milton, 'Mr Behan Makes Fun of the I.R.A.,' *Evening Standard*, 15 October 1958, p.13.

Simpson, Alan, *Beckett and Behan and a Theatre in Dublin* (London: Routledge and Kegan Paul, 1962).

Sinfield, Alan, *Literature, Politics and Culture in Postwar Britain* (Oxford: Basil Blackwell, 1989).

Smyth, Gerry, *Decolonisation and Criticism: The Construction of Irish Literature* (London: Pluto Press, 1998).

——, 'The Right to the City: Re-presentations of Dublin in Contemporary Irish Fiction,' in Liam Harte and Michael Parker (eds), *Contemporary Irish Fiction: Themes, Tropes, Theories* (Basingstoke, UK: Macmillan, 2000), pp 13–34.

Stillinger, Jack, *Multiple Authorship and the Myth of Solitary Genius* (Oxford: Oxford University Press, 1991).

Storey, Mark (ed.), *Poetry and Ireland since 1800: A Source Book* (London: Routledge, 1988).

Sullivan, T.D., A.M. and D.B. (eds), *Speeches from the Dock* (Dublin: Gill and Macmillan, 1968).

Swift, Carolyn, *Stage by Stage* (Dublin: Poolbeg Press, 1985).

Synge, J.M., *Prose*, ed. Alan Price (Oxford, UK: Oxford University Press, 1968).

——, *The Aran Islands* (Oxford, UK: Oxford University Press, 1979).

——, *Collected Works III*, ed. Ann Saddlemyer (Gerrards Cross, Bucks, UK: Colin Smythe, 1982).

——, *Collected Works IV*, ed. Ann Saddlemyer (Gerrards Cross, Colin Smythe, 1982).

Swinnerton, Frank, *The Georgian Literary Scene: A Panorama* (London: Hutchinson, 1935).

Tambling, Jeremy, *Confession: Sexuality, Sin, the Subject* (Manchester, UK: Manchester University Press, 1990).

Taylor, John Russell, *Anger and After: A Guide to the New British Drama* (London: Penguin, 1963).

Terdiman, Richard, *Present Past: Modernity and the Memory Crisis* (Ithaca, NY, USA: Cornell University Press, 1993).

Tone, Wolfe, *The Autobiography*, ed. R. Barry O'Brien (1826; reprinted London: T. Fisher Unwin, 1893).

Tschumi, Bernard, *Architecture and Disjunction* (Cambridge, MA, USA: MIT Press, 1996).

Tynan, Kenneth, 'The End of the Noose,' *The Observer*, 27 May 1956, p.11.

——, 'New Amalgam,' *The Observer*, 19 October 1958, p.19.

Uíbh Eachach, Vivian and Ó Faoláin, Dónal (eds), *Féile Zozimus: Volume 2 – Brendan Behan: The Man, The Myth, The Genius* (Dublin: Gael Linn, 1993).

Wall, Richard, '*An Giall* and *The Hostage* Compared,' *Modern Drama*, 18 (1975), pp 165–72.

Waters, Maureen, *The Comic Irishman* (Albany: State University of New York Press, 1984).

Watt, Stephen, *Joyce, O'Casey, and the Irish Popular Theater* (Syracuse, NY: Syracuse University Press, 1991).

Wellworth, George, *The Theatre of Protest and Paradox: Developments in the Avant-Garde Drama* (London: MacGibbon and Kee, 1965).

Wilde, Oscar [C.3.3.], *The Ballad of Reading Gaol* (London: Leonard Smithers, 1898).

Wolfreys, Julian, *Victorian Hauntings: Spectrality, Gothic, the Uncanny and Literature* (Basingstoke: Palgrave, 2001).

Woolf, Virginia, *Orlando: A Biography* (London: Penguin, 1993).

Wordsworth, William, *Wordsworth's Literary Criticism*, ed. W.J.B. Owen (London: Routledge and Kegan Paul, 1974).

Worton, Michael and Still, Judith (eds), *Intertextuality: Theories and Practices* (Manchester: Manchester University Press, 1990).

Yeats, W.B., *Autobiographies* (Dublin: Gill and Macmillan, 1955).

——, *Essays and Introductions* (London: Macmillan, 1961).

Young, Steven, 'Fact/Fiction: Cruiskeen Lawn, 1945–66,' in Anne Clune and Tess Hurson (eds), *Conjuring Complexities: Essays on Flann O'Brien* (Belfast: Institute of Irish Studies, 1997), pp 111–18.

Index